THE TEICHMAN FAMILY EDITION

THE JEWISH EXPERIENCE: 2,000 YEARS

A COLLECTION OF SIGNIFICANT EVENTS

THE TEICHMAN FAMILY EDITION

THE JEWISH

A SHAAR
PRESS
PUBLICATION

EXPERIENCE: 2,000 YEARS

A COLLECTION OF SIGNIFICANT EVENTS

RABBI NACHMAN ZAKON

Published by SHAAR PRESS
and Distributed by MESORAH PUBLICATIONS, LTD.
4401 Second Avenue / Brooklyn, NY 11232 / (718) 921-9000 / www.artscroll.com

Distributed in Israel by SIFRIATI / A. GITLER
6 Hayarkon Street / Bnei Brak 51127 / Israel

Distributed in Europe by LEHMANNS
Unit E, Viking Industrial Park, Rolling Mill Road / Jarrow, Tyne and Wear, NE32 3DP / England

Distributed in Australia and New Zealand by GOLDS WORLD OF JUDAICA
3-13 William Street / Balaclava, Melbourne 3183, Victoria / Australia

Distributed in South Africa by KOLLEL BOOKSHOP
Shop 8A Norwood Hypermarket/ Norwood 2196 / Johannesburg, South Africa

ISBN: 1-57819-496-2

Printed in the United States of America by Noble Book Press
Custom bound by Sefercraft, Inc. / 4401 Second Avenue / Brooklyn NY 11232

עֲטֶרֶת זְקֵנִים בְּנֵי בָנִים וְתִפְאֶרֶת בָּנִים אֲבוֹתָם

The crown of elders is grandchildren,
and the glory of children is their parents

(Proverbs 17:6)

The Teichman Family of Los Angeles

dedicates this volume to the memory of

our parents and grandparents,

ז״ל *Sam Teichman* — שמואל ב״ר יששכר דוב ז״ל

ע״ה *Lujza Teichman* — ליבה ברײנדל בת ר׳ יהושע הלוי ע״ה

ע״ה *Rose Teichman* — רחל בת ר׳ אלכסנדר סנדר ע״ה

ז״ל *Isaac Kae* — יצחק אײזיק ב״ר אברהם חיים ז״ל

Their birthplace was the Chassidic metropolis of Munkatch. From its awesome dynasty of great Rebbes, they absorbed the ideal that what is holy is good, and none of us is whole as long as a fellow Jew is in need or pain. We are proud of the legacy they left us to preserve. The Teichman legacy survived the Holocaust. It is carried on in America with pride and dedication by their children and grandchildren.

The name Munkatch evokes visions of greatness in Torah, greatness in Chassidus, greatness in the courageous defense of Torah life, and greatness in kindness and generosity.

The very names of its holy Rebbes still evoke reverence and aspirations to live up to the splendor of their ideals:

הגה״צ אדמו״ר ר׳ צבי אלימלך מדינוב זצוק״ל

הגה״צ אדמו״ר ר׳ אלעזר מלאנצוט זצוק״ל

הגה״צ אדמו״ר ר׳ שלמה זצוק״ל

הגה״צ אדמו״ר ר׳ צבי הירש זצוק״ל

הגה״צ אדמו״ר ר׳ חיים אלעזר זצוק״ל

Generations after their passing their memories are still strong and their works, such as *B'nei Yisas'char*, *Darchei Teshuvah*, and *Minchas Elazar*, to name a few, are still classics of Halachic and Chassidic learning.

They were towering figures during the times of turmoil, when authentic Judaism was under fire and Jews needed their warmth, strength, and wise leadership.

תנצב״ה

Pre-War Munkatch is no more — but its soul lives and thrives in the person and under the leadership of the present Rebbe, Reb Moishe Leib שליט״א. The *tishen*, the yeshivos, the *batei midrash* — all of this recalls the glories of the past and proves that *Klal Yisrael* remains eternal. Our people's triumph over exile and obstacle is the theme of this book. It is also the theme of Munkatch and many other communities that outlived the Holocaust — and will survive until the final Redemption, may it come speedily in our time.

Preface

Rabbi Nachman Zakon envisioned this work as a look at some of the highlights of Jewish history as it played out alongside major world events. We are confident that the reader — young or old — will find it enlightening and enjoyable. It can be savored in one long sitting or in snippets, from cover to cover or by turning pages randomly. It includes food for thought, items of interest, and focus on perspectives, as well as a fascinating array of photographs and illustrations.

This book was written with the conviction that the history of the Jewish people is the world's great creation — and this book is a list of its ingredients. The author is an American-born educator, who made *aliyah* many years ago. He has taught about the sweep of Jewish history for many years and in this work he collects "time capsules" of events and personalities that formed what we are today.

We are confident that **The Jewish Experience: 2,000 Years** will be a favorite for many years to come.

Acknowledgments

We are grateful to the **Teichman Family of Los Angeles,** who dedicated this book as a means of uniting Jews with their history. The Teichmans have had a significant share in shaping that history in contemporary times. They are men of vision and generosity, whose loyalty to Jewish causes wherever they are has won them the admiration and gratitude of multitudes. They are justly proud of their origins in the Chassidic metropolis of Munkatch and they remain loyal to the values and teachings of their forebears and spiritual leaders.

Rabbi Raphael Butler is a longtime friend and colleague whose guidance and suggestions were instrumental in shaping the book.

Many people contributed to turning Rabbi Zakon's manuscript into this finished product. We are deeply grateful for their generous expenditure of time and expertise.

Those who edited, researched, and enhanced the contents are **Rabbi Menachem Davis, Charlotte Friedland, Rabbi Shmuel Klein, Rabbi Moshe Gelbein, Rabbi Moshe Kolodny, and Mindy Stern.**

The esthetic beauty of this work is a tribute to the graphics professionals who invested a wealth of energy in its design and production. The demanding tasks of design and layout were performed with distinction by **Hershy Feuerwerker,** assisted by **Avrohom Kay, Rivky Grossman, Leah Weiner, Frady Vorhand, and Tzini Hanover**. The project was directed by **Eli Kroen**. The best compliment we can give them is the joy of seeing their work.

The flow of the work was coordinated by **Zissel Keller.**

We are sure that, in expressing our gratitude to them all, we speak for the many thousands of people who will enjoy this beautiful book.

The Publishers

Author's Dedication

Every Jew reading this book is a miracle — the result of ancestors, grandparents, and parents who miraculously withstood waves of hatred, persecution, and assimilation. They were ancestors who remained fiercely loyal to Torah and to their Jewish identity. Read this book, and you will discover how great a miracle you really are!

This book is dedicated to my ancestors, particularly my very special parents.

לזכר נשמות
אהרן יוסף בן יוחנן הכהן
בריינדל רייזל בת נחמן

Nachman Zakon
Jerusalem

3597
165 B.C.E.

Greek coin picturing
Antiochus IV, the Greek ruler
of *Eretz Yisrael* defeated by
the Hasmoneans at the time
of the Chanukah story

Pottery oil lamp used during
the time of the Second Temple

JEWS RECAPTURE JERUSALEM TEMPLE — THE MIRACLE OF CHANUKAH

Antiochus, the Syrian-Greek ruler of *Eretz Yisrael*, forbade the Jews from practicing Judaism, on pain of death. Galvanized into action, the Jews went to war against him. In the city of Modiin, Mattisyahu, son of Yochanan, the *Kohen Gadol* (high priest), and the leader of the Jews, called his people to armed revolt against the religious persecution. After a series of fierce battles, the small army of the Hasmoneans, under the leadership of their general, Mattisyahu's son Yehudah HaMaccabee, defeated the vastly superior forces of the Syrian-Greek army.

After their victory, the Jews entered the Temple, which had been desecrated, determined to immediately rededicate the *Beis HaMikdash*. They built a new Menorah and searched throughout the magnificent Temple compound for pure oil with which to light it. After a thorough search, only one small, sealed bottle was found. It was definitely pure because it still bore the seal of the *Kohen Gadol* and it contained enough oil to last a single night. With great rejoicing they lit the Menorah's lamps. Miraculously, the one

2

Burial cave of Chanah and her seven sons, who gave their lives during the rule of the Syrian-Greeks

day supply of oil lasted a full eight days, enough time to produce new oil. Every year, Jews throughout the world celebrate Chanukah to commemorate this great miracle and the miraculous military victory that allowed the Jews of that time to freely practice the *mitzvos*.

Mattisyahu's sons governed the Jewish people and continued the battles against the Syrian-Greeks, until the final decisive victory nearly a quarter century later in 148 B.C.E. The first leader was Yehudah. Despite his bravery, he perished in battle and was succeeded by Yonasan, who, after a short period of rule, was taken captive and killed. The last son of Mattisyahu to govern the Jews was Shimon. Under his leadership the Jews enjoyed an era of peace, security and prosperity — the first golden age of the Jews since the destruction of the First Temple.

A coin minted by Yonasan,
a Hasmonean ruler

3685
76 B.C.E.

SHLOMZION BECOMES QUEEN

Upon the death of her husband, King Yannai, who was a descendant of the Hasmoneans, Shlomzion (Salome Alexandra), a *very* righteous woman, became queen of the Jews. Together with her brother, Shimon ben Shetach, who was the *Av Beis Din* (chief justice of the Jewish high court), Shlomzion strengthened Torah observance throughout *Eretz Yisrael*. During her reign, which is considered to be one of the great eras of the Second Temple, the land was blessed and the people prospered.

3695
66 B.C.E.

CIVIL WAR

Queen Shlomzion had two sons: Hyrkanus, the older son, and Aristobulus, the younger. After Shlomzion's death each coveted the throne. Hyrkanus enlisted the aid of Aretas, king of Arabia, and his armies. They marched on Jerusalem and besieged the city, attempting to defeat Aristobulus and his soldiers who were inside the city. During the siege an agreement was reached by the two sides: In exchange for a payment of 2,000 *drachmae*, each day two lambs would be raised, in a basket, up the walls of the besieged city, so that the daily Temple sacrifice *(korban tamid)* would not be interrupted. One day, at the urging of a renegade Jew, Hyrkanus' men sent up a pig instead of a lamb. The *Kohanim* standing on the wall drew up the basket, unaware of the terrible exchange that had taken place. When the pig dug its hooves into the walls of Jerusalem, an earthquake shook the land of Israel.

3698
63 B.C.E.

ROMAN LEGIONS INVADE JERUSALEM

Both Hyrkanus and Aristobulus turned to the Roman general Pompey to enlist his aid against the other. Pompey chose to side with the man whom he knew Rome could easily control — Hyrkanus. Pompey's legions entered Jerusalem while Aristobulus retreated to the Temple Mount. After two months of struggle, the Roman legions overran the Temple area. In a day of ferocious bloodshed they slaughtered thousands of people, many of them *Kohanim*. Aristobulus was captured and forced to march in Pompey's victory parade in Rome. Hyrkanus was appointed ruler. Unfortunately, the brothers' decision to invite Rome to settle their disagreement resulted in Rome gaining power over *Eretz Yisrael*. The independence achieved in the Jewish victory over the Syrian-Greeks in the miracle of Chanukah came to an end. The Jewish state was placed in the charge of the Roman governor of Syria, Gabinius.

HILLEL APPOINTED PRINCE *(NASI)* — THE AGE OF *TANNAIM*

Hillel, a descendant of King David, traveled to *Eretz Yisrael* to study with the great scholars Shemaya and Avtalyon. He was coming from Babylonia, where great Jewish communities and yeshivos had been established by the exiles after the destruction of the First Temple.

One cold winter day Hillel did not have the money to pay the admission fee to attend the lecture being given by these great teachers. In his strong desire to learn Torah, he climbed to the roof of the lecture hall and lay down on the skylight, his ears pressed to it to hear his teachers' words. Hillel was so engrossed in the lecture, he did not notice the snow beginning to fall. As the snow piled up he continued listening attentively. He was found the next morning, buried under the snow, unconscious.

Hillel's appointment as *Nasi* came about many years later when he came to the Temple for Pesach. That year, *Erev Pesach* was on the Sabbath, an unusual occurrence. Only Hillel knew the answers to the questions that were puzzling the Jewish leaders as to what to do in this rarely occurring situation. Seeing Hillel's vast knowledge, the leaders of Jewry at the time, known as the Bnei

44 B.C.E.

On the 15th of March, Julius Caesar is assassinated.

3728
32 B.C.E.

5

Beseira (children of Beseira), stepped down, telling Hillel that because of his greater wisdom he should take their place.

Hillel is one of the great scholars called *Tannaim*. The *Tannaim* are the rabbis whose teachings are recorded in the Mishnah.

Many people came to study Torah in Hillel's yeshivah; his students were known collectively as "*Beis Hillel*" (the Academy of Hillel). Alongside Hillel's yeshivah was "*Beis Shammai*" (the Academy of Shammai). Like Hillel, Shammai was one of the most outstanding students of Shemaya and Avtalyon. He and Hillel were the two great leaders in their time. His students were known as "*Beis Shammai*." The Mishnah lists hundreds of cases in which *Beis Shammai* and *Beis Hillel* disagreed over points of Jewish law.

3742
19 B.C.E.

The so-called "Herod's Gate" in Jerusalem

HEROD RENOVATES JERUSALEM TEMPLE

Rome appointed Herod, a non-Jew who had been a servant, as the king of *Eretz Yisrael*. He was a brutal dictator who killed members of his own family, including his own sons, and wiped out the remaining descendants of the Hasmoneans. The Jews living in *Eretz Yisrael* at the time were crushed under his harsh decrees.

Herod ordered the murder of many Torah scholars. Though he allowed the Torah sage Bava ben Buta to survive, Herod had him blinded.

Some time later, Herod tested Bava ben Buta's loyalty to the regime. Entering the scholar's room and presenting himself as a simple Jew, he tried to convince Bava ben Buta to curse the evil King

Herod. He urged him again and again, assuring the sage that they were alone in the room and that he had nothing to fear. Bava refused. The king then let Bava ben Buta know that he was, in fact, Herod himself. Herod then confessed that had he known that the sages were so guarded in their speech, he would not have killed them.

Overcome with guilt and remorse for having killed the sages, he asked Bava ben Buta what he could do to atone for his deed. Bava ben Buta advised him to use his vast resources and energies to refurbish the Temple.

Herod vigorously pursued this project, employing 10,000 laborers, and three years later the renovated Temple stood as one of the great wonders of the ancient world.

64 C.E.

The city of Rome burns for six days.

A coin minted by Herod

Tablet in the Temple of Herod warning the gentiles not to proceed beyond the court assigned to them

3826
66 C.E.

JEWISH REVOLT AGAINST IMPERIAL ROME

After Herod's death in 4 B.C.E. (3757), his descendants continued to rule over various parts of *Eretz Yisrael* until 44 C.E. (3804), when Roman Procurators began to rule over the Jews directly, with an iron hand. As a result of the ruthless policies of these commissioners, especially those of Florus, the last Procurator, the Jews found their conditions unbearable. Many felt they had no choice but to rebel against their cruel overlords. In 66 C.E., anti-Roman fighting broke out in Jerusalem, with the Jews taking over some fortified positions.

The Roman Governor of Syria, Cestius Gallus, entered Jerusalem with his army, planning to dislodge the insurgents, but was totally unsuccessful. During their retreat, they were attacked by Jewish soldiers from Jerusalem who killed 6,000 of them and captured vast amounts of weapons. Upon returning to Jerusalem, the Jews of the city declared their independence from Rome. They appointed regional military commanders and fortified major cities in *Eretz Yisrael*. Soon, however, the Romans sent their best general, Vespasian, with 60,000 soldiers to stop the revolt.

3827
67 C.E.

ROMANS SURROUND JERUSALEM

The Jewish revolutionary armies could not withstand the overwhelming numbers of Roman legionnaires. Though the Jewish soldiers defended themselves bravely, Vespasian and his army were able to destroy city after city. Finally he arrived at Jerusalem and placed it under siege. No food or supplies could get in or out; the Jews were trapped! But the city had enough stores of food, grain and other essentials to withstand a long siege.

Unfortunately, unity among the trapped Jews was sorely lacking. Differences of opinion among the Jews about how to proceed with the war against the Romans erupted into bitter battles and even bloodshed. The storage centers of food, so vital to the city's ability to withstand a Roman siege, were burned to the ground by Jewish zealots hoping that the lack of food would force the Jews to leave the city and fight the Roman attackers. With the food gone and Jerusalem sealed off by the Romans, the citizens of Jerusalem suffered extreme hunger and thirst. People died in the streets from hunger. The situation was desperate, the destruction of Jerusalem imminent.

The rabbinical leader of Jerusalem, Rabbi Yochanan ben Zakkai, recognized that it was crucial to Jewish survival that he meet with Vespasian. He pretended to be dead and escaped the city on a burial stretcher. Once outside the city walls, he met with Vespasian. When Rabbi Yochanan saw the general, he addressed him by the title Caesar. Moments later, Vespasian received a message from Rome confirming Rabbi Yochanan ben Zakkai's statement: The Senate had appointed Vespasian as the new Caesar. In gratitude, Vespasian told Rabbi Yochanan ben Zakkai that he would grant him any request. Rabbi Yochanan ben Zakkai made three requests that would ensure the survival of the Jewish people long past the destruction of Jerusalem — and the fall of Rome. His first request was to spare the city

Did you know that?

- At the time of the Destruction of the Temple, Rome had a Jewish population of 50,000, with eleven synagogues.

- To celebrate his great victory, Titus built a towering monument in Rome. It still stands today, and is known as the Arch of Titus. On it is the inscription, *Judea Capta* (Judea is captive). Carvings on the Arch depict Titus' victory parade, and include images of Temple vessels that he had brought to Rome, and of Jewish captives being forced to march by their Roman victors.

- The man who destroyed the *Beis HaMikdash* did not go unpunished: Titus died a slow and painful death, brought about by a parasite that slowly ate away at his brain.

- One wall of the Temple compound miraculously withstood the blazing fires of destruction — the Western Wall, still standing in Jerusalem, the holiest place in the world for the Jewish people. Today, thousands visit and pray there daily.

of Yavneh and its Torah scholars. In the coming years, Yavneh became a primary center for the continuation of Judaism and Jewish studies. His second request was that Rome not kill the descendants of Rabban Gamliel (who was a descendant of Hillel and thus of the Davidic dynasty). This ensured that Jewish leadership would continue. Third, he asked that Vespasian provide a medical team that would heal the righteous Rabbi Tzadok, who had prayed and fasted for forty years that the Temple not be destroyed. His inspiration would be needed in the difficult times ahead.

Tomb of the *Tanna* Rabbi Yochanan ben Zakkai

The Arch of Titus in Rome, showing the Menorah and other spoils of the Temple

ROME CONQUERS JERUSALEM AND THE TEMPLE IS BURNED

The new Caesar of Rome, Vespasian, put his son Titus in charge of the five Roman legions, comprising 80,000 men, that would destroy the great capital city of the Jews. The city's brave defenders were extremely weak and exhausted due to starvation. On the 17th of Tammuz the city's protective wall was breached. In an orgy of destruction the invaders slaughtered old men, women and children. The city was systematically destroyed, neighborhood by neighborhood, house by house. Its inhabitants were put to death or exiled. The valiant defense of the Temple continued for three weeks, until the 9th of Av. On the afternoon of the 9th of Av, the Romans set fire to the structure, with many defenders trapped inside. The fire burned a full day until dusk on the 10th of Av.

Some historians date the destruction of the Temple as 68 C.E.

3830
70 C.E.

Did you know that?

- Tishah B'Av, the ninth of Av, is the eternal day of tragedy. On that day, the spies in the desert gave their terrible report, both Temples were destroyed, Beitar was conquered by the Romans, they plowed the Temple area, the Jews were expelled from Spain in 1492, and World War I began.

An aerial view of the Masada fortress

3833 73

THE FALL OF MASADA

Masada was a fortress built on a mountaintop rising 1,300 feet into the Judean Desert sky, about thirty-five miles south of Jerusalem. In this seemingly impregnable fortress were 967 men, women and children, bravely determined to resist the Romans, despite the fall of Jerusalem. To get to the top of the mountain, the Romans built a ramp of rocks and sand. After a long siege and fierce battle, the Tenth Legion conquered Masada — but there were no people, only the desert wind and empty buildings! Finally they found two old women and five children. All the others had killed one another, rather than be tortured and murdered by the Romans.

Did you know that?

Archaeologists excavated Masada in 1963. They uncovered a square pit too small to be a basement. Puzzled, they airlifted two Jerusalem rabbis to Masada by helicopter. The rabbis measured the pit and authoritatively confirmed that the archaeologists had uncovered a *mikveh* built by the defenders of Masada. Also discovered were a synagogue and fragments of Hebrew scrolls.

3888 128

Did you know that?

🐍 Only those volunteers strong enough to rip a tree from the ground while riding on horseback were allowed to enlist in Bar Kochba's army.

🐍 The Romans numbered their army units in sequence. However, after the humiliation of having their entire Twenty-Second Legion wiped out by Bar Kochba's men, this number was never used again.

3894 134

Did you know that?

🐍 Beitar fell on the 9th of Av, the same date the First and Second Temples were destroyed.

🐍 For fifteen years the slain of Beitar lay in the field, unburied. During this time, miraculously, their bodies did not decompose. When the Jews were finally allowed to bury the bodies, the Rabbis composed the fourth blessing of Grace After Meals, to thank God for preserving the bodies and enabling them to be buried.

BAR KOCHBA REVOLTS

The Roman emperor Hadrian enacted laws forbidding the Jews to practice Judaism. The observance of the Sabbath, circumcision, *tefillin*, and other *mitzvos* was punishable by death. The Jews' response to this persecution was an attempt to gain religious freedom from the Romans. Amassing a large army, Shimon bar Koziba, a courageous and pious Jew who was a strong leader and military genius, defeated the Romans in battle after battle, liberating *Eretz Yisrael* and finally recapturing Jerusalem. He set up an independent Jewish state, minting new coins that had religious themes and Hebrew letters. The great *Tanna*, Rabbi Akiva, fully supported Bar Koziba, renaming him Bar Kochba, which means Son of a Star. Rabbi Akiva believed that Bar Kochba was worthy of leading the Jewish people to the ultimate redemption.

FALL OF BEITAR

The Romans saw the Bar Kochba revolt as a serious threat to their empire. Emperor Hadrian sent a total of eight legions to reconquer Jerusalem and crush the rebellion. When Jerusalem fell to the Romans the Jews retreated to the city of Beitar. The rebellion continued for over three years. The spiritual force that protected the army of Bar Kochba and the city of Beitar was Bar Kochba's uncle, Rabbi Eliezer HaModai. His fervent prayers and meditations enabled the city to resist the might of the Roman Empire. The Talmud relates that once, when Rabbi Eliezer was immersed in prayers, a man — later discovered to be a spy — whispered something to him. The spy did this deliberately, to cast suspicion on Rabbi Eliezer. Bar Kochba thought that his uncle was a spy for the Romans and had him killed. Without the merit of Rabbi Eliezer the city fell to the Romans, and Bar Kochba himself was killed during the bitter battle for the city. Over half a million Jews were slaughtered. A river of blood ran from Beitar down to the sea. As a warning against future rebellions, the Romans did not allow the dead to be buried.

RABBI AKIVA EXECUTED

3894 134

Rabbi Akiva openly defied the Roman laws against teaching Torah. He reasoned that just as a fish out of water dies, so the Jewish nation without Torah study would perish. For this crime the Romans imprisoned the great sage, who was 120 years old at the time, and sentenced him to death by torture. As the Romans tore the flesh off his body with iron combs, Rabbi Akiva started reciting the prayer *"Shema Yisrael"* with great joy, despite the terrible pain. His students asked him how he could do this. He told them that all his life he had wanted to fulfill the command to love God, even if it meant dying for His sake, and now he had been given this great opportunity. With the final word of *Shema* — God is one — Rabbi Akiva died of his wounds. The story of his heroic death has echoed down through the centuries as an example of Jews dying a martyr's death *al kiddush Hashem* — to sanctify God's Name.

Did you know that?

- Rabbi Akiva was one of ten great Jewish leaders who were cruelly tortured and killed by the Romans. These ten martyrs were called the *Asarah Harugei Malchus*, which means "the ten killed by the government." The Jews remember them every year in special prayers said on Yom Kippur and Tishah B'Av.

Tomb of Rabbi Akiva in Tiberias. The tablets on the side tell the story of his martyrdom.

Tombs of Rabbi Akiva
and Rabbi Moshe Chaim
Luzzatto in Tiberias

Focus: Rabbi Akiva

Akiva the son of Yosef, an unlearned shepherd whose father had converted to Judaism, worked for a wealthy man, Kalba Savua. Kalba Savua's daughter, Rachel, saw this shepherd's outstanding character traits and recognized his great potential. She offered to marry him if he would commit himself exclusively to Torah study. Akiva was undecided: after all, he didn't even know *alef-beis*, he couldn't even read! While pondering his future, he noticed water dripping on a rock. The drops of water had eaten away the hard stone. This caught Rabbi Akiva's imagination and he said to himself: "If water can make an impression on hard stone, the Torah will have the power to impress itself on my uneducated mind." Thus, one of the greatest sages in Jewish history started his schooling at the age of 40.

Rachel's father was opposed to his daughter's choice of a husband. He told her that if she insisted on marrying the shepherd Akiva he would not give her any money to help support them. As the daughter of a wealthy man, she was used to a very high standard of living: nice clothes, plenty of food, a beautiful house. She turned her back on all these things in order to marry Akiva. Many years later, Rabbi Akiva told his thousands of students, "My Torah and your Torah belong to her."

At the very beginning Akiva studied the *alef-beis* with the youngest children. Twenty-four years later, he had become a prominent teacher and leader, with over 24,000 students of his own. He survived the destruction of the Second Temple and lived on to become one of the key personalities who rebuilt the Jewish community after the Temple had been destroyed.

One of the powerful ideas Rabbi Akiva stressed is the *mitzvah* of *"Ve'ahavta le're'acha kamocha* — love your fellow Jew as you love yourself."

16

MISHNAH COMPLETED

3960 200

The Written Torah given at Sinai was accompanied by an Oral Torah, which explained the *mitzvos* and added further laws. For centuries, this Oral Torah was passed down from generation to generation, father to son, *rebbi* to student. Rabbi Yehudah HaNasi sensed that due to the upheavals of exile and Roman persecution, some of the Oral Torah would have to be written down or it would be forgotten. He called together the greatest rabbis of his time, and they gathered the teachings of the *Tannaim,* the sages who lived during and just after the Second Temple period. Rabbi Yehudah HaNasi composed the Mishnah based on that compilation of teachings.

The Mishnah is a compendium of teachings on and disputes about Jewish law, and covers topics as varied as the Sabbath and Festivals, the Temple service, charity, civil matters, agriculture, the laws of ritual purity, and marriage and divorce laws. The Mishnah is composed of six sections called *sedarim*. Each section deals with a different set of laws. These *sedarim* are subdivided into sixty-three individual books called *masechtos* (tractates). The *masechtos* are further divided into chapters called *perakim* and finally into paragraphs called *mishnayos*. There are approximately 3,000 *mishnayos* in the entire Mishnah.

Did you know that?

🐌 Many Jewish schools run competitions, with the top prize going to the student who has memorized the most *mishnayos*. There are students who have memorized thousands of them.

Tomb of the *Tanna* Rabbi Meir
in Tiberias

Focus: The Mishnah

The Six *Sedarim* of the Mishnah are:

Seder Zeraim — the laws of agriculture

Seder Moed — the laws of Jewish holidays and the Sabbath

Seder Nashim — the laws pertaining to relationships between men and women

Seder Nezikin — laws of damages, courts, and property

Seder Kodashim — the laws of the Temple

Seder Taharos — the laws of ritual purity and impurity

Emporer Marcus Aurelius Antoninus

Focus: Rabbi Yehudah HaNasi

Rabbi Yehudah was born on the same day that Rabbi Akiva was murdered by the Romans. His father, Rabbi Shimon ben Gamliel the Second, defied the Roman laws against practicing Judaism and circumcised his firstborn son, naming him Yehudah. About the same time a baby was born to a Roman family. He grew up to be the emperor of Rome, Marcus Aurelius.

Rabbi Yehudah HaNasi, leader of the Jews in his time, and Marcus Aurelius, known in the Talmud as Antoninus, had a strong bond of friendship that lasted throughout their lifetimes and benefited the Jews greatly.

Rabbi Yehudah was a very wealthy man, whose fortunes rivaled those of some of the kings of his day. Though his riches would have enabled him to enjoy amazing luxuries, he never indulged himself. Instead, he used his great wealth to help others.

Rabbi Yehudah is rarely called by his name or by his official title, *Nasi* (Prince). Instead, he has been titled by the Jewish people *"Rabbeinu HaKadosh,"* our holy teacher, or simply *"Rebbi,"* for his role as the Jewish leader who had the Oral Torah written down. In effect, Rebbi became the teacher of the Oral Torah to all future generations.

Women praying at the tomb of the *Tanna* Rabbi Shimon bar Yochai in Meron

Mount Meron, where the famed *Tanna* Rabbi Shimon bar Yochai is buried

JEWS BARRED FROM BUILDING NEW SYNAGOGUES

With the spread of Christianity, the Roman Empire and its emperors became devout Christians. As a result, Rome passed various laws against the Jews, among them a decree that made it illegal to build new synagogues anywhere in the Roman Empire. By 418 Jews were barred from holding public office anywhere in the empire.

4175 415

410 C.E.

Rome is sacked by barbarians, marking the beginning of the fall of Rome.

4215 455 DEATH OF YAZDEGERD THE SECOND

Yazdegerd the Second, ruler of Persia, made it illegal to observe the Sabbath. The sages prayed for relief from the king's decree, and soon after, a serpent entered the king's chamber and swallowed him. Upon his ignominious death, the Jews were once again permitted to keep the Sabbath.

4235 475 TALMUD COMPLETED

After the *Tanach* (the Bible), the most important book of the Jewish people is the Talmud. It has preserved the Jews as a nation even though they had no land, government, or army. Through good times and bad, the Talmud provided the Jews with the inspiration and wisdom to survive centuries of exile. The Talmud — also known as *Shas* (an acronym for *Shishah Sedarim*, Six Orders) or *Gemara* (which means "learning") — discusses all aspects of Jewish life and law. It records the discussions, arguments, and teachings of the *Amoraim*, the Sages who lived for several generations after the Mishnah was compiled, and who explained the laws of the Mishnah. Additionally, the *Gemara* contains many passages of stories and moral teachings called *Aggadata*.

In contrast with the Mishnah which was compiled in *Eretz Yisrael*, the *Amoraim* studied in yeshivos in Babylonia as well as in *Eretz Yisrael*. The Jerusalem Talmud was compiled by Rabbi Yochanan in *Eretz Yisrael*, and the Babylonian Talmud was compiled by the last of the *Amoraim*, Rav Ashi and Ravina, in Babylonia. The Talmud remains the major subject of study by Jewish students, adults and scholars. It is studied over and over again, and every review brings a new dimension of understanding and discovery of knowledge and wisdom.

Did you know that?

🐜 NASA scientists claim that the moon takes 29.530588 days to circle the earth. This figure was arrived at through the use of sophisticated, high-tech computerized measuring equipment. The Talmud, written before computers were available, taught that it takes 29 days, 12 hours, 39 minutes, and 43⅓ seconds, or 29.530594 days to circle the earth, differing from the NASA figure by .000006, or six-millionths of a day — just a second and a half!

First page of Tractate *Sotah* from the Munich manuscript of the Talmud (Munich Codex Hebr. 95).
This is the oldest surviving manuscript of the entire Babylonian Talmud. It was written by
Shlomo ben Shimshon in the year 1342 (5102).

Focus: The *Amoraim*

There are many great men whose teachings appear in the Talmud; they are called *Amoraim*. The *Amoraim* were great scholars, knowledgeable in all areas of Torah wisdom. They were also people of outstanding ethical and moral character. Below is some information from the Talmud about these amazing men.

Rav and Shmuel: Rav never walked more than a few steps without being involved in Torah study and wearing his *tzitzis* and *tefillin*. Though he was the much respected founder of the yeshivah of Sura in Babylonia, he remained humble. Rav considered learning Torah so important that he regarded its public study above the bringing of the daily sacrifices in the Temple! Rav's real name was Abba. The name Rav was given to him as a sign of respect.

Rav is very often mentioned in the Talmud disagreeing with his colleague, Shmuel, who headed the yeshivah of Nehardea in Babylonia. The Talmud establishes guidelines for when there is a disagreement between these two great Torah scholars: When they argue about matters of ritual, the law follows the opinion of Rav. If they argue about a civil matter, the law is decided according to Shmuel's opinion. Shmuel taught the rule that it is forbidden to mislead someone, Jew or non-Jew.

Rav Yochanan and Reish Lakish: When his father passed away, Rabbi Yochanan inherited large vineyards in the north of *Eretz Yisrael*. However, working in the vineyards would have distracted him from his Torah studies, so he sold them. This illustrates his devotion to Torah learning. Rabbi Yochanan is considered the compiler of the *Talmud Yerushalmi*.

Rabbi Yochanan's greatest student was Reish Lakish. Reish Lakish had, as a very young man, left his Jewish studies to become a bandit. Rabbi Yochanan recognized the enormous potential in this young man, and convinced him to return to his studies. Rabbi Yochanan was proved right when the former bandit became a challenging and diligent student. On every law that Rabbi Yochanan taught, Reish Lakish would ask twenty-four questions. He would review his studies forty times. Reish Lakish's diligence and success made him one of the most respected *Amoraim* of the age, known for his unusual sharpness of mind. He married Rabbi Yochanan's sister, becoming the brother-in-law of the man who changed his life.

In the many places where the Talmud records the disputes between Rabbi Yochanan and Reish Lakish in Jewish law, the law follows Rabbi Yochanan, with only three exceptions.

Abaye and Rava: The yeshivah in Pumbedisa, which had been started by the *Amora* Rabbi Yehudah and had become the primary Babylonian yeshivah, was looking for a new *rosh yeshivah* to replace the one that had passed away. There were four eligible candidates who met the rigid requirements in Torah knowledge, wisdom, and character traits for this prestigious and influential position. The four were: Abaye, Rava, Rabbi Zeira and Rava bar Masna. Abaye was chosen. His breadth of Torah wisdom was acquired despite his being orphaned at birth and growing up impoverished and weak. One of Abaye's great Talmudic sayings is that a person should always be willing to participate in community activities. Abaye also taught that in every generation there are thirty-six *tzaddikim* who merit to perceive the Divine Presence.

Rava established the yeshivah in Mechoza. Upon the passing of Abaye, Rava was appointed *rosh yeshivah* of Pumbedisa, and he then moved the yeshivah to Mechoza. Throughout the Talmud's pages, one can find Abaye's statements being challenged by Rava. In all the arguments between them the Talmud teaches us that the law follows Rava's opinion, except for six times when the law is in accordance with Abaye. In fact, whenever any *Amora* disagrees with Rava, the law follows Rava.

Once, to test the powers of the rabbis, the king demanded that Rava make it rain in the summer, a season when it never rains in Babylonia. Rava prayed and rain it did!

Rava taught that God created the Evil Inclination, but He created the Torah as its antidote. He also said that someone who embarrasses another person publicly has no share in the World to Come.

Hillel the Second: The Jewish calendar is based on lunar months, and the basic year has 354 days. In order to ensure that the festivals occur in their proper seasons, a complex system based on a nineteen-year cycle is employed. Leap years, which occur seven times in each 19-year cycle, have thirteen months. In addition, the calendar is designed so that certain holidays do not fall on specific days of the week (the first day of Rosh Hashanah, for instance, can never occur on a Sunday, Wednesday, or Friday).

Until 359 C.E. (4119) the court in *Eretz Yisrael* determined when the months began — based on witnesses sighting the new moon — and when to intercalate a leap year. In 4119, when it became apparent that the courts would no longer be able to meet in *Eretz Yisrael*, Hillel the Second used the traditional formulas and calculations to create a Jewish calendar for every year. No other calendar of the ancient world has so accurately kept time to the present.

ETHIOPIA INVADES KINGDOM OF JEWISH CONVERTS

4285 525

In the 6th century, the Himyarites, a tribe living in southern Arabia, converted to Judaism together with their king. They lived in what is today Yemen. Dhu Nuwas was the last Jewish king of the Himyarites. He executed Christian merchants in retaliation for the Christian Byzantine Empire's mistreatment of the Jews. The Byzantine emperor, Justinian the First, persuaded the king of Ethiopia to invade the Jewish kingdom. The Ethiopians invaded and destroyed it.

REOPENING OF PUMBEDISA YESHIVAH

4349 589

After the period of the *Amoraim,* the first four generations of Rabbis who headed the yeshivos of Pumbedisa and Sura in Babylonia were known as *Savoraim,* "the Explainers." The next era, which began in 589, was that of the *Geonim* (singular, *gaon*). As heads of the Babylonian yeshivos, the *Geonim* provided leadership to the Jewish nation. The first *gaon,* Rabbi Chanan, reopened the yeshivah in Pumbedisa, which had been closed for about half a century due to Persian persecution. The last *gaon* was Rabbi Hai Gaon, who lived about 350 years after the start of the *Geonic* period. The leadership of the *Geonim,* and the many answers to questions in Jewish law addressed to them by Jewish communities throughout the Diaspora, spread the teachings of Torah and Talmud throughout the far corners of the world.

570 C.E.

Mohammed, founder of the Moslem religion, is born.

Focus: Three great *Geonim*

Rabbi Saadia Gaon: Rabbi Saadia lived in the beginning of the 10th century. Born in Egypt, he was the first non-Babylonian to be chosen as *gaon.* Through his writings and position he successfully fought the Karaites, apostate Jews who believed only in the Written Torah and not in the Oral Torah as recorded in the Talmud. He translated the Scriptures into Arabic and wrote a commentary, in Arabic, on many of its books. Through his efforts, many Karaites returned to practicing Judaism. A prolific writer, his most famous work, *Emunos V'Dei'os,* is the first book written on the Torah *weltanshauung* to be arranged by topics. It was vital in helping Jews in his time to resist assimilation.

Rabbi Sherira and Rabbi Hai: Rabbi Sherira and his son, Rabbi Hai, were the last of the *geonim.* Father and son, each

lived for almost a hundred years. Rabbi Sherira was born in 900 and spanned the entire 10th century; Rabbi Hai died in 1038 at the age of 99. Their leadership was the last great flash of light before Babylonia ceased to be the Torah center of the Jewish world. Rabbi Sherira and Rabbi Hai were brilliant scholars whose students and teachings passed the tradition on to the newly developing Torah centers in Europe. Rabbi Sherira Gaon wrote *Iggeres Rabbeinu Sherira Gaon,* an essay tracing Jewish history from the era of Moshe Rabbeinu to his own time. Rabbi Hai's greatness earned him the honor of being called "The Father of Israel." Students came from all over the civilized world — including Italy, Spain, Egypt, and *Eretz Yisrael* — to study under this great *gaon* in the yeshivah of Pumpedisa.

23

4374 614

Did you know that?

- *Eretz Yisrael* is surrounded by Arab Moslems numbering in the tens of millions.

- Arab Moslems bow in the direction of Mecca, their holy city, during the five times a day they pray.

- The first caliph, Abu Bekr, Mohammed's successor, taught the Moslems the religious principle of *jihad,* holy war. Moslems believe that those killed in *jihad* will go straight to heaven. Today many Arab countries refer to their fight against Israel's existence as a *jihad.* The most dangerous type of terrorist, a suicide bomber, is willing to die along with the Jews he kills, because he has been promised that he will go to heaven for his murders.

JERUSALEM REOPENED TO JEWS

When the Bar Kochba revolution failed with the capture of Beitar, all Jews living in Jerusalem were expelled from the city and the Jews were forbidden to live there. When the Persians captured Jerusalem from the Byzantine (Eastern Roman) Empire, Jews were once again allowed to settle in the holy city. It took almost 500 years before Jews were once again living in Jerusalem.

Focus: Islamic Expansion

In the 7th century, under the leadership of Mohammed, the founder of Islam, and his successors, the Arab armies established a Moslem empire in the Middle East. Refusing to convert to Islam, the Jewish communities suffered terribly at the hands of Mohammed's brutal armies. However, once the empire was established and the wars of conquest came to an end, the Jewish communities began to flourish. The Jews living in the empire became international traders of silks, spices, perfume and other goods. They transported their wares by caravans and ships across the deserts and seas of the Middle East, reaching all the corners of the empire.

4397 637

715 C.E.

Spain is conquered by the Moslems.

ERETZ YISRAEL CONQUERED BY THE MOSLEM EMPIRE

Emperor Haracilius lost *Eretz Yisrael* to the Arab armies. It wasn't until the 20th century, over 1,300 years later, that the Moslems lost control over all of *Eretz Yisrael*. It passed from them to the British in 1917.

4500 740

THE KINGDOM OF THE KHAZARS

In what is today southern Russia, there once lived a tribe of fierce pagan warriors. Their king, Bulan the Second, called together representatives of Christianity, Islam and Judaism to prove to him which was the true religion. His discussions with them convinced him to become a Jew. The Khazar king and about 4,000 of his people converted to Judaism. The Khazars ruled an area stretching over vast territory, from the Black Sea to the Caspian Sea, for the next 300 years.

Generations later Rabbi Yehudah HaLevi used this episode as the basis of his classic work of Jewish philosophy, the *Kuzari*. It is written in the form of a discussion between the king of the Khazars and his Jewish mentor.

Rabbi Yehudah HaLevi was born in Toledo, Spain and was one of the great Hebrew-Spanish poets, whose poetry became part of the prayers of the Jewish people. His most famous liturgical composition, *"Tzion Halo Sishali,"* is recited on Tishah B'Av, as part of the *kinnos*. In this dirge Rabbi Yehudah HaLevi expresses the yearning of the Jewish people to return to *Eretz Yisrael*. He also wrote the Sabbath song *"Yom Shabbason."*

Did you know that?

- At first, the Khazar king spoke only to representatives of Islam and Christianity. But when he learned that both were outgrowths of Judaism, he rejected them and asked that a rabbi be sent to speak with him instead.

THE FOUR CAPTIVES

4720 960

Traveling the high seas in the 10th century was extremely dangerous. Rabbi Abraham ibn Daud in his *Sefer HaKabbalah* relates that, nevertheless, four great scholars set out on a journey to raise funds for the yeshivos in Italy. During their voyage pirates overran their ship. Captured and taken prisoner, they were to be sold as slaves. Jewish prisoners were particularly valuable, as Jewish communities paid huge sums to buy captives and set them free, fulfilling the important commandment of *pidyon shevuyim*, redeeming captives.

Each of the four rabbis was sold at a different port in a different country. Rabbi Moshe was ransomed in Cordoba, Spain together with his son Chanoch; Rabbi Chushiel was ransomed in Tunisia, North Africa; and Rabbi Shmaryahu in Alexandria,

Egypt. (The identity of the fourth rabbi is unknown.) The tragedy proved to be fortuitous for the Jewish people: Each rabbi helped build a vibrant Jewish community and established superior levels of Jewish learning in his new home.

4760
1000

THE BISHOP OF MAINZ AND RABBI AMNON

Rabbi Yitzchak of Vienna, in his classic *Or Zarua*, relates that *U'Nesaneh Tokef*, a central prayer of the High Holidays, was written as a result of a tragic encounter between the bishop of Mainz, in Germany, and Rabbi Amnon, a leader of the Jews in his generation.

The bishop and Rabbi Amnon would often discuss religious philosophy. Time and time again, the bishop tried without success to convince the rabbi to convert to Christianity. At the conclusion of one of their meetings, the bishop demanded that Rabbi Amnon convert. Rabbi Amnon told the bishop that he needed three days to consider the matter. Rabbi Amnon, of course, was not even thinking of converting, but he hoped that after three days the bishop would forget his demand.

Upon arriving home, though, Rabbi Amnon was distraught, for he realized that he had committed a terrible blunder: He had given the bishop the impression that he considered betraying his God. For three days Rabbi Amnon prayed and fasted to atone for his misleading words. At the end of the three-day period he was brought forcibly to the bishop. Rabbi Amnon said that his tongue should be cut out, as punishment for uttering words that could be construed as blasphemous. The bishop responded that the tongue was not at fault; however, his feet would be cut off, for they had refused to come.

After each limb was removed, the bishop asked Rabbi Amnon if he would agree to convert. Bleeding and in terrible pain, Rabbi Amnon steadfastly refused. The bishop then ordered his hands and arms to be cut off, again asking him to agree to become a Christian. Despite this horrific ordeal, Rabbi Amnon would not renounce his Judaism.

Rabbi Amnon was sent home on a stretcher. A few days later, on Rosh Hashanah, he asked to be brought to the synagogue. Lying on his stretcher, he was placed near the *chazzan*. When the *chazzan* was about to begin reciting the holy "*Kedushah*" prayer, Rabbi Amnon motioned for him to stop. The synagogue was hushed as Rabbi Amnon, in a loud voice, recited the intense, emotional prayer he had composed, inspired by his *kiddush Hashem* — sanctifying of God's Name — in the face of the bishop's cruel tortures. His body, overcome by the wounds inflicted upon it, expired, as he finished. His prayer, *U'Nesaneh Tokef,* is one of the most emotional parts of the Rosh Hashanah and Yom Kippur *Mussaf.*

RABBEINU GERSHOM, LIGHT OF THE EXILE, PROHIBITS POLYGAMY

4760 1000

Rabbeinu Gershom, the undisputed leader of Ashkenazic Jewry, was known by the honored title *Meor HaGolah*, Light of the Exile. He convened a gathering of rabbis in Germany, at which a number of important regulations (*takanos*) were enacted as binding on all of Ashkenazic Jewry and their descendants. Anyone breaking these regulations would be harshly punished by excommunication, called "*cherem d'Rabbeinu Gershom.*" The most famous regulation was the prohibition of polygamy, something which, until this time, had been permitted, though rarely practiced. Other *takanos* prohibited divorcing a wife against her will, reading other people's mail, or shaming Jews who had converted to Christianity under duress.

Rabbeinu Gershom headed the yeshivah in Mainz, Germany. Because of his great stature and that of his students, who became the teachers of the famed Rashi, his yeshivah made Germany — *Ashkenaz* as it was called by the Jews — the preeminent Torah center of its day. Students came to his yeshivah from as far away as Italy, Spain and Babylonia. The establishment of Rabbeinu Gershom's yeshivah created a new center of Torah study, in addition to those in Babylonia and elsewhere. Ultimately, Europe became the center of Jewish learning and creativity until the Holocaust.

Did you know that?

Tragically, Rabbeinu Gershom's own son was forced to convert to Christianity. Upon his death, his father observed a double period of *shivah* — one for his son's physical demise and one for his son's spiritual demise.

4787
1027

RABBI SHMUEL HANAGID APPOINTED GRAND VIZIER

Did you know that?

§ Rabbi Shmuel HaNagid often was forced to use his genius to defend himself and his fellow Jews against the jealousy and hatred of the Arabs that he ruled. The following is one such incident.

§ Once, while Rabbi Shmuel was walking with the king, an Arab shopkeeper directed a long stream of curses against Rabbi Shmuel. The enraged king ordered Rabbi Shmuel to have the man's tongue cut out. Some weeks later, the king was walking with Rabbi Shmuel again when they encountered the same man. This time he greeted Rabbi Shmuel with blessings and words of praise. The king asked Rabbi Shmuel why he hadn't carried out the royal orders. Rabbi Shmuel's reply was that he had indeed fulfilled the king's decree. By sending the man gifts and talking with him, he had "cut out" the man's evil tongue — and replaced it with a good one. Rabbi Shmuel's wisdom had turned an enemy into a lifelong friend.

§ Shmuel HaNagid lived at the same time as the author of the great mussar classic *Chovos HaLevavos*, Duties of the Heart, written originally in Arabic by Rabbi Bachya ben Yosef ibn Pekuda.

§ In Arabic Shmuel HaNagid was known as Ibn Nagdela, which means "The Prince."

Rabbi Shmuel was a student of Rabbi Chanoch, who had been one of the four captives. When Rabbi Shmuel's native city, Cordoba, Spain, was torn by civil war, its vibrant Jewish community was destroyed. Shmuel became a spice merchant in the port city of Malaga, in the Berber kingdom of Grenada. A brilliant student of Rabbi Chanoch in Talmud studies, he also received a thorough secular education, and was proficient in mathematics, languages, poetry and science. In Malaga, he composed letters for illiterate gentiles, which they then presented to the ruler's top minister and adviser, the Vizier Ibn al Arif. The vizier, impressed by the contents and writing style, recognized Rabbi Shmuel's great talents and wisdom and appointed him his personal secretary. Rabbi Shmuel's new position required that he move to Grenada, where the palace was located.

The vizier gave King Chabus of Grenada excellent advice. What the king didn't know was that much of that advice came from the Jew, Rabbi Shmuel. As a result of Rabbi Shmuel's wisdom, the kingdom of Grenada became powerful and prosperous. Before Ibn al Arif died, he advised the king to appoint Rabbi Shmuel as the new vizier of the kingdom. Rabbi Shmuel came to be called "Shmuel HaNagid," or Shmuel the Prince. In this powerful and prestigious position, he used his influence, wealth and power to help Jews in many countries. In his own city he established a yeshivah in which he personally delivered lectures. Adjoining the yeshivah was a large library containing *sefarim* painstakingly written by hand. Rabbi Shmuel supported synagogues and yeshivos in the faraway lands of Babylonia, Sicily, and *Eretz Yisrael*; he also distributed charity to the poor in the city of Grenada.

When King Chabus died and his son, Badis, inherited the throne, Rabbi Shmuel became even more powerful. Like Joseph in the Torah, he was master of the kingdom in every way but in title. King Badis left all affairs of state in the hands of Rabbi Shmuel. The king was too busy enjoying himself to be bothered with running his kingdom. Rabbi Shmuel was a diplomat, statesman, commander in chief of the army, and a warrior who commanded soldiers in the battlefield.

Despite all his responsibilities, he continued his pursuit of Torah knowledge. He authored halachic works and composed prayers in the form of Hebrew poetry (*piyutim*). He carried on extensive written debates with Rabbi Yonah ibn Janach on issues of Hebrew grammar.

BIRTH OF RASHI

"What does Rashi say?" This is one of the first questions a young child learning *Chumash* hears his *rebbi* ask. It is often the first question a Torah scholar will ask when beginning to study a topic in the Talmud. Known as the teacher of the Jewish people, Rashi speaks to the young boy, and to the greatest sages of the age — each on his own level.

Rashi was born in Troyes, France to a father who, through his extraordinary piety, merited such an exceptional son. Once Rabbi Yitzchak was traveling on a ship with a beautiful gem. As a businessman he had invested heavily in the purchase of the stone, and anticipated making a large profit through its sale. While on the ship he was approached by gentiles who wished to purchase the stone to adorn their temple, but he refused their offers. Thinking Rabbi Yitzchak was merely bargaining for a higher price, they offered larger and larger amounts of money. However, Rabbi Yitzchak did not want his diamond to beautify a house of idol worship. Recognizing that the potential buyers were determined to get the gem even if it meant robbing it from him, he flung it into the ocean. Not long afterwards, in the same year that the great leader of Ashkenazic Jewry, Rabbeinu Gershom Meor HaGolah, passed away, Rabbi Yitzchak's son Rashi was born. His father called the baby Shlomo. Rashi's full name, Rabbi Shlomo Yitzchaki (son of Yitzchak), represents the acronym formed by the first letters of his name — Rashi.

At that time, the great Torah centers were in Worms and Mainz. Rashi traveled from his birthplace, Troyes, to study in

4800
1040

Did you know that?

§ Until recently visitors to the city of Worms could see the synagogue where Rashi studied. It stood for nine centuries. When it celebrated its 900th anniversary in 1934, Germany was already under Nazi rule. Four years later, on Kristallnacht, the synagogue was set ablaze by the Nazis. It was reconstructed in 1961.

§ Rashi earned his living as a wine merchant, growing grapes and making wine.

these cities. He returned to his hometown at age 25, an accomplished scholar, and he married there. Rashi spent the rest of his life as leader of the yeshivah he founded in Troyes, learning, teaching, and writing his exhaustive commentaries, which explain almost *every* phrase in the Five Books of Torah, the Books of the Prophets and the Writings, and the Talmud.

Rashi's commentary is unique in its ability to explain even the most difficult texts. Young students and great scholars study Rashi, and hundreds of books have been written to explain the deeper meaning of his "simple" comments. He was called the "father" of all commentators.

Rashi's last years were marred by the tragedy of the murderous rampage of the first Crusaders, who massacred the Jewish communities of Worms and Mainz.

He had several daughters, who were married to the best of his students. His grandsons became the great Talmud scholars, the *Baalei HaTosafos;* among them were Rabbeinu Tam and Rashbam.

Rashi passed away at the age of 65, but he lives on today, and in all generations, through his teachings, which are studied wherever Torah is taught.

Rashi's study in Worms, which was set afire by the Nazis on the night of November 9, 1938

LEGENDS ABOUT RASHI

§⌾ When Rashi's mother was pregnant, and walking down a narrow alleyway in Troyes, a horseback rider almost trampled her. Miraculously, the wall behind her opened. She stepped back into the wall and the horseman passed her by, leaving her unharmed. Until World War II, there was a place in the wall of the city which was known as the spot were the wall had opened for Rashi's mother.

§⌾ One of the leaders of the first Crusade, Godfrey of Boullion, the Duke of Lorraine, visited Rashi before setting out to capture *Eretz Yisrael* for the Christians with his army of thousands. Perhaps the duke wanted to boast about his future triumph. Rashi told him that he would return to Troyes with only one escort. Angry and outraged at Rashi's impertinence, the duke told Rashi that should his forecast not be fulfilled to the letter, he would be put to death. The duke's army won a great victory and slaughtered all the Jews and Moslems they found in Jerusalem. Godfrey left his force in *Eretz Yisrael*, where they built forts and controlled the land for over eighty years. The duke returned to Troyes escorted by *two* officers — not one — and looked forward to carrying out his promise to kill Rashi, since his prediction had not come true. However, as Godfrey entered the gates of the city a massive stone fell from the arch and crushed the skull of one of his two men, killing him instantly. The Duke entered Troyes with one soldier at his side, just as Rashi had foretold.

A page from the first printed edition of Rashi's commentary on *Chumash*, issued from the press of Abraham ben Garton at Reggio di Calabria, Italy in 1475. This is the earliest dated Hebrew printed book.

The Rif was 27 years old when Rashi was born. For more on the Rif, see 4848 / 1088.

4827 1066

MASSACRE IN GRENADA

Upon the passing of Rabbi Shmuel HaNagid, his son Rabbi Yosef became the new prince of Grenada. Like his father before him he was a *talmid chacham* and knew many languages. Tragically, he was not as capable as his father in defusing the tensions and neutralizing the hatred that developed against him. The fact that he was an influential and powerful non-Moslem greatly angered the Arab community.

One Sabbath, an enraged Arab mob broke into his elegant mansion, slaughtering him and most of his family. They hung his body on the city gate and then proceeded to kill as many of the city's Jews as they could find. Two thousand Jews died that Sabbath *al kiddush Hashem*, sanctifying God's Name.

4848 1088

RABBI YITZCHAK OF FEZ FLEES TO SPAIN

Rabbi Yitzchak was a *rosh yeshivah* in the city of Fez, Morocco. He is called the Rif, acronym of the words Rabbi Yitzchak of Fez (Alfasi). At the age of 75, slanderous lies were told about him to the government and he was forced to flee to Spain. Though this was a difficult move for the Rif, Spanish Jewry benefited. Rabbi Yitzchak had a monumental impact upon them through both his writings and his students, most particularly the Ri Migash, who became the mentor of Rambam's father.

The Rif's students, and their students after them, became the preeminent leaders of Spanish Jewry. Nearly all of Rabbi Yitzchak's halachic opinions are accepted as binding by the great Sephardic halachic authorities, such as Rambam and Rabbi Yosef Karo (author of the *Shulchan Aruch).* The Rif wrote a *sefer* called *Sefer HaHalachos,* which is still studied earnestly in yeshivos and study halls over 900 years later. The *Sefer HaHalachos* of the Rif records the final decisions of the *Gemara,* without the discussions that led up to them. Since he focused only on those issues and halachos that were practiced by Jews of his time, he omitted laws of the *Beis HaMikdash* and the agricultural laws of *Eretz Yisrael.* In complete editions of the Talmud, the commentary is printed in the back of each tractate in *Moed, Nashim* and *Nezikin,* as well as in the tractates of *Berachos* and *Chullin.* Essentially, the Rif is a halachic distillation of the Talmud, and is considered an integral part of advanced Talmud study.

Horns of Hittin, site of an important battle between the Crusaders and the Moslems for control of *Eretz Yisrael*

JERUSALEM CAPTURED DURING THE FIRST CRUSADE

4510 1099

The Crusaders were Christians determined to free the "Holy Land" — *Eretz Yisrael* — from the hands of its Moslem rulers. One thousand mounted knights in shining armor, backed by tens of thousands of Christian soldiers, breached the walls of Jerusalem after a five-week siege. Many of the Arabs in the city were slaughtered, and thousands were sold as slaves. The few hundred Jews living in the city sought refuge in their synagogue, but the Crusaders found them. The Crusaders then locked them in and set fire to the building. No one escaped.

Did you know that?

- The Bishop of Cologne saved the Jews in his city. He personally ordered the gates of the city locked to prevent the Crusaders from entering Cologne.

- In the month of Adar the Jews of Narbonne, France were miraculously saved from the Crusaders. They celebrated the 20th of Adar — the day they were rescued — as an additional Purim.

33

The Crusaders took over the city and established a kingdom in *Eretz Yisrael*. For a half century no Jew or Moslem was allowed to live in Jerusalem. The mosques of the city were turned into churches. A cross was placed on the golden dome looming over the Western Wall, and the mosque beneath it became a cathedral. Off and on, the Christians ruled in parts of *Eretz Yisrael* for almost two centuries.

Ruins of one of the fortresses
built by the Crusaders in *Eretz Yisrael*

Focus: The Crusades

Holy War! Whether it was the battle cry of the Moslem *jihad* or the Christian Crusaders, it meant a bloodbath for thousands of innocent, usually Jewish, victims. For more than 200 years the Crusaders passed in wave after wave over the Jewish com-munities of Europe, killing, destroying, and terrorizing the Jews. The Crusaders were an army of kings, priests, soldiers, bandits, riffraff, and criminals who were marching to *Eretz Yisrael* to free it from Moslem control. On their march to the

Holy Land they often forced the Christian religion on Jews, who were treated like outsiders in their own European lands. Using torture and terror, they would force Jews to accept Christianity. If they refused they could be put to death and their property looted, with every Crusader stealing whatever he could. In the face of these barbaric and primitive hordes of Christians, most of the Jewish people rose to their great challenge and bravely resisted baptism, keeping the Jewish faith and remaining loyal to Torah, *mitzvos*, and *Hashem echad*, our one God.

The death toll of the Crusades was staggering. Tens of thousands of Jews in France, Germany and England were killed, and hundreds of Jewish communities were destroyed. The Jews in the city of Worms were murdered by Crusaders on Rosh Chodesh Sivan, as they were saying *Hallel* in the castle where they took refuge. In York, England, the Jews fled to the city tower. With no escape, they were surrounded by Crusaders demanding that they convert. On Friday evening, *Shabbos HaGadol*, March 18, 1190 — knowing that the Crusaders would kill the adults and allow some children to survive, to be raised by the Church as Christians — the Jews put their families to death and killed themselves. Among the many that died that day was Rabbeinu Yom Tov of Joigny, one of the Tosafists and himself a student of the great Tosafist Rabbeinu Tam. Many other *Baalei*

Tosafos were also caught in the storm of the Crusades.

King Richard the First of England, known as Richard the Lionhearted, led the third Crusade. His coronation was an excuse for the citizens of London to rampage, killing the Jews in the city. A student of Rabbeinu Tam, the Tosafist Rabbi Yaakov of Orleans, lost his life that day. In addition, the communities of Mainz and Speyer in Germany, Metz and Troyes in France, and Norwich in England were decimated by the Crusaders. And that is just a partial list.

To commemorate those who died defending their Jewish faith, and the communities that were lost, the prayer *Av HaRachamim* (Father of Mercy) was added to the Sabbath prayer services, following the *Haftarah* reading. It is recited to this very day.

One of the results of the Crusaders' persecutions was that Jewish citizens began to be looked upon as aliens with no civil rights, who could be exiled or killed at will. City after city exiled its Jews, usually confiscating their possessions and canceling debts owed to them by their gentile neighbors. The Jews were exiled from Paris in 1192, England in 1290, Milan in 1320, Zurich in 1349, Hungary in 1360, and Strasbourg, Germany in 1386. As a result of these persecutions, Jews started to move into Poland and Russia. At that time the Eastern European gentiles did not mind having Jewish neighbors.

Did you know that?

❧ On July 8, 1984, the bodies of the martyrs of York were reinterred in the city's Jewish cemetery. That evening, a bolt of lighting struck the oldest cathedral in York, causing devastating damage.

The tower of York, known as Clifford's Tower, as it appears today

4512 1101

Did you know that?

- The Aruch lived at the same time as Rashi and they wrote letters to each other.

- The Aruch was a successful doctor.

COMPLETION OF FIRST MAJOR TALMUD DICTIONARY

In the city of Rome Rabbi Nassan ben Yechiel completed the *Aruch,* a dictionary of over 3,000 words found in the Talmud. The *Aruch* did not only translate, it also provided analyses of many subjects in the Talmud, and was a major contribution to Talmud study. The author was the leader of the Jewish community in Rome and one of the famous scholars who studied in the great Torah centers that flourished in Italy during the 12th and 13th centuries. Bari and Otranto were Italian cities about which Jews said that "from Bari the Torah would spread, and the law of God from Otranto."

4904 1144

BLOOD LIBEL IN NORWICH

Did you know that?

- Apion, an anti-Semite who lived in Hellenistic Egypt, recorded what was probably the first blood libel. He wrote that when the Greeks took over the *Beis HaMikdash* at the time of the Chanukah story, they discovered a fat Greek boy who told his "liberators" that the Jews captured a Greek youth every year and kept him prisoner in the Holy of Holies, fattening him up to sacrifice him on Yom Kippur.

- In Lincoln, England, the child supposedly murdered by the Jews was raised to the status of sainthood — Little Saint Hugh.

In Norwich, England a boy named William was found dead on Pesach. The Jews were accused of torturing the child and using his blood to bake matzah! The accusation of Jews killing Christians for their blood has been brought against the Jews in many different cities and countries of the Diaspora, even into the 1900's, the "modern era." Almost always, the blood libels resulted in pogroms against the Jews. In the rare instances where the murders were thoroughly investigated, it was determined that the dead child had been killed by fellow Christians looking for an excuse to harm the Jews.

Focus: The Tosafists

Open a volume of Talmud. On the page are two columns surrounding the Gemara text. These are the two pillars of Talmud study: Rashi on the inner column and Tosafos on the outer side. Tosafos compare the text on the page with other Talmud passages, analyzing and resolving apparent contradictions. Unlike Rashi, which is the work of one person, Tosafos is the collected and edited Torah teachings of over a hundred scholars. Some of the leading Tosafists were grandsons and students of Rashi. They were the leaders of Jewry in the lands of England, France, and Germany in the 12th and 13th centuries.

Many of the Tosafists, their families and their communities, suffered at the hands of the Crusaders. Despite this, the great, pious, and brilliant *Baalei Tosafos* left a rich and vast legacy of wisdom for all the generations that followed.

Rabbeinu Tam is mentioned by name more often than any other Tosafist. His name was Rabbi Yaakov ben Meir, and he was called "Tam" because he was compared to our forefather Jacob, whom the Torah describes as *ish tam*. His explanations, questions, and answers on the Talmud text are evidence of his powerful mind and vast Torah knowledge. Rabbeinu Tam was a very wealthy man who employed many Jewish and non-Jewish servants. He had many halachic disagreements with his grandfather Rashi. One of the best known is in the order of the Scriptural passages that are placed in the *tefillin*. All men wear *tefillin* with the verses in the order dictated by Rashi. Some people, however, mostly Chassidim and Sephardic Jews, wear two pairs of *tefillin* during the morning prayers. They begin with "Rashi *tefillin*" and then, toward the end of the prayers, remove those and put on a pair of "Rabbeinu Tam *tefillin*."

Rabbi Shmuel ben Meir, another grandson of Rashi who was a Tosafist, wrote an important commentary on various tractates of the Talmud. His commentary on those portions of Tractate *Bava Basra* where we do not have a commentary from Rashi appears in standard Talmud editions. He also wrote a commentary on the *Chumash*, known by his acronym — Rashbam. He explains the verses using the simplest meaning of the text. His commentary on the last chapter of Tractate *Pesachim* is printed on the Talmud page directly under that of his grandfather.

Another Tosafist, **Rabbi Yehudah HaChassid**, was one of the first of the German Kabbalists called the *Chassidei Ashkenaz*. The *Chassidei Ashkenaz* led a life of asceticism inspired by mys-

Standard page of the Talmud:
(1) Talmud text in center (2) Rashi (3) Tosafos

ticism. Rabbi Yehudah fasted almost every day, eating only at night. He wrote *Sefer Chassidim*, a guide to ethical behavior. A number of the directives that appear in his will — which is known as *Tzavaas Rabbi Yehudah HaChassid* — have become widely accepted. The custom that a man does not marry a woman with the same name as his mother is due to Rabbi Yehudah HaChassid's ruling.

The **Ri, Rabbi Yitzchak of Dampierre**, a nephew and student of Rabbeinu Tam and descendant of Rashi, is, after his uncle, the next most frequently mentioned Tosafist in the commentary. He had sixty students. Each one knew an entire *masechta* of Talmud by heart. During the *shiurim* in the yeshivah any one of these sixty would be called upon to analyze a point being discussed.

4907 1147

RABBEINU TAM ATTACKED BY CRUSADERS

On the second day of Shavuos, Crusaders burst into the house of Rabbeinu Tam. They rampaged through the home of the holy *tzaddik* — the most famous of the Tosafists — stole all his possessions, desecrated his *Sefer Torah*, and wounded him. Miraculously, he escaped with his life.

4910 1150

RAMBAM'S FATHER LEAVES CORDOBA, SPAIN

The Koran, the Moslem book of Mohammed's teachings, divides the world into two parts: those who believe in Mohammed the prophet and those who do not. Those who do not, according to one interpretation of the Koran, should be put to death unless, of course, they are willing to become Moslems. Unfortunately, Moslem Spain, with its large Jewish population, was conquered by the Almohads, fanatic Moslems who interpreted the Koran strictly and demanded that the Jews of the realm convert to Islam. Many outwardly did, practicing Judaism in secret. Others chose to move to places where they could be Jews openly. Rabbi Maimon left Cordoba, taking his family, including his young son, who would grow up to be the world famous Rambam.

RAMBAM ARRIVES IN EGYPT

4925 1165

In the Arab world he was recognized as the best physician of his time. To the Jews, Rabbi Moshe ben Maimon, Rambam — an acronym of the first letters of his name — (known in English as Maimonides) was one of the greatest rabbis that ever lived. The epitaph on his gravestone in Tiberias, Israel reads: "From Moshe (Rabbeinu) to Moshe (ben Maimon) there was no one like Moshe."

This well-known picture is supposedly a likeness of the Rambam

Newly constructed entrance to the tomb of Rambam. The fourteen pillars at the sides each represent one section of his famed *Yad HaChazakah*.

Did you know that?

🐚 The Rambam's *Sefer HaMitzvos,* (which lists all the Torah commandments), *Moreh Nevuchim,* (Guide to the Perplexed) and Commentary on the Mishnah were all written in Arabic. The Hebrew versions that have been used for centuries are translations. *Sefer HaMitzvos, Moreh Nevuchim* and portions of the Mishnah commentary were translated by Rabbi Shmuel ibn Tibbon, a contemporary of the Rambam. Though he never met the Rambam, they wrote to each other, and the Rambam advised him on how to do the translation.

Did you know that?

§ The thirteen statements of *Ani Maamin* (Principles of Faith) are based on those formulated by Rambam in his introduction to *Cheilek,* part of his Commentary on the Mishnah.

§ The Rambam wrote over ten medical texts, including one on poison, one on asthma, and an alphabetical listing of drugs.

Born in Spain, as a young boy the Rambam and his family became exiles, fleeing from persecution. After more than ten years of wandering within Spain, the family settled in Fez, Morocco, only to be forced to leave once again. Traveling to *Eretz Yisrael* by ship, a severe storm put them in danger of sinking, but miraculously they survived. The Rambam annually observed the day that his life was spared as a day of penance, rejoicing, feasting and giving alms to the poor, in gratitude to God.

Rambam left *Eretz Yisrael*, after a short visit to the holy sites there, and arrived in Fustat, the old city of Cairo, Egypt. Within a few years of his arrival, Rambam suffered loss after terrible loss. Two of his sons, his wife, and his father all passed away.

The Rambam was very close to his younger brother, David, who was a merchant dealing in expensive gemstones and other luxury items. Very often David traveled by ship, buying goods in distant lands, hoping to sell his wares in other ports for a

The tomb of Rambam in Tiberias

handsome profit. Unfortunately, on one of his trips the boat he was on sank in the Indian Ocean. This tragedy marked a great change in the life of Rambam. David had supported Rambam from the fortune he had amassed as a successful and prosperous merchant. While his brother was alive Rambam did not have to work for a living, and spent his time studying Torah. When his brother passed away, Rambam became a practicing doctor in order to support himself.

His fame spread and he became a physician attending to the Sultan, his many wives and his children. The Arabs said of Rambam that he was such a good doctor that if the moon would be his patient, he could heal it of its spots.

Because of his great Torah knowledge, Rambam became the leader of Egyptian Jewry, given the special title *Nagid*. As *Nagid*, Rambam was responsible for the physical and spiritual well-being of all Egyptian Jewry.

A page of Rambam's *Mishneh Torah,* printed in Rome, before 1480

Focus: The great books of Rambam

Mishneh Torah: A summary of all Torah law, the *Mishneh Torah* is divided into fourteen books, which is why it is also called the *Yad HaChazakah* (Strong Hand) — for the numerical value of the Hebrew word *Yad* is fourteen. The *Mishneh Torah* contains all the rulings discussed in the Talmud, including laws about building the *Beis HaMikdash*, *korbanos* (offerings) and Jewish kings. It took Rambam ten years to write. Over the centuries, it has been the most intensely studied of Rambam's works, and one of the most important Jewish books ever written. There are well over 300 *sefarim* published to explain Rambam's *Mishneh Torah*.

Commentary on the Mishnah: The Rambam managed to complete this work even though he was suffering the hardships of being a refugee — writing parts of the book on ships, and parts wandering from one strange land to another.

Moreh Nevuchim (*A Guide to the Perplexed*): A book of Jewish philosophy and commentary on Scripture, which he wrote at the end of his life. He did so to help Jews in his time who had questions about their faith.

Sefer HaMitzvos: A description of all 613 commandments. The book contains two lists: one, a list of the positive commandments, those that God wants us to do; the other, a list of all He doesn't want us to do, the negative commandments. It also explains the rules that determine how Rambam identified which are the 613 commandments. The book was written as an introduction to his *Mishneh Torah*.

Iggeres Teiman: The Rambam wrote a lengthy letter to the Jews of Yemen (*Teiman*), who were suffering cruel persecution. The letter strengthened their faith and inspired them to remain loyal to their religion. The Rambam's teachings had great influence on the traditions of Yemenite Jewry.

4929 1168

A member of India's
Bnei Israel community

Did you know that?

🐝 Binyamin of Tudela describes the Bnei Israel, a Jewish sect in India known as the Black Jews, who claim that their community on the Indian continent was founded by exiles from the First Temple. They survived until the modern era, when about 800 of them made *aliyah* to *Eretz Yisrael.*

In 1205, when Rambam died, the Ramban was ten years old. For more on the Ramban, see 5023 / 1263.

BINYAMIN OF TUDELA, THE JEWISH MARCO POLO, ARRIVES IN BAGHDAD

Rabbi Binyamin ben Yona of Tudela traveled extensively, for thirteen years. His trips took him from Spain to the ends of the known world. He may even have been the first European traveler to describe the Far East.

Medieval travel was difficult. Roads were unpaved and not policed, and travelers risked attack by wild animals and roving bands of bandits. Nevertheless, on camelback, boat, and horseback, Binyamin managed to visit hundreds of places, including Italy, Greece, Persia, India and *Eretz Yisrael*. His diary of his travels is a valuable historical resource. He describes the rabbis and lay leadership of each community, and details the Jews' living conditions and sources of income. He records facts, figures, interesting stories, and paints vivid pictures of the places he went to and the Jewish communities he visited.

4976 1215

THE JEWISH BADGE

Over the years the Christian Church came up with many ways to make the Jews appear different and alien. Sometimes they were forced to live in special parts of the city — usually surrounded by walls — which they were not allowed to leave after sunset. These areas were called ghettoes. In 1215 Pope Innocent III passed a law requiring all Jews to wear a badge, a colored piece of cloth sewn onto their clothes. Over the centuries, this idea caught on as a popular way to degrade the Jews. Jews were forced to wear all kinds of silly clothing: horned hats, yellow "dunce caps," red badges, yellow badges, green caps.

This practice disappeared by the beginning of the 1800's, but it was revived in Nazi Germany, where the vast majority of Jews were assimilated and virtually indistinguishable from their gentile neighbors. Starting in 1939, the Nazis forced German Jews to wear a yellow six-pointed Jewish star, the Magen David, with the word "Jude" printed on it, at all times. A Jew not wearing the badge could be arrested, or worse. Wearing the badge made the Jews easily identifiable targets to be terrorized, beaten and humiliated by the anti-Semitic Germans. In all the countries invaded by the Germans the Jews were forced to wear the yellow star.

Did you know that?

- The idea of forcing a minority population to wear a badge was first invented by Caliph Haroun al Rashid, who, in 807, ordered all Christians in his domain to wear a blue badge!

A Jewish family of Prague, wearing the Jew badge

1215 C.E.

Magna Carta is signed by King John of England.

5002 1242 KING OF FRANCE ORDERS THE TALMUD BURNED

The Catholic Church confiscated hundreds of copies of the Talmud from yeshivos, synagogues, and the Jews of France. Printing was unknown at that time, and each volume had been painstakingly copied by hand. The manuscripts filled twenty-four wagons. By the order of King Louis IX these wagons were brought to Paris and publicly burned before Christian spectators. This tragedy occurred after a debate the king had forced on the Jews. The brilliant Tosafist Rabbi Yechiel of Paris and other French rabbis had been compelled to defend the Talmud before the king's court.

Did you know that?

- After his death King Louis IX was made a saint by the Church. He is quoted as having said, "The best way to argue with a Jew is to plunge a sword into him."

- Rabbi Yonah of Gerona was so moved by the great tragedy of the destruction and public humiliation of the Talmud that he wrote a *sefer* called *Shaarei Teshuvah*, "Gates of Repentance," which became a *mussar* classic.

- Rabbi Yechiel continued to teach in Paris, probably from memory. In 1260 he and many of his students immigrated to *Eretz Yisrael*, where he led a yeshivah in Acre for five years, until his death.

A 12th-century manuscript of the Talmud, Tractate Bava Kamma. This manuscript was written by Yitzchak bar Chaninai of Gerona, Spain.

People of the Book:
Famous Jewish Commentators 1100 - 1400

Talmud and Halachah Commentators

RABBEINU NISSIM (RAN)

In most tractates, Ran's commentary explains Rif's decisions (see 1088). It helps explain the Talmud's intent and is vital to understanding the law. He also wrote independent commentaries on many other tractates. Ran's commentary on Tractate *Nedarim* is published alongside the text of the Talmud and is the primary commentary on that tractate. Rabbeinu Nissim's halachic responsa are frequently cited in later works. The collection of his essays on Jewish thought, *Derashos HaRan*, is a seminal work that deeply influenced many thinkers, including Rabbi Don Isaac Abarbanel.

OR ZARUA

Rabbi Yitzchak of Vienna's work, *Or Zarua*, was a halachic guide popular among Ashkenazic Jewry. His student was the leading Rabbi of Germany, Rabbi Meir of Rothenburg, known as Maharam (see 1286).

ROSH

Rabbi Asher ben Yechiel was born in Germany, where he studied under Rabbi Meir of Rothenburg. After Rabbi Meir died in prison, Rabbi Asher, his outstanding student, became the leader of German Jewry. Afraid that the authorities would put him in prison, as they had done to his mentor, he fled the country of his birth, arriving in Barcelona, and made his way to the home of Rashba, Rabbi Shlomo ibn Aderes (see page 50). They had corresponded with each other, and Rashba greeted Rosh with the great honor due to a *talmid chacham*. Rosh was appointed Rabbi of the Spanish city Toledo, and when Rashba died the Jews of Spain turned to the Rosh to be their new leader.

In his commentary, Rabbi Asher recorded his halachic conclusions of the Talmud's discussions, and commented on the

Rosh

Did you know that?

§ Due to poverty Ibn Ezra was forced to travel all over Europe. During his journeys he traveled from Spain to Rome to France (where he met Rabbeinu Tam, the famous Tosafist), and even as far as England!

§ Ibn Ezra wrote books on Hebrew grammar, astronomy, and mathematics.

§ The Rambam had such a high regard for Ibn Ezra's Torah commentary that he instructed his son to study it.

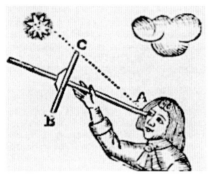

Jacob's staff — an astronomical device invented by Ralbag

Did you know that?

§ Ralbag invented an instrument to measure the position of the stars and planets. It is called "Jacob's staff" and was used extensively by astronomers and navigators, including the early explorers of the New World. This invention, and his book on astronomy, were influential in laying the foundation for the development of modern astronomy. He also wrote books on mathematics. Astronomers named a crater on the moon in Ralbag's name. The crater's name is "Rabbi Levi."

discussions to explain how he arrived at his decisions. These decisions, which appear in virtually *every* standard edition of the Talmud since 1520, contain rulings that greatly influenced later halachic codes. The Rosh is used by Talmud scholars to analyze the Talmud as well. Rabbi Asher also wrote a Tosafos-style commentary called *Tosafos HaRosh;* a Mishnah commentary; an ethical work, *Orchos Chaim;* and a Torah commentary. His responsa are frequently cited by later authorities.

Torah Commentators

IBN EZRA

Rabbi Avraham ibn Ezra, who was born in Spain, was a great Torah scholar, Hebrew poet, and a master of Hebrew grammar. His commentary on all the Books of the Bible, printed in the standard texts of *Tanach*, is known for its linguistic and grammatical analysis. In composing his commentary, Ibn Ezra drew on the works of Rabbi Saadia Gaon and other commentators and grammarians whose commentaries had been written in Arabic. He is the only surviving source for many of these comments. He also wrote some of the songs *(zemiros)* sung at the Sabbath meals.

RADAK

An orphan at age 10, Rabbi David Kimchi was raised and educated by his older brother, Rabbi Moshe. Although his commentary was written on the entire *Tanach*, we have only the sections on Genesis, Prophets, Psalms, Proverbs and Chronicles. His commentary, one of the most popular on Scripture, is "required reading" for any serious student. Radak also wrote *Sefer Michlol* on Hebrew grammar, and *Sefer HaShorashim,* a Hebrew dictionary. These were popular not only with Jewish scholars, but also among non-Jews who wanted to learn Hebrew.

RALBAG

Rabbi Levi ben Gershon lived in Provence. He wrote philosophical works as well as a commentary on the Scripture. Generally, his commentary presents the simple meaning of the text, its philosophical underpinnings, and practical lessons to be learned.

5023 1263
RAMBAN'S GREAT DEBATE

Ramban (Nachmanides), Rabbi Moshe ben Nachman, was called upon by King James I of Aragon, Spain to debate a Jewish apostate, Pablo Christiani, who would present Christian arguments against Judaism. Ramban requested from the king that he be allowed to speak openly, with complete freedom of speech, without fear of being made to suffer for anything he said. The king granted Ramban's request. Ramban, one of the greatest Jewish scholars, defeated his opponent with convincing and logical arguments. It was apparent to all the spectators that Ramban possessed a greater knowledge of the Bible, and he was acknowledged as the victor. After the debate, King James awarded Ramban a prize of 300 gold coins.

Ramban

Did you know that?

§ Ramban wrote his first *sefer* when he was 15 years old.

Acre, the port where Ramban first set foot in *Eretz Yisrael*

A woodcut depicting a disputation between monks and rabbis

Focus: Ramban

Though Ramban had been guaranteed safety after his debate with Pablo Christiani, his victory upset the Church authorities. He was forced to leave his Spanish homeland, where he had been born and had lived for seventy years. Though elderly, Rabbi Moshe ben Nachman undertook the dangerous and treacherous journey, over land and sea, to *Eretz Yisrael*. During his lifetime in Spain, Ramban had become one of the greatest rabbis there. Because of his superior knowledge in all branches of Torah, Talmud, Kabbalah and Jewish law, he was acknowledged as Spain's premier halachic authority. The many *sefarim* he wrote are used as basic texts today when studying Torah. After Rashi, Ramban's commentary on *Chumash* is the one most studied. He wrote novellae on the Talmud, and a number of important philosophical works and halachic essays on topics such as mourning and family purity. His glosses to Rambam's *Sefer HaMitzvos* are considered indispensable for a complete understanding of that work.

Arriving in *Eretz Yisrael*, Ramban visited Jerusalem. In a letter to his family, he describes the holy city as a small town of about 2,000 people. On the Sabbath only a *minyan* of Jews were found in the entire city! They met for prayer in a private house. Ramban acquired a building to serve as a synagogue, and Torah scrolls were brought from the town of Shechem to establish a proper place of worship.

Ramban stayed in Jerusalem for a very short time, from Elul until after Yom Kippur, but the synagogue he established was used by the Jews of Jerusalem for centuries. Its site houses a synagogue that is still in use today! Through his efforts, the Jerusalem Jewish community started to grow once again.

Ramban settled in Acre, which had a large Jewish community. It was there that he completed his commentary on *Chumash*.

EMPEROR RUDOLPH IMPRISONS THE MAHARAM

5046 1286

Rabbi Meir, the leading halachic authority of Germany, made his decision. Stories of horrifying massacres of Jews in German cities and the harsh rule of the German government provided the impetus. Moreinu HaRav Meir (literally: our teacher, Rav Meir — the Maharam) decided to leave his city, Rothenburg, and the German lands forever. In those days, Jews were not allowed to leave Germany, so plans were made for Rabbi Meir and his family to escape secretly. As they were on the road to freedom, a Jew who had converted to Christianity recognized the famous rabbi and informed his archbishop, who had the Maharam arrested. By order of the German emperor, Rabbi Meir was imprisoned in the Ensisheim Fortress.

The emperor realized that he had captured the most important rabbi in Germany. The Maharam had written over 1,500 responses to questions of Jewish law sent to him from all over Germany and other lands. He had studied under the last of the French Tosafists and had himself written the Tosafos printed in Tractate *Yoma*. His decisions on Jewish law were binding throughout Germany, and he was the author of several special prayers. He was the teacher of the greatest halachic authorities of that generation.

The emperor knew that he could extort large amounts of money from the Jews as ransom for Maharam's release. When Maharam learned of the emperor's evil plan, he sent a message from prison to the Jewish community that under no circumstances should they pay the ransom. What would prevent the emperor from imprisoning him again to get more money, or imprisoning other rabbis for ransom, he argued. If this money were paid, rabbis would live in constant fear of being imprisoned. As a result of his heroic decision, Maharam lived in prison for seven years, until his death. Despite his imprisonment, he continued to answer questions and to teach. He communicated with the outside world through his student, Rabbi Shimshon ben Tzadok, who visited him in jail.

Even after Maharam's death, the frustrated emperor would not release his body to the Jewish community without ransom. For fourteen years Maharam was not given a Jewish burial, until Alexander ben Shlomo Wimpen, a Frankfurt Jew, paid the entire ransom from his personal fortune. He requested in return that he be buried next to this great man. Both their graves were miraculously preserved when the Nazis vandalized the ancient cemetery.

Tombstone of Rabbi Meir of Rothenburg

People of the Book: More Famous Jewish Commentators 1200 - 1400

Talmud and Halachah Commentators

RASHBA

Rabbi Shlomo ibn Aderes (Rashba), a student of Ramban and Rabbi Yonah of Gerona, wrote a Talmud commentary on seventeen tractates that has become an integral part of serious Talmud study. The Rashba lived his entire life in Barcelona, Spain. In the second half of the 13th century, he became the communal leader of all Spanish Jewry. His great wisdom was recognized internationally and he received questions from Jewish communities in many different countries. Over 3,000 of these questions and answers were published. Many of the answers were quoted by later halachic codes and are very important in establishing Jewish religious practices. His *Toras HaBayis* and *Avodas HaKodesh* are fundamental to students of Jewish law. Among his prominent students was Rabbi Yom Tov ibn Asvilli (Ritva), who write novellae on the Talmud, responsa, and a defense of Rambam's *Guide to the Perplexed*.

RABBEINU YAAKOV (THE BAAL HATURIM)

When Rabbeinu Yaakov, the son of Rosh, wrote his halachic code, he classified all Jewish laws practiced since the destruction of the Temple into four sections, called "The Four *Turim*" (rows). His work is referred to as the *Tur* for short. (See Rabbi Yosef Karo, 1570, for more on the four sections.) Almost all books published on Jewish law since his time follow the four categories of the *Tur*. Rabbeinu Yaakov quotes great halachic authorities up to his day, both Ashkenazic and Sephardic, with explanation where needed, and gives the final ruling. His code, and its decisions, was the basic halachic authority for the Jews for over a century, and is still a basic reference work utilized by today's rabbis. His brief Torah commentary is famous for, among other things, its brilliant *gematrios,* calculations of the numerical values of Torah words and phrases from which lessons are derived. In addition, he wrote a longer, comprehensive *Chumash* commentary.

MEIRI

Rabbi Menachem HaMeiri of Perpignon (in southern France) wrote *Beis HaBechirah,* an extensive commentary on the entire Talmud. For many centuries his work was unavailable, essentially lost to the Jewish community. In the 20th century, the only complete manuscript copy of this commentary was discovered in the Duckl Library in Parma, Italy and it was published. Written in a straightforward style, it is a collection and summary of different interpretations of Talmud passages by many of the greatest early Talmudic authorities. Rabbi Menachem also wrote commentaries to Proverbs and Psalms; *Chibur HaTeshuvah* on repentance; and *Magen Avos,* an exposition on many of the customs of the Jews of Provence.

Torah Commentator

RABBEINU BACHYA

Weaving together four different styles of interpreting the *Chumash* — the simple meaning, Midrash, philosophy, and Kabbalah — Rabbeinu Bachya ben Asher's commentary has been a very popular work for centuries. His *Kad HaKemach* is an encyclopedia on moral and ethical topics.

THE BLACK DEATH

5108 1348

When the bubonic plague hit Europe, it spread quickly and viciously. Over the next few years it killed over one quarter of Europe's population. Tens of millions of people lay dead in cities and towns all across Europe. A terrified continent called it "the black death."

It was noticed that one group — the Jews — seemed to have fewer people dying of the plague. Looking for someone to blame for the illness and deaths, the Christians accused the Jews of causing all the horror by poisoning the wells of Europe. As a result of this false accusation, superstitious mobs in Spain, Switzerland, Bavaria, Germany, Poland, and Austria killed the Jews who lived in their cities. Whole Jewish communities were

1338 C.E.

Hundred Years War between England and France begins.

Seal of the Jewish community of Regensburg, 1356

burned alive by their gentile neighbors. In Strasbourg 2,000 Jews were set aflame in the cemetery on the Sabbath. Sometimes the Jews, facing violence and torture and the possibility of having their children kidnaped and raised as Christians, chose to die by their own hands, and set their communities ablaze in a holy fire. Six thousand Jews in Mainz, Germany perished this way. In a period of three years, a total of 300 Jewish communities were destroyed and tens of thousands of Jews were murdered. In Strasbourg the City Council came to the defense of the Jews. Then the citizens of Strasbourg replaced the council with new members, who authorized the murder of all the Jews of the city.

Although Pope Clement VI declared the Jews innocent of causing the plague, his proclamation was largely ignored. Even though the Jews drank from the same "poi-

The attack against the Jews of Strasbourg in 1348

The interior of the Strasbourg Synagogue

soned" wells as their Christian neighbors, the superstitious mobs believed that the Jews were protected from the poison because of incantations they mumbled over the water before they drank it. This incantation was the *berachah* (blessing) a Jew recited before drinking.

Actually, it was true that the Jews were less affected by the plague than their gentile neighbors. This was because the medieval towns were filthy. People threw garbage into the streets and rarely washed themselves — a perfect environment for the spread of disease. However, the Torah life of the Jews demanded cleanliness. Thus, Jews washed their hands upon awakening and before eating, and they bathed before the Sabbaths and Festivals. In addition, Jewish dead were accorded immediate burial. These practices helped protect the Jews from the disease.

5155
1395

THE JEWS LEAVE FRANCE

On September 17, 1394 Charles VI of France ordered the expulsion of the Jews from the kingdom, and they were forced to leave between January and March of 1395.

This was not the first time Jews were prohibited residence in France. In 1291, Jews fleeing expulsion from other countries were denied entry by Philip the Fair. In 1311, he ordered the "permanent expulsion" of the Jews of France. However, this order was rescinded by his son, Louis X, in 1315.

The Jews were once again expelled from France in 1322, but were "readmitted" by Charles V — without his formally reversing the expulsion decree — in 1359.

While the order of 1394 was not new, it succeeded in ultimately forcing the Jews from most of France.

5202
1442

CONTACT WITH JEWS IS RESTRICTED

For the better part of his reign, Pope Eugenius VI had been favorable to the Jews. His personal physician was a Jew. In 1434, he guaranteed the Jews of Germany the right to freely practice their religion and ordered that they be protected against forced conversion.

However, in 1442, perhaps in an effort to show his loyalty to Christian ideals, he issued an edict that severely curtailed the rights of the Jews — first in Leon and Castile, and later throughout Italy.

The Papal bull prohibited Christians from hiring Jews as maids or servants, and it forbade Jews from constructing new synagogues, lending money on interest, serving in public office, working on Sundays and Christian holidays, and from testifying in court against Christians. In Italy, the Jews were also prohibited from studying any religious works other than the five Books of the Torah.

Rather than submit to these unbearable limitations, many Jews fled the areas under Papal control.

Over the course of the next year, the Jews made many efforts to have the order overturned. Indeed, in December 1443 the measures were retracted.

THE PRINTING OF THE FIRST JEWISH BOOK

5235 1475

Before printing was invented, all books were copied by hand. Today, it takes a *sofer,* a scribe, approximately one year to finish writing a *Sefer Torah*. Imagine how long it would take to copy the entire Talmud! Handwritten manuscripts were very expensive and most books were found only in the libraries of rich individuals or the city synagogue. Printing made more books available to more people, because many books could be produced in much less time and for much less money.

The first printed *sefer* was Rashi's *Chumash* commentary, produced on a printing press in Italy.

The Reggio di Calabria edition of Rashi, printed in 1475; this was the first dated printed Torah work

First page of the Soncino Bible,
printed around 1492 in Naples

First page of the Book of Joshua, printed in 1488

SPAIN ESTABLISHES THE INQUISITION

5241 1481

For almost a century before 1481, many Jews in Spain had been forced to convert to Christianity. Though these Jews went to church and acted like Christians, at home many of them continued doing the *mitzvos*, lighting candles in closets and praying secretly in basements. These people were called Marranos by their suspicious gentile neighbors. Marrano is a pejorative word; it means "pig." The Church established the Inquisition to find Jewish converts to Christianity who were still practicing their Judaism. Through torture, imprisonment, and terror they hunted down these innocent people. Altogether, the Inquisition was responsible for the burning to death of 32,000 Jews. The Inquisition's jurisdiction over Jews who had resisted and not converted was to begin in 1492.

The home of Samuel Abulafia in Toledo, dating to the 14th century. It was styled like a fortress, with few windows.

An Inquisition trial. Witnesses against the accused wore masks to protect their identity.

The seal of the Inquisition, Seville, 1800

The auto-da-fé at Lisbon

Did you know that?

- Converts to Christianity — even those who were forced converts — who were found guilty of practicing Judaism were burned alive at a grand public ceremony called the *auto-da-fé.*

- The Spanish Inquisition was officially abolished by Queen Mother Maria Christina of Spain in 1834. A schoolteacher burnt to death in 1826 was the Inquisition's last victim.

Corozas (the hats) and *sanbenitos* (the aprons), worn by those condemned by the Inquisition as they went to *the auto-da-fé*

THE TALMUD IS PRINTED

5243 1483

Joshua Solomon Soncino, who also printed the first Hebrew *Siddur* and *Tanach*, began printing the Talmud in Italy. The first volume, Tractate *Berachos*, was printed in 1483.

RABBI OVADIAH BERTINORO SETTLES IN JERUSALEM

5248 1488

Born in Italy, Rabbi Ovadiah, who eventually became the Rabbi of an Italian city called Bertinoro, left Italy in 1486 for *Eretz Yisrael*. Traveling at that time was a dangerous affair, requiring a voyage on the high seas — where pirates were a constant threat — and long journeys on camel caravans through the desert. After a very difficult and arduous two-year journey which took him through Italy, Sicily, Rhodes, Greece and Egypt, Rabbi Ovadiah arrived in *Eretz Yisrael*. He made his way to Jerusalem, where he was appointed Chief Rabbi of *Eretz Yisrael*. There he completed his famous commentary on the Mishnah, which came to be known as "Rav" — an acronym of Rabbeinu Bertinoro. In straightforward language, he explains the *mishnayos*. This commentary has appeared in almost every standard edition of the Mishnah since the commentary was written.

5252 1492

THE JEWS ARE EXPELLED FROM SPAIN

The burning of Jews in Nuremberg, Germany, 1493. Spain was not the only country to persecute the Jews.

By the order of Spain's King Ferdinand and Queen Isabella — the same pair who sent Columbus on his journey to discover America — hundreds of thousands of Jews were ordered to convert to Christianity or leave their homes by the 9th of Av. Hundreds of communities that had existed in Spain for over 500 years ceased to exist when the Jews left Spain to become refugees overnight.

Interior of the El Transito Synagogue at Toledo, Spain

A group of Marrano families in Portugal early in the 20th century

Focus: The life of Rabbi Don Issac Abarbanel

A descendant of King David, Rabbi Don Issac Abarbanel was the leader of Spanish Jewry at the time of the Expulsion from Spain. He wrote classic commentaries on Scripture, the Passover Haggadah, Tractate *Avos*, as well as philosophical works. Among his writings were many defenses of Judaism against Christian scholars. Some of his works deal with the ultimate coming of the Messiah, encouraging his fellow Jews not to lose hope in the face of persecution.

He was recognized as an international diplomat and financial genius, and he negotiated treaties between European powers. In 1490, the year that the cruel and dreaded priest Torquemada became head of the Inquisition, Abarbanel was appointed the royal treasurer, helping to finance Ferdinand and Isabella's war against the Moslems. Though he offered the king and queen a bribe of 30,000 golden ducats to abolish the decree, he was unsuccessful in preventing the Expulsion. The king and queen offered to exclude him and allow him to stay, but he turned them down and left Spain with his Jewish brethren.

Arriving in Italy, he worked for the king of Naples, but when Naples was conquered by Charles of France in 1495, he was forced once again to flee, eventually settling in Venice.

Interior glimpse of the synagogue at Cordoba, which has been converted to a church

5252 1492

COLUMBUS DISCOVERS THE NEW WORLD

Did you know that?

- On his famous expedition that brought him to the New World, Columbus used navigation tables and navigation instruments created by Rabbi Abraham Zacuta.

- On his voyage, Columbus took a Jewish interpreter who was the first white man to set foot in the New World. His name was Luis de Torres. Torres was also the first person to introduce tobacco to Europe.

- Columbus set sail hours after the edict expelling the Jews from Spain took effect. It was the 9th of Av, the anniversary of the destruction of the Temple in Jerusalem. He landed in the New World on Hoshana Rabbah.

Christopher Columbus, believed by many to have been himself a Marrano (secret Jew), discovered the New World, which came to be called America. As this new continent opened up to settlement, many Jewish Marranos fled there to escape the long arm of the Inquisition and practice their Judaism openly. Over the centuries the New World continued to be a haven for Jewish refugees fleeing persecution. Millions of Jews from Europe, Arab lands, and, most recently, from the Soviet Union and Iran, arrived in America, to rebuild their lives in freedom.

Rabbi Yosef Karo, who wrote the *Shulchan Aruch,* was 4 years old when Columbus discovered America. For more on Rabbi Yosef Karo see 5330 / 1570.

A depiction of Columbus landing in the New World

Abraham ben Samuel Zacuta

JEWS EXPELLED FROM PORTUGAL

5257 1497

Many of the refugees from the Spanish Expulsion found safe haven in neighboring Portugal. The respite was short-lived, however, because in December of 1496 the king of Portugal ordered the Jews in his country to convert to Christianity or leave within ten months. During Pesach 1497, the Portuguese forcibly baptized Jewish children and raised them as Christians. When the Jews fled the country, they were unable to take their children with them.

THE *EIN YAAKOV* IS PUBLISHED

5275 1515

Rabbi Yaakov ibn Chaviv extracted many of the stories and ethical passages of the Talmud, known as *Aggadata,* and collected them in *Ein Yaakov,* first published in Salonica, Greece. It became very popular throughout the world. The work was actually completed by Rabbi Yaakov's son, Rabbi Levi ibn Chaviv.

THE OTTOMAN TURKS CONQUER *ERETZ YISRAEL*

5276 1516

The Ottoman Turks ruled *Eretz Yisrael* for the next four centuries, until the British defeated them in 1918.

An illuminated *Megillah* from the 16th century

5284 1524

PURIM CAIRO

The Jews of Cairo were ordered to pay a huge sum of money to their ruler, Ahmed Pasha, by 28 Adar. Failure to pay would be punished by a massacre of the Jewish community. On the day the money was due, Ahmed Pasha was assassinated by one of his officers, and the decree was annulled. To mark the salvation of the Jewish community, the Cairo Jews celebrated every year on the 28th of Adar, and the day became known as Purim Cairo.

ATTEMPT TO REINSTATE *SEMICHAH* AND SANHEDRIN

5298 1538

From the time the Jews received the Torah, the High Court, later known as the Sanhedrin, was the ultimate authority interpreting Jewish law. Among other responsibilities, it decided questions of halachah that were in doubt and established the Jewish calendar.

Each member of the Sanhedrin had received *semichah*, "ordination," by someone who had himself received *semichah* in an unbroken chain from Joshua, who was ordained by Moses. By the 1500's the chain had long been broken, and no one had been ordained for centuries.

Rambam rules that the sages living in *Eretz Yisrael* may renew the *semichah* by agreeing to bestow *semichah* on a specific person. Relying on this opinion, Rabbi Yaakov Beirav, hoping to reestablish the Sanhedrin, gathered the sages of Safed, and they bestowed *semichah* on him. He, in turn, ordained several people, including Rabbi Yosef Karo. The legitimacy of the *semichah* was contested by the great Jewish scholars of Jerusalem led by Rabbi Levi ibn Chaviv, and the *semichah* initiated by Rabbi Yaakov Beirav eventually ceased.

1540 C.E.

Nicholas Copernicus publishes his theory that the sun is the center of the solar system.

When Copernicus publicized his theory the Maharal of Prague was 28 years old. For more on the Maharal see 5369 / 1609.

Focus: The life of Rabbi Joseph Joselman Loanz of Rosheim

Throughout history, there have been influential Jews who used their good offices to assist their brethren. They are known as *shtadlanim*. A *shtadlan* uses influence and connections to intercede with government authorities to prevent hostile actions and legislation against the Jewish community, sometimes at great personal risk and sacrifice. Rabbi Joseph Joselman Loanz of Rosheim was one of the most famous *shtadlanim* in Jewish history. Among his many accomplishments: He saved German Jewish communities from being destroyed during the Peasant Wars (1524-26), by bribing the battling peasants. He delayed the expulsion of Jews from Saxony, and was a victor in a debate held before German Protestant princes in Frankfurt. In 1544, he obtained from Charles V a guarantee against charges of ritual murder. In 1546, he obtained a promise from Charles V that his soldiers would face the death penalty for molesting Jews.

A document signed by Rabbi Joseph Joselman of Rosheim

Focus: The life of Donna Gracia Nasi

Known as the Grand Widow of Constantinople, Gracia used her power and prestige to help Marranos escape the Inquisition, and financed their building new lives as Jews in different countries. Gracia's early years were full of adventure. She was born in Portugal under the Christian name Beatrice de Luna. In a harrowing journey, pursued by the Portuguese Inquisition, she escaped their deadly clutches and arrived in Antwerp. Eventually she fled to Venice, where her sister denounced her to the Venetian authorities, and she was imprisoned. Through the efforts of her influential nephew, Don Joseph Nasi — a Marrano who had escaped Spain, and had become a powerful figure in the Turkish Empire — she was released. Donna Gracia joined her nephew in Constantinople and spent the rest of her life doing many deeds of *tzedakah*, supporting yeshivos, founding schools, and ransoming Jews captured by pirates. She also helped support many Torah scholars, and established a Hebrew printing press in Belvedere, near Constantinople.

5302 1542

THE PRESENT-DAY WALLS OF JERUSALEM ARE BUILT BY SULTAN SULEIMAN

Legend has it that the Sultan's father appeared to him in a dream, threatening dire consequences if he did not build a wall around Jerusalem. The Turkish ruler heeded his departed father's message, and shortly thereafter completed rebuilding and reinforcing the walls around Jerusalem. His majestic walls still surround the Old City, rising, in some places, as high as a three-story building. The walls were built with eight entrance gates. The most unique of these gates is *Shaar Rachamim*, the "Gate of Mercy," which was sealed shut by the Arabs, because tradition says that Elijah the Prophet will pass through this gate to herald the coming of the Messiah. When that time comes, may it be soon, the gate will surely open to accommodate Elijah's mission.

The walls of Jerusalem

The walls of Jerusalem

Focus: The sages of Safed

Safed is a picturesque town with narrow alleyways and stone-paved steets, situated on a hilltop in the Galil. In the early 1500's a concentration of great sages lived and learned there. Here are a few of the most famous:

Rabbi Yitzchak Luria Ashkenazi (Arizal): Rabbi Yitzchak was born in Jerusalem in 1534. His father died when Yitzchak was young and his mother took him to live with his wealthy uncle in Cairo. Recognizing Yitzchak's outstanding abilities, his uncle provided for his livelihood so that he could devote himself to his studies. After marrying his first cousin, his uncle's daughter, Rabbi Yitzchak began an intensive program, spending the entire week in solitude, immersed in prayer and study, and returning home only on the Sabbath. He was among the Torah giants of his day, but he is best known for his mastery of the Kabbalah, the Torah's mystical teachings.

At the age of 36 the Arizal moved to the city of Safed, where he lived for only eighteen months, until his passing at the age of 38 in 1572. His most devoted pupil, Rabbi Chaim Vital, recorded his vast teachings, which became the basis for all future study by *mekubalim* (scholars of Kabbalah). The synagogue in which the Ari prayed and studied, as well as the fresh spring-water *mikveh* he

used, still stand and are visited by thousands of people each year.

Rabbi Moshe Alshich: Rabbi Moshe was one of the select few who received the *semichah* that had been revived in Safed by Rabbi Yaakov Beirav (it was conferred upon him by Rabbi Yosef Karo), and he was appointed as *dayan* of the *beis din* of Safed. On the Sabbath, Rabbi Moshe would deliver riveting lectures on the Torah, replete with brilliant insights and ethical teachings. These lectures evolved into the *sefer Toras Moshe*, or, as it is more commonly known, *Alshich*.

Rabbi Shlomo Alkabetz: Late Friday afternoon the Arizal and his disciples would dress in pure white Sabbath clothes. They would leave the synagogue and assemble outside to greet the "Sabbath Queen." They were led in song by Rabbi Shlomo Alkabetz and together with him would sing the *Lecha Dodi* prayer he had composed. *Lecha Dodi* was adopted by Ashkenazic Jews as the central prayer in the service which ushers in the Sabbath. At the last stanza, the congregation turns around to the synagogue entrance to symbolically welcome the incoming Sabbath. Rabbi Alkabetz was a great Kabbalist and author. He wrote *Menos HaLevi*, a commentary on the Book of Esther, as a Purim gift for his future father-in-law.

Outskirts of the mountain city of Safed

Tomb of the great Kabbalist
Rabbi Yitzchak Luria, know as the
Ari HaKadosh, or *Arizal,* in the
ancient cemetery of Safed

Tomb of Rabbi Shlomo
Alkabetz, author of *Lecha
Dodi,* in the ancient
cemetery of Safed

1551 C.E.
Suleiman the
Magnificent conquers
Persia.

5325 1565 THE *SHULCHAN ARUCH* PUBLISHED

What are a Jew's obligations on the Sabbath? What are the laws governing marriage? All the thousand and one questions a Jew asks about how to perform the *mitzvos* are answered in the *Shulchan Aruch,* written by Rabbi Yosef Karo in Safed. Rabbi Yosef organized Jewish law by subject, and broke it down into chapters and numbered paragraphs, to make the study of Jewish law accessible to everyone. The name *Shulchan Aruch* means "Set Table": everything is ready for consumption. The influence of the *Shulchan Aruch* continues to be as strong today as it was when it was first published.

Rabbi Yosef Karo was born in Spain and, at the age of 4, fled with his family to Constantinople, Turkey. Over the centuries, the Sephardic Jewish community, which originated in Spain, and the Ashkenazic Jewish community, which originated in France and Germany, had developed differences in Jewish custom. One of the best known differences in custom is that Sephardic Jews eat rice and legumes on Passover, while Askenazic Jews are prohibited by custom from doing so.

Not long after the publication of the *Shulchan Aruch*, Rabbi Moshe Isserles of Poland, known as the Rema, added to the *Shulchan Aruch* additional notes that are called "The *Mapah — The Tablecloth*." The Rema was an Ashkenazi, and he added his comments to clarify those instances when the *Shulchan Aruch* differed from the Ashkenazic custom. The *Shulchan Aruch* and the *Mapah,* printed together, became — after the Torah and the Talmud — the book that has had the most powerful impact on the Jews throughout our long history.

The *Shulchan Aruch* is divided into four units:

Orach Chaim: Daily laws, the Sabbath and Festivals

Even HaEzer: Laws of marriage and divorce, etc.

Choshen Mishpat: Civil law

Yoreh Deah: Jewish dietary laws, the laws of family purity, usury, charity, Torah study, visiting the sick, death and mourning, and other laws

A page of the standard *Shulchan Aruch:*

(1) Text of the *Shulchan Aruch*

(2) Rema's notes

(3) *Taz,* the commentary by Rabbi David HaLevi (see Halachah Commentators, p. 89)

(4) *Magen Avraham*, the commentary by Rabbi Abraham Gombiner (see Halachah Commentators, p. 90)

All questions of modern living can be answered by studying and applying the appropriate passages in the *Shulchan Aruch.* The halachah as recorded in the *Shulchan Aruch* and its commentators is the authoritative code of Jewish life, regulating all of Jewish experience. Rabbinic ordination is conferred on students upon achieving mastery of major parts of the *Shulchan Aruch* and its commentaries.

Focus: The life of Rabbi Yosef Karo

Rabbi Yosef Karo was born in Spain in 1488, and he lived there until he was expelled, with the entire Jewish community, on the fateful 9th of Av, 1492. First seeking refuge in Portugal, the family was soon forced to flee once again. Yosef spent his early childhood growing up as a refugee in Constantinople. Despite his difficult beginnings, Rabbi Yosef developed his abilities to the point where his writings had monumental impact on the Jewish people.

He began writing the *Beis Yosef*, a comprehensive commentary on the *Tur* (see More Famous Torah Commentators 1200-1400), at the age of 35, diligently working, perfecting it, and completing it after thirty-two years. At the age of 48 Rabbi Karo left Turkey to settle in Safed. There he was granted the newly reinstated *semichah* ordination by his teacher and mentor, Rabbi Beirav. A master scholar, halachic authority and Kabbalist, Rabbi Yosef was chosen to succeed Rabbi Beirav in the prestigious position of *Av Beis Din* — Chief Judge of Safed — after Rabbi Beirav's passing. Rabbi Yosef Karo also wrote *Kesef Mishneh*, a commentary on Rambam's *Mishneh Torah; Maggid Meisharim;* and responsa (written responses to halachic inquiries). The *Shulchan Aruch*, Rabbi Karo's most renowned work, was published when he was 76. He passed away in 1575 at the age of 87.

Tomb of Rabbi Yosef Karo, author of the *Shulchan Aruch,* in the ancient cemetery of Safed

The Rema Synagogue in Cracow

The Rema

Focus: The life of Rabbi Moshe Isserles (the Rema)

For centuries after his death in 1572, the Rema's grave was a pilgrimage site for the Jews of Poland. On Lag B'Omer, his *yahrtzeit*, crowds would gather there. On his tombstone is inscribed the epitaph: From Moses to Moses there was no one like Moses. He achieved worldwide recognition through his comments on Rabbi Yosef Karo's *Shulchan Aruch*, and they established him as the accepted halachic authority for all of Ashkenazic Jewry. He also wrote other halachic and philosophical works, as well as responsa.

As a young man the Rema's Torah genius was recognized and he was appointed to the Cracow Rabbinical Court, a position usually reserved for much older men. He corresponded on halachic issues with the greatest sages of his age.

In the Rema's synagogue in Cracow, which was built in his lifetime, there was a *Sefer Torah* that was written in the Rema's own hand and read only on special occasions. Jewish tourists in Europe today make both the Rema's synagogue and his tomb in Cracow important stops on their tours.

VAAD ARBA ARATZOS — THE COUNCIL OF THE FOUR LANDS

5340
1580

For almost 200 years the Jews in Poland were governed by the Council of the Four Lands. This Jewish Parliament, as the Poles called it, was recognized by the Polish government as the body through which the Jews were governed. The Council collected taxes, established schools, and made regulations. Disputes between Jews were settled by the courts, which applied Jewish law to all its cases.

5350 1590

A scene from "The Merchant of Venice"

THE MERCHANT OF VENICE

William Shakespeare's play, "The Merchant of Venice," portrays Shylock as a ruthless Jewish merchant who wants to remove a "pound of flesh" from a gentile who was unable to repay his debts. Oddly enough, at the time this anti-Semitic play was written, there were no Jews living in England, and Shakespeare most probably never met a Jew in his life!

5356 1596

PRAYERS IN THE AMBASSADOR'S HOME

The Moroccan emperor's ambassador to Holland was a Jew by the name of Don Samuel Polack. The first public Jewish worship in the city of Amsterdam took place in his home.

MAHARAL PASSES AWAY

5369
1609

Rabbi Yehudah Loewe ben Betzalel, known as Maharal (an acronym of Moreinu HaRav Loewe) was born in 1526. He had been Chief Rabbi of Moravia, and was installed as Chief Rabbi of Prague in 1598. His intelligence and knowledge earned him the friendship and admiration of Emperor Rudolf II of Austria. He authored dozens of works, including a supercommentary on Rashi's Torah commentary, a treatment of the Aggadic portions of the Talmud, and many ethical and philosophical works. Using a blend of philosophy and Kabbalah, he explains many of the ethical teachings and stories found in the Talmud and expounds their deeper meanings. He is among the most influential thinkers in Jewish history, and has impacted virtually every stream of Jewish thought. Maharal advocated a system of education where students would first master all of Scripture, then all of Mishnah, and only then begin the study of Talmud. He also instituted the *Chevra Mishnayos* — groups of adults who study the Mishnah. This idea, which originated in Prague, spread throughout Europe.

Statue of Yehudah Loewe ben Bezalel, Maharal of Prague

Focus: The *Golem* of Prague

One of the most fascinating legends in Jewish history concerns the Maharal and his creation, the *Golem*. According to this legend, the Maharal gathered a select few men under a star-studded sky. After much personal preparation, studying holy works and repeatedly immersing in a *mikveh*, they were ready to harness powerful spiritual forces. The Maharal shaped earth into the form of a man and, using Kabbalistic secrets, transformed the mound of earth into a living being, a large, strong man lacking the power of speech — a *Golem*! The Maharal named the *Golem* he created Yosef. The *Golem*'s mission was to pro-

tect the Jews from all attempts by anti-Semites to discredit or destroy them through secret plots, blood libels, or attacks. According to the legend, over the course of many years the Maharal and his secret weapon, the *Golem*, prevented many catastrophes from befalling Jewish communities. When the Maharal decided that there was no further need for the *Golem* he ordered it to accompany him to the attic of the large Prague synagogue called the Altneuschul, where he transformed it back into lifelessness. The Maharal descended from the attic, which was then sealed permanently.

Did you know that?

§➤ One of the few large synagogues not destroyed during the Holocaust was the Maharal's Altneuschul. The Nazis' repeated attempts to destroy it mysteriously failed.

§➤ At the entrance of Prague's city hall stands a monument erected to Maharal.

Exterior view of Altneuschul in Prague

Did you know that?

🔊 The name Altneuschul means "Old
New Synagogue." The reason for
this strange name is that it was once
the "new" synagogue of Prague.
Later on, another synagogue was
built, so that the building that used
to be the *newest* synagogue was
now the *old new* synagogue.

🔊 Another reason for the unique name
is that it comes from the Hebrew
words *al t'nai*, "on condition." This is
based on a tradition that stones
from Jerusalem were used in its
construction, "on the condition" that
when Mashiach comes, the stones
will be returned to the Holy City.

Interior view of Altneuschul in Prague

An alley in the Jewish section of old Prague, known as the Shames-Gasschen

5376
1616

EXECUTION OF THE "FRANKFURT HAMAN"

In 1614, Vincent Fettmilch led a wild group of townspeople in an attack against the Jewish ghetto of Frankfurt. At the time of the attack, the Jews were praying in the synagogue. Fettmilch's pogrom — which was conducted against the wishes of the emperor — wiped out most of the Jewish population, destroyed the synagogue, and devastated the ghetto. Over 1,000 survivors were led to the cemetery, and from there ordered to leave the city and never return. Everything the Jews owned had to be left behind. Ultimately the emperor had Fettmilch arrested and executed, with his head hung publicly on a spike. His home was destroyed by the authorities and his family exiled from Frankfurt.

The Jews were finally allowed to return to their homes on the 19th of Adar, 1616. To celebrate, the Jews instituted the 20th of Adar as a special local Purim.

1616 C.E.

Outbreak of Thirty Years' War in Europe.

1620 C.E.

Pilgrims arrive at Plymouth Rock. They came to the New World seeking religious freedom.

Expulsion of the Jews from the ghetto in Frankfurt, in the 1600's

THE SH'LAH ARRIVES IN *ERETZ YISRAEL*

5381
1621

Despite his success, fame and secure position, the 60-year-old Rabbi Yeshaya Horowitz, Chief Rabbi of Prague, decided to undertake the dangerous and difficult journey to *Eretz Yisrael*. In the 17th century, when one left Europe to move to *Eretz Yisrael*, it meant that he would have almost no contact with the family left behind. To provide guidance for his sons and grandchildren, who were remaining in Europe, Rabbi Horowitz wrote a book that eventually served as a guide not only for his children but for the entire family of the Jewish people: *Shnei Luchos HaBris*. This work includes ethical teachings, many based on Kabbalah, halachic decisions, and guidelines for the observance of various customs. The author became known as the Sh'lah, the acronym of his famous work!

The Sh'lah traveled to Israel by way of Italy. As he crossed the Mediterranean, his ship was nearly captured by pirates. He then traveled overland by caravan to the cities of Aleppo and Damascus. Finally, after a year of travel, he arrived in Jerusalem, where he became Chief Rabbi of the Ashkenazic community.

MANHATTAN BOUGHT FROM THE NATIVE AMERICANS

5386 1626

Did you know that?

- When the Native Americans were first discovered, some scholars thought that they were the lost ten tribes of Israel.

- In the 20th century, New York City had a few Jewish mayors. Under Mayor Abe Beame, Gracie Mansion, the mayoral residence, even had a *mezuzah*.

> The great Talmudic commentator, Maharsha, was 71 years old when Manhattan was bought from the Indians. For more on Maharsha see Famous Jewish Commentators 1500 - 1600.

Peter Minuit bought the island of Manhattan from the Brooklyn tribe of Native Americans for about $24 worth of cloth and trinkets. For millions of Jewish immigrants fleeing the persecution and terror of Europe centuries later, the island of Manhattan was their first stop and new home in the New World, and it became one of the major population centers for Jewry. New York City — of which Manhattan is part — is the city with the largest Jewish population in the world. The island Peter Minuit bought has become the home of hundreds of synagogues and Jewish schools.

5402 1642

Rabbi Yitzchak Aboab

Did you know that?

🎵 The Jewish military unit in Recife was exempt from duty on the Sabbath.

1632 C.E.

Construction of the Taj Mahal, one of the world's most beautiful buildings, is begun in India. It took twenty-two years to complete.

RABBI YITZCHAK ABOAB DA FONSECA APPOINTED FIRST RABBI IN THE NEW WORLD

Fleeing the Inquisition, some Marranos chose to immigrate to the New World, especially to Brazil. Originally a Portuguese colony, Brazil had been conquered by the Dutch, and under Dutch rule the Marranos were able to openly practice their Judaism. Many Jews were attracted to this haven of religious freedom. The major Jewish community was in the town of Recife, which was known as the "port of the Jews." The Jews exported the newfound wealth of the New World — tobacco, reptile skins, cotton and sugar. The Amsterdam Jewish community sent Rabbi Yitzchak Aboab to act as the Rabbi of Recife. He arrived with an additional 600 Jewish pioneers to strengthen the Recife Jewish community. When the Portuguese reconquered Brazil, the Inquisition was reinstated. The practice of Judaism was outlawed and Rabbi Aboab returned to Amsterdam.

People of the Book:
Famous Jewish Commentators 1500 - 1600

Talmud Commentators

MAHARSHAL

Rabbi Shlomo Luria (Maharshal), a descendant of Rashi, founded and led the yeshivah in Lublin. His commentary on the Talmud, *Chochmas Shlomo*, is printed at the back of standard editions of the Talmud, appearing beneath the commentary of Maharsha and alongside that of Maharam. Using manuscripts and early editions, Maharshal took great pains to accurately establish the text of the Talmud, Rashi and Tosafos. He also wrote the *Yam Shel Shlomo*, in which he analyzes earlier authorities' understanding of Talmudic passages and reaches halachic conclusions. Though Maharshal wrote *Yam Shel Shlomo* on sixteen Talmudic tractates, only seven of these are extant.

MAHARAM

Rabbi Meir ben Rabbi Gedaliah (Maharam) of Lublin named his Talmudic commentary *Meir Einei Chachamim* — "Enlightening the Eyes of the Wise." It is printed in the back of the standard editions of the Talmud, alongside that of Maharshal. This commentary gives clear explanations of many passages of the Talmud and Tosafos. Maharam also wrote halachic responsa that are frequently cited by later authorities. There is a tradition that Maharshal had blessed Maharam's father Rabbi Gershom that the latter's wife would give birth to a son who would light up the Jewish Diaspora with his wisdom. By the time he was 30, Maharam was both Rabbi and *Rosh Yeshivah* of the large Jewish community of Cracow. Among his most prominent disciples was R' Yeshaya Horowitz, the Sh'lah.

MAHARSHA

Rabbi Shmuel Eliezer Eidels' commentary on the Talmud is printed in the back of standard editions of the Talmud above those of Maharam and Maharshal. His commentary is divided into two parts: *Chidushei Halachos*, which focuses primarily on Tosafos, and *Chidushei Aggados,* which provides profound explanations of the stories and ethical teachings of the Talmud. He is known as "Eidels" in tribute to

Did you know that?

🐍 Rabbi Yom Tov Lipman Heller undertook to make sure that the taxes imposed on his community were collected fairly, and that the wealthy citizens paid a greater share. A number of wealthy people were infuriated, and slandered him to Emperor Ferdinand II, claiming that he was fomenting a revolution. On 5 Tammuz 1629 he was tried before a court of Christian clergymen and condemned to death. After much intervention, his sentence was changed to forty days imprisonment and a heavy fine. He returned home on *Erev Yom Kippur*. He wrote the story of his imprisonment in *"Megillas Eivah - The Scroll of Enmity."* He instructed his descendants to read *Megillas Eivah* each year, on the 1st of Adar, the day he was elected to the Rabbinate of Cracow fourteen years after his release.

his mother-in-law, Eidel, who supported his yeshivah in Posen for twenty years.

Mishnah Commentator

TOSAFOS YOM TOV

Rabbi Yom Tov Lipman Heller was a student of the Maharal. As a young man, he was appointed to the prestigious position of judge of the Rabbinical Court in Prague. He then served as Rabbi of various cities, gaining a reputation as a fighter for justice who refused to show special favor to the wealthy and influential community leadership. In 1644, Rabbi Yom Tov was appointed Chief Rabbi of Prague, where he implemented a policy of demanding that the rich pay a higher proportion of the government taxes imposed upon the Jewish community than the poor. His commentary on the Mishnah, *Tosafos Yom Tov*, provides an in-depth analysis of the Mishnah. He also wrote many other works.

5408
1648

THE MASSACRES OF "TACH VETAT" [ת״ח ות״ט]

"Tach VeTat" stands for the catastrophic Jewish years 5408-5409. During these years the violent Cossack Bogdan Chmielnicki led a barbaric Cossack peasant army against the Jews and Poles. They burnt people alive, killed children in their mother's laps, cut limbs off people and left them to die a slow death. It was said that during the Cossack slaughter the rivers of Nemirov turned red with Jewish blood. There was no end to the many sadistic types of death to which they subjected their unfortunate victims, especially Jews. The Jews in Poland and Ukraine sought refuge in the Polish towns. At Tulchin the Poles handed over Jews as ransom for their own safety. In Nemirov the city was able to withstand Chmielnicki's attack. Chmielnicki retreated and attacked again after first disguising his men as a Polish army unit. The city's residents, seeing the advancing Polish soldiers, cheered and unlocked their gates. Chmielnicki entered the city and slaughtered 6,000 Jews and set the synagogue ablaze. The *Sifrei Torah* were cut up and turned into boots for his men. During these terrible years over 100,000 Jewish people perished and hundreds of Jewish communities were obliterated. To commemorate those terrible times, the rabbis chose the day of the slaughter at Nemirov, the 20th of Sivan, to be a fast day for Polish Jewry.

Did you know that?

- In Kiev, capital of Ukraine, a monument stands to honor the great hero of Ukrainian history, Bogdan Chmielnicki.

- "Mordechai Purim" was celebrated by the Jews of Mezibozh on the 12th of Teves. On that day a man by the name of Mordechai and his wife Esther saved the town from being attacked by Chmielnicki.

FIRST JEWS ARRIVE IN NEW AMSTERDAM

5414 1654

When the Portuguese took control of the Dutch colony in Brazil, they outlawed the practice of Judaism. Five thousand Jewish refugees left Brazil on sixteen vessels, one of which, the St. Charles, carrying twenty-three Jewish passengers, set sail for North America.

When they arrived in the Dutch colony of New Amsterdam, on the island of Manhattan, these first Jews were not made to feel welcome. In fact, the Dutch colonial governor of New Amsterdam, Peter Stuyvesant, made clear his distaste for these new immigrants. In his correspondence to the Dutch West India Company, he requested that "this deceitful race … not infect the new colony."

His employers, the Dutch West India Company, having shareholders who were Jewish, ordered him to allow the Jews to settle and to grant them civil and religious freedom. Despite Stuyvesant's anti-Semitic objections, the Jewish community flourished and grew.

> When the Jews first came to New York, Rabbi David Segal, known as the *Taz* (an acronym of *Turei Zahav,* the name of his commentary on the *Shulchan Aruch*) was 62 years old. For more on the *Taz* see Famous Commentaries of the 1600's - 1700's.

5416 1656

JEWS ALLOWED BACK TO ENGLAND

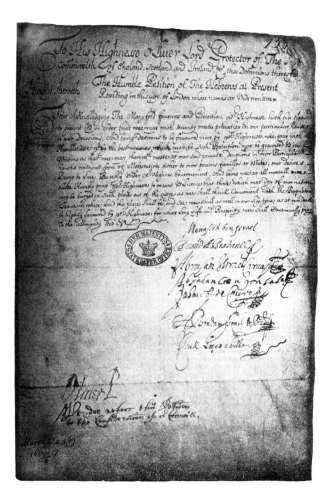

A petition from the Jews of England to Oliver Cromwell

The Jews were expelled from England by Edward I in the year 1290. Over 16,500 left the country, and for over three centuries there was no Jewish community there.

In 1655 Menasseh ben Israel, a Dutch Jewish rabbi and writer, convinced Oliver Cromwell, the Lord Protector of England, to allow the Jews to return. (Jews were not given the right to be naturalized English citizens until 1753.) Menasseh believed that the ultimate redemption of the Jewish people could not come about until the fulfillment of the prophecies of the Books of Deuteronomy and Daniel — that the Jews would be exiled to the ends of the earth.

By negotiating with the English to open their country to Jewish settlement, he felt he would be spreading the Diaspora further and hastening the coming of the Messiah. He also hoped to provide a new land to which the refugees from the Chmielnicki massacres could immigrate.

Menasseh convinced Cromwell that it was important to the Christian religion, as well, that Jews be allowed to live in England.

With permission granted for Jewish settlement, twenty Marrano families openly declared their Judaism and, with a *Sefer Torah* sent from Amsterdam, opened a synagogue on Creechurch Lane in London. Over the coming centuries the Jews of England became a major Diaspora Jewish community.

Centuries later, in 1917, the Balfour Declaration, in which Great Britain agreed to help establish a Jewish

Did you know that?

❧ The famous artist Rembrandt painted a portrait of Menasseh ben Israel as well as many other scenes of daily Jewish life.

homeland in Palestine — and which led to the founding of the State of Israel — was a direct result of the influence of England's Jewish community.

Focus: Menasseh ben Israel

Born a Marrano in Portugal and given the name Manoel Dias Soerio, Menasseh and his family escaped the Inquisition and moved to Amsterdam, where they returned to publicly practicing Judaism. Amsterdam had become a safe haven for many Jews seeking freedom to practice Judaism openly. Its liberal laws allowed its Jewish inhabitants to freely engage in commerce, and many of the Jews there amassed wealth and power. In a short time the influence of the Jews turned Holland into a world

power. Menasseh grew up in this thriving, free Jewish community. He became a rabbi, established the first Hebrew printing press in Amsterdam, and wrote a number of scholarly works. Among his many published writings were works on philosophy, matters of faith, and mysticism. One of his most popular books was *Consiliadore*, which uses traditional Jewish sources to resolve apparent contradictions in Scripture. Menasseh wrote his books in Hebrew, Portuguese, Spanish and Latin.

Menasseh ben Israel

Menasseh ben Israel pleading before Oliver Cromwell on behalf of resettling Jews in England
(from a painting by Solomon A. Hart)

5424 1665

SHABSAI TZVI DECLARES HIMSELF THE MESSIAH

In over 1,500 years, since Bar Kochba's failed revolt following the destruction of the Second Temple, no one had succeeded in claiming to be the Messiah. Until Shabsai Tzvi.

Shabsai Tzvi (from an old etching formerly in the art collection of the Berlin Jewish community)

The prophets had foretold that the time would come when the Messiah would gather the Jews from their exile. In this era, the persecution of Jews would come to an end, the Temple would be rebuilt, and a new commonwealth set up, governed by Torah law. No enemies would arise to destroy it. Indeed, the world would be at peace, with no war anywhere on earth; weapons would be recast and used for peaceful purposes. All this would happen under the leadership of a Jewish leader, the Messiah, a descendant of King David.

With a combination of charisma and gall, Shabsai Tzvi and his "prophet," Nathan of Gaza, capitalized on the Jews' faith and perpetrated a grandiose hoax of epic proportions.

On Shavuos 1665, in Gaza City, Nathan proclaimed Shabsai Tzvi as the long awaited Messiah of the Jewish people – and himself as the Messiah's prophet. Both of the men seemed trustworthy; and with proclamations, pronouncements, and letters sent throughout the Diaspora, they spread word of their arrival.

Many great rabbis saw through this hoax and strongly opposed Shabsai Tzvi. In many places they succeeded in stopping people from accepting the false Messiah, but Shabsai Tzvi's popularity continued to grow. Jews had suffered for centuries in exile and the thought that the Redemption was at hand was very tempting.

Excitement gripped the Jewish world. Rumors of miracles and reports that the Ten Lost Tribes were assembling to march spread like wildfire, reaching as far as Europe. People fasted and prayed, sold their homes and liquidated their businesses in anticipation of the ultimate return to the land of Israel.

In the city of Amsterdam, a European commercial center, international trade was disrupted by the Jewish community's reserving almost every available ship in anticipation of their voyage to Israel – as soon as the word would be given.

Non-Jews were greatly agitated by Shabsai Tzvi's announcements. The Pope sent a delegation to Jerusalem to investigate. Though many exceptional individuals tried to challenge the populace's belief

Rabbi Yaakov Sassportas,
a leading early opponent of Shabsai Tzvi

that Shabsai Tzvi was Messiah, their voices were drowned out by the masses who held firmly to the belief that the Messiah had come.

Shabsai Tzvi thoroughly acted the part of "King of the Jews." Establishing his court in Smyrna, Turkey, he appointed ambassadors to be sent to the Diaspora, received delegations, accepted gifts and tributes, and divided up the territories of the globe among his close associates.

In Gaza, he declared the abolishment of the observance of the 17th of Tammuz – a day of fasting and mourning which marks the day the Babylonians and the Romans breached the walls of Jerusalem, three weeks before the destruction of the Temples. Instead, the Jews of Gaza

Shabsai Tzvi in prison, 1666
(from a 17th century etching)

rejoiced and sang *Hallel*. Shabsai Tzvi later abolished the Tishah B'Av observance — the fast which commemorates the anniversary of the destruction of the two Temples — and all other fasts connected to the Temple destruction. Ultimately, he even permitted the eating of non-kosher food!

The Sultan of Turkey, alarmed by Shabsai Tzvi's popularity and actions, had him placed under arrest and taken to the fortress at Gallipoli.

Nathan, ever a public-relations genius, explained to confused Jews that the Messiah's imprisonment was an integral part of the Messianic process, and that the Jews needed to repent yet more before he could take power.

Remarkably, Shabsai Tzvi managed to continue his "royal" activities even in prison, continuing to receive Jewish delegations.

It was the Sultan who finally brought this cruel hoax to an end. He had Shabsai Tzvi brought before him, and offered him a choice: conversion to Islam or immediate execution.

At the age of 40, the false Jewish Messiah renounced his faith and became the Moslem Aziz Mehmed Effendi, with a position in the Sultan's courts as "keeper of the palace gates."

5448 1687 VICTORY IN POSEN

The Jews of Posen were attacked by an anti-Semitic mob. After a fierce three-day battle in which many lives were lost, the Jews emerged victorious. This was among the few times during the Middle Ages that a Jewish community succeeded in defending itself.

People of the Book:
More Famous Jewish Commentators
1500 - 1600

Torah Commentator

MIZRACHI

The Mizrachi is a "supercommentary" – a commentary to a commentary — that analyzes Rashi's commentary on the *Chumash*, providing sources and resolving apparent difficulties. Rabbi Eliyahu Mizrachi, who authored the work, was the Chief Rabbi of Turkey, where he was active in assisting refugees from the Spanish Inquisition. In addition to being a leading Torah scholar, he was a recognized authority in mathematics, astronomy, and philosophy, and wrote books on these subjects. In addition to his Rashi commentary, he wrote responsa and novellae.

Halachah Commentators

A number of the standard commentaries on the *Tur* (see More Famous Jewish Commentators 1200 – 1400) and the *Shulchan Aruch* (see 5325/1565) were composed during this period. Among them were:

BACH

Rabbi Yoel Sirkis was Rabbi in Cracow for twenty-one years. He was well-to-do and personally supported a number of the students in his yeshivah. *Bayis Chadash* (of which Bach is an acronym), his commentary on the *Arbah Turim*, appears in all standard editions of the *Tur*. He also corrected errors in Talmudic texts, and wrote responsa and works on Kabbalah.

TAZ

Rabbi David HaLevi was an outstanding disciple of the Bach, and became his son-in-law. His commentary on the *Orach*

Chaim and *Yoreh Deah* portions of *Shulchan Aruch, Turei Zahav* (hence the acronym *Taz*), appears on the innermost column of each page of the standard *Shulchan Aruch*. He was one of the thousands of refugees who were forced to flee the Chmielnicki massacres — first to Lublin, then to Moravia. Following the Cossack uprising, he returned to Lemberg, where he served as Rabbi until his death in 1667. Toward the end of his life, he sent his son and his stepson to investigate Shabsai Tzvi's claim to be the Messiah.

SHACH

One of Rabbi Shabsi HaCohen's enduring contributions to Judaism was made at a relatively young age. He began his work, *Sifsei Cohen*, a commentary on the *Yoreh Deah* portion of the *Shulchan Aruch,* at the age of 18. It was completed and published when he was only 24, and was recognized and referred to even by his senior contemporaries. Indeed, Rabbi Shabsi was a prodigy who, at the age of 12, was accepted into the yeshivah of Rabbi Yehoshua ben Yosef of Cracow. Some years after publishing his first work he wrote a commentary on the unit of *Shulchan Aruch* dealing with civil laws, *Choshen Mishpat*. These commentaries are printed alongside the text in all standard editions of the *Shulchan Aruch*. Rabbi Shabsi's personal life was marred by the tragedies of the Chmielnicki massacres, which he survived as a refugee. Though his life was short — he passed away at the age of 41 — his works continue to have an impact even to this day.

MAGEN AVRAHAM

Rabbi Avraham Gombiner's father was killed in the Chmielnicki massacres. For many years, Rabbi Avraham taught young schoolchildren, until the residents of Kalisch, where he was living, recognized his great scholarship and appointed him one of the city's *dayanim*, rabbinic judges. His *Magen Avraham* is a comprehensive treatment of the *Orach Chaim* section of the *Shulchan Aruch*. It appears in the outer column in standard editions of the *Shulchan Aruch*. He wrote *Zayis Raanan*, an extensive commentary on *Yalkut Shimoni*.

BACK TO JERUSALEM: 1,000 JEWS AND RABBI YEHUDAH HACHASSID

5461
1700

A dramatic journey began when Rabbi Yehudah left Shidlitz, Poland, with thirty families, to resettle in Jerusalem.

The group traveled through Hungary, Germany, and Italy, where, inspired by Rabbi Yehudah's charismatic personality and sense of mission, additional families joined them. By the time they left for Jerusalem, Rabbi Yehudah had a following of 1,000 men, women, and children. This was the largest *aliyah* of Ashkenazic Jews in centuries. Half of the party perished during the journey; the survivors arrived on Wednesday, the 4th of Cheshvan. Tragically, Rabbi Yehudah passed away the next Monday. He had lived in Jerusalem for less than a week.

The people who accompanied Rabbi Yehudah tried, but failed, to establish a permanent community. They incurred huge debts to the Arabs in order to acquire living quarters and food. After repeated unsuccessful attempts to get the debts repaid, the Arabs burst into the synagogue, pillaging the sanctuary. They then used the area as a garbage dump. The Ashkenazic Jews were banished from the city, their homes converted into Arab shops. The Arabs considered all Ashkenazic Jews responsible for the unpaid debt. They harassed Ashkenazic Jews, and ordered that no Ashkenazic Jew be permitted to take up residence in Jerusalem as long as the debt remained unpaid. This decree prevented Ashkenazic Jews from living in Jerusalem for over 100 years, until 1820, when the students of the Gaon of Vilna repaid the debt.

5478
1718

THE EMERGENCE OF THE BAAL SHEM TOV

Rabbi Yisrael ben Eliezer, later known as the Baal Shem Tov (or by the acronym Besht), was born in Elul 1698.

Orphaned at a very young age, Yisrael was always inspired by his father's last words to him: "Remember, God is with you and therefore never be afraid." Rabbi Yisrael became a teacher's assistant in the town *cheder*. As part of his job he would pick up the children and escort them to school. The children loved going to school with him, as he would sing with them as they marched. He married at the age of 20 and spent many years isolated in the Carpathian Mountains. There he studied Torah, becoming a great scholar, knowledgeable in Talmud, Midrash, *Tanach* and Jewish law. In addition he studied the deep mysteries of the Torah in the Kabbalah. Rabbi Yisrael's spiritual attainments were great, and he was able to cure the sick through Kabbalistic amulets and blessings. He became known as a miracle worker and was acknowledged as a very holy Jew. People called him "Baal Shem Tov — Master of the Good Name."

All this time, Rabbi Yisrael kept his greatness hidden and concentrated on personal growth. When he was 36 years old, he began to reveal his new way of serving God to the Jews of Ukraine. His teachings, called Chassidus, were firmly rooted in Torah, and stressed the emotional dimension of Judaism and the need for joy in the service of God. His approach succeeded in strengthening the spirit of many Jews and he attracted disciples from throughout Greater Poland and beyond. Within decades, Chassidus had spread from Mezibozh, the small *shtetl* where the Baal Shem Tov lived, to Poland, Russia, Hungary and Eastern Europe, and even to Lithuania, where it was opposed by the Gaon of Vilna. By the turn of the 20th century, there were millions of Chassidic

1714
Gabriel Fahrenheit invents the thermometer.

Jews. Today, there are large, vibrant Chassidic communities throughout the world.

Though Chassidic teachings attracted many great Torah scholars, it was embraced particularly by the poor and humble Jews, who were touched by the Baal Shem Tov's boundless love for them. He emphasized age-old Torah concepts: the importance of praying with feeling and doing *mitzvos* with joy; God's love for every Jew; and the belief that a holy *tzaddik* can offer advice and help to his followers, and bring them closer to God. Chassidim used singing and dancing to inspire themselves to be better Jews. The Baal Shem Tov also encouraged the study of certain aspects of Kabbalah. Because of the importance of *Eretz Yisrael*, he himself attempted a trip there, but returned to Europe, unable to complete the voyage.

He passed away on Shavuos 1760/5520.

Through his *talmidim*, Chassidus continued to spread and grow. The disciple who succeeded the Baal Shem Tov as leader was Rabbi Dov Ber, known as Maggid of Mezeritch. It was he who became the teacher of great disciples who spread Chassidus throughout Eastern Europe. Other disciples of the Besht include Rabbi Yaakov Yosef of Polnoye, author of *Toldos Yaakov Yosef*, in which the teachings of the Baal Shem Tov were first put into print; and Rabbi Menachem Mendel of Vitebsk, who immigrated to *Eretz Yisrael* with 300 Chassidim.

The teachings of the Baal Shem Tov gave Jews the courage to stand firm, proud, and fiercely committed to Judaism despite the hardships of poverty and anti-Semitism they suffered in Christian Europe.

Rabbi Yisrael ben Eliezer,
known as the Baal Shem Tov

Beis HaMidrash of the
Baal Shem Tov in Mezibozh

5481 1721 THE VILNA GAON IS BORN

A true child prodigy is rare. There is, perhaps, one in each generation. And when Eliyahu ben Rabbi Shlomo Zalman was born on the first day of Pesach 5481, the Jewish people were blessed with a child prodigy who was one in many centuries, and whose influence and contributions continue to guide, enlighten, and inspire.

Commonly referred to as the "Vilna Gaon," the genius of Vilna, the Gra (an abbreviation for Gaon Rabbi Eliyahu) never had a position as a rabbi of a congregation or of a city. However, through his students, his writings, and his personal example he became the teacher of the Jewish people, and he influenced all the generations of Jews from his time to the present, to live lives dedicated exclusively to Torah study and the pursuit of Torah knowledge. His best-known student, Rabbi Chaim Volozhiner, encouraged by the Gra, founded the yeshivah in Volozhin, which became the model for all of today's yeshivos.

The Great Synagogue in Vilna

During the Vilna Gaon's lifetime, the Chassidic movement was growing throughout Eastern Europe. The Gra was opposed to the teachings of Chassidus and the changes in practice that the Chassidim were advocating. He even signed a ban against them. As a result, the Chassidic movement attracted much opposition as it spread into Lithuania.

The Gaon's written legacy includes commentaries on virtually all areas of the Written and Oral Torah, including Scripture, Mishnah, Talmud, *Zohar* and other Kabbalistic works, and *Shulchan Aruch*. In addition, he pointed out printers' errors that had become common in the Talmud and Midrash text. His *Ayil Meshulash* is a work on geometry. He passed away on the 5th day of Succos, 1797.

An entrance to the ghetto of Vilna

The Vilna Gaon

Focus: The Gaon of Vilna

When only a small child, not yet 6 years old, Eliyahu stepped up to the front of the Great Synagogue in Vilna and delivered a Talmudic speech of such brilliance and magnificence that it astonished the entire congregation. Very soon he surpassed his teachers and began learning on his own. Studying day and night, he devoted his entire life to the study of all branches of Torah knowledge. In order to better understand certain areas of Torah, he also mastered mathematics, natural science and astronomy. He towered far beyond all Torah scholars in his generation and was the acknowledged Torah giant of his age. Despite his mental acuity, pho-tographic memory, and respected family backround, the Gaon remained humble. Shortly after his marriage he decided to journey through Europe disguised as a poor man. Dressed as an impoverished Jew he traveled and wandered for five years. Decades later, toward the end of his life, the Gaon once again left Vilna. His intense love for *Eretz Yisrael* inspired him to attempt the long and dangerous journey. Unfortunately, after two months, circumstances compelled him to return to Vilna, his journey aborted. After the Gaon's death some of his students completed their mentor's journey, immigrating to *Eretz Yisrael* in the first decades of the 1800's.

Did you know that?

- When the Gra was a youngster, he wouldn't play see-saw. He disliked a game where, in order to get to the top, you had to push someone else down.

- A Berlin professor, stumped by a particularly complex mathematical problem, presented it to the Gra, who immediately solved it.

- Surrounded by the Russian army, the Jews of Vilna gathered in the syna-gogue to pray for heavenly protection. The Gra told them that no one would be hurt. At that moment, a cannonball hit the building but caused only mini-mal damage to the roof.

- The Gra knew *Tanach* so well that he could say it by heart — backwards!

- In the last moments of his life the Gra took hold of his *tzitzis* and cried, "How great is the reward for this *mitzvah*, bought for a few pennies! But after a man's death, all the money in the world can't buy the reward of a *mitzvah*."

- At the Gra's request, he was buried next to Graf Potocki, a righteous convert who took the Jewish name Avraham ben Avraham. The son of a Polish count, Avraham converted to Judaism and was burned at the stake by the Church, when he refused to return to Catholicism.

- The Gra never slept for more than two hours a day, and never for more than half an hour at a time.

5500
1740

MESILLAS YESHARIM IS PUBLISHED

Rabbi Moshe Chaim Luzzatto was 33 years old when his very popular work on Jewish ethics, *Mesillas Yesharim*, "The Path of the Just," was published.

The slim volume explores man's purpose and offers guidance on how one can attain spiritual fulfillment.

Mesillas Yesharim was reprinted innumerable times and translated into many languages. At the turn of the 20th century, it could be found in Jewish homes throughout the world, a classic text that was universally accepted.

Tomb of Rabbi Moshe Chaim Luzzatto, author of *Mesillas Yesharim*. He is buried next to Rabbi Akiva.

Focus: Rabbi Moshe Chaim Luzzatto – Ramchal

Rabbi Moshe Chaim Luzzatto, also known by his acronym, Ramchal, was born in Padua, Italy in 1707. As a child he received a broad Torah education and was considered a genius by his family and teachers.

While still in his teens, he wrote books on Hebrew language, grammar and usage, and rhetoric that drew comprehensively from all the books of the Bible, the Talmud, and Biblical commentaries.

At about that time he began to study Kabbalah, the mystical writings of the *Zohar* and the writings of the students of the holy Ari of Safed. Ramchal gathered a group of about ten students whose purpose was to study all facets of the Torah, including the *Zohar*, in a pure and holy environment. When the Ramchal was 20 years old a *Maggid* – a heavenly messenger – came to teach him the secrets of the Torah, which he was instructed to write down and teach to his students.

When the rabbis of Venice heard about Ramchal's group studying the *Zohar* and his claim that he was taught by a *Maggid*, they wrote to Ramchal's mentor, Rabbi Yeshayahu Bassan, protesting Ramchal's activities. They suspected that Ramchal was a secret follower of the false Messiah Shabsai Tzvi, who had died in 1676, but whose mystical Messianic movement was still very much alive.

Ramchal, however, was not a follower of Shabsai Tzvi, and did not cease his study of Kabbalah. However, he was forced to hand over many of his writings to Rabbi Bassan. These works were hidden from public view and were not published.

A strong controversy developed around Ramchal and his teachings. Many rabbis believed that a person who was so young and who was learning outside of *Eretz Yisrael* should not study the *Zohar*, and could not have had a *Maggid* speak to him. (Ramchal pointed out that the Ari learned from a *Maggid* at a young age, while still in Egypt,

aand that Rabbi Yosef Karo had also learned from a *Maggid* while living in Turkey.) As a result of the controversy, Ramchal left Padua and moved with his family first to Frankfurt and then to Amsterdam. He supported himself by working in the diamond trade for a few hours a day, and learning Torah the rest of the time. In Amsterdam he wrote the book that was to become – long after his lifetime – the most widely accepted *mussar* (ethical) work of the last 150 years: *Mesillas Yesharim*.

In 1743, at the age of 36, Ramchal moved with his family to Acre in *Eretz Yisrael*, believing that his Kabbalah studies and teachings could reach greater heights in the Holy Land.

In 1747 a plague struck the city of Acre, and Ramchal — who was only 40 at the time — and his family perished. He was buried on a hilltop outside Tiberias, near the grave of Rabbi Akiva.

After the controversy quieted down, and with the passing of the Shabsai Tzvi movement, the Jewish people rediscovered Ramchal and began to study his books. The Vilna Gaon was so impressed with the *Mesillas Yesharim* that he wanted to leave Vilna to meet its author, but Ramchal was no longer alive. In the mid-1800's, Rabbi Yisrael Salanter, founder of the *mussar* movement, said that all *mussar* works are good, but that the *Mesillas Yesharim* was the best. Many of the Chassidic Rebbes similarly praised Ramchal and his writings.

More recently, Rabbi Chaim Friedlander, *mashgiach* of the Ponevezh Yeshivah, wrote glosses on and arranged for the publication of several manuscripts of Ramchal that had been held in libraries for nearly 200 years.

To date, over twenty of Rabbi Moshe Chaim Luzzatto's works have been published, and he is acknowledged throughout the Jewish world as one of the outstanding Torah giants of the 18th century.

5511 1751 RABBI YAAKOV OF EMDEN AND THE AMULETS OF RABBI YONASAN EYBESCHUETZ

Rabbi Yonasan Eybeschuetz's great Torah scholarship had earned him the position of Chief Rabbi of the Jewish community of Metz and then of the three sister-cities of Altona, Hamburg, and Wandsbeck. In addition to his vast knowledge of Talmud and Jewish law, he was also learned in matters of Kabbalah — the mystical aspects of the Torah. As the community's Rabbi, he was often approached by people in need, and he wrote Kabbalistic amulets for them to wear.

These amulets came to the attention of Rabbi Yaakov of Emden (Holland), whose father, the Chacham Tzvi, had been one of the most outspoken opponents of Shabsai Tzvi. Continuing his father's tradition, he worked tirelessly to stamp out any remnants of Shabsai Tzvi's influence among the Jews. Rabbi Yaakov, an outstanding scholar in his own right, examined some of the amulets and he became convinced that Rabbi Yonasan believed in Shabsai Tzvi.

Rabbi Yaakov demanded that Rabbi Yonasan Eybeschuetz be removed from his office as Chief Rabbi and be disqualified from the rabbinate. The resulting dispute as to whether Rabbi Yonasan was innocent or guilty of believing in Shabsai Tzvi is one of the famous as well as sad controversies of the 18th century. The affair became so public that the king of Denmark personally involved himself in the dispute. Though Rabbi Yonasan was declared innocent and remained the Chief Rabbi, the matter was not laid to rest.

Despite their differences, both are recognized as righteous men of the highest order, whose dispute was motivated by the quest for truth and for the good of the Jewish community.

Both Rabbi Yaakov of Emden and Rabbi Yonasan Eybeschuetz have left rich legacies of halachic and homiletic writings. Indeed, Rabbi Eybeschuetz's *Urim VeTumim* and *Kereisi U'Pleisi* are masterpieces of halachic literature.

People of the Book:
Famous Commentators of the 1700's

Tanach Commentator

METZUDAS DAVID
AND METZUDAS TZION

These two important commentaries to *Neviim* and *Kesuvim*, the Scriptural Books of the Prophets and Writings, are printed in standard editions of these books. They are clearly written and simple to use. *Metzudas David* explains the basic meaning of the verses, while *Metzudas Tzion* explains difficult words used in the text. They were published by Rabbi Yechiel Hillel Altschuler, who completed the commentary his father, Rabbi David Altschuler, had begun.

Talmud Commentators

PACHAD YITZCHAK

Pachad Yitzchak, the first Talmudic encyclopedia, was written by Rabbi Isaac Lampronti, one of the great Torah scholars of Italian Jewry. The author alphabetically arranges concepts and topics discussed in the Talmud and presents the opinions and interpretations of his rabbinic predecessors and contemporaries.

PNEI YEHOSHUA

Rabbi Yaakov Yehoshua Falk, Rabbi of Frankfurt-am-Main, lay in the rubble of a building that had blown up when gunpowder stored within it had exploded. Though his family did not survive, Rabbi Yaakov Yehoshua did. He wrote his famous work, *Pnei Yehoshua*, to show his gratitude to God for saving him from almost certain death. In this work, which is a staple of advanced Talmud study, he analyzes the Rashi and Tosafos on the Talmud and offers insights, highlights, questions, and resolutions.

Did you know that?

🖙 Rabbi Akiva Eiger once spoke harshly to a student. Later, the student moved and Rabbi Akiva Eiger did not know his whereabouts. Fifteen years later, teacher and student met and Rabbi Eiger remembered to ask the young man's forgiveness.

🖙 As Rabbi of his city, Rabbi Akiva Eiger was in charge of the local hospital. For his work, the government gave him an award.

🖙 In addition to being an extraordinary Talmud scholar, Rabbi Akiva Eiger was also a man of great kindness and piety. Here is a story told about him: Once, a carriage in which he was riding fell into a ditch during a storm. The wagon driver stepped into the mud and water and pushed the wagon back onto the road. Rabbi Akiva Eiger offered the wagon driver a pair of dry socks. The driver thanked his passenger. Now he wouldn't have to finish the trip in wet socks. It was only at the end of the journey that the driver realized that Rabbi Akiva Eiger had given him his own pair of socks!

GILYON HASHAS

Rabbi Akiva (Ginz) Eiger was an outstanding scholar and acknowledged leader of his generation. He was known not only for his vast knowledge but for his awesome piety and modesty as well.

Even during the lifetime of the Gaon of Vilna, Rabbi Eiger was offered the position of Rabbi of Vilna. His commentaries on the Talmud are required study for anyone who seeks to understand the Talmud in depth. His hundreds of halachic responsa are published in *She'eilos U'Teshuvos Rabbi Akiva Eiger*. His glosses on the *Shulchan Aruch* are still studied intensively. *Gilyon HaShas,* his glosses on the Talmud, offers cross-references to Talmudic and post-Talmudic sources, often posing difficult questions or raising apparent contradictions. The questions he raises continue to challenge the greatest Talmud scholars, who try to find resolutions to these issues. In addition, his Talmudic novellae are considered paradigms of clear, analytical thought.

5513
1753

THE MAGGID MEETS THE BAAL SHEM TOV

The leader of Chassidus after the Baal Shem Tov was Rabbi Dov Ber, known as the Maggid of Mezeritch. Legend has it that, suffering from poor health, he came to the Baal Shem Tov for a cure. He was already an outstanding Talmud scholar, Kabbalist, and "maggid" (itinerant preacher) when he chose to become a student of the Baal Shem Tov. Though he lived only thirteen years after the passing of the Baal Shem Tov, the Maggid developed the great disciples who spread Chassidus throughout Eastern Europe. His many students became great Chassidic Rebbes and founded Chassidic dynasties throughout Europe.

Focus: Chassidic Rebbes and Dynasties

RABBI YISRAEL BAAL SHEM TOV (the "Besht"), born 1698, died 1760: Founder of Chassidus.

FAMILY OF THE BAAL SHEM TOV

▸ **Udel**, his daughter, a wise and righteous woman to whom he entrusted many confidential matters.

▸ **Rabbi Moshe Chaim Ephraim**, son of Udel, grandson of the Baal Shem Tov, born 1748, died 1800. Grew up in the house of the Baal Shem Tov. Author of *Degel Machaneh Ephraim* on the *Chumash*, a primary source for the teachings of the Baal Shem Tov. Served as Rabbi in Sadilkov most of his adult life.

▸ **Rabbi Baruch**, son of Udel, grandson of the Baal Shem Tov, born 1753, died 1811. As a child he was beloved by the Baal Shem Tov. After the passing of his grandfather, he became Rebbe in Mezibozh and was influential in the spreading of Chassidus.

▸ **Rabbi Nachman of Breslov**, son of Feiga, grandson of Udel, great-grandson of the Baal Shem Tov, born 1772, died 1811. Although his Chassidim did not choose a successor to him, Breslover Chassidus remains strong and growing.

▸ **Rabbi Avraham Gershon Kitover**, brother-in-law of the Baal Shem Tov, founder of the Chassidic community in Jerusalem. He first traveled to *Eretz Yisrael* in 1742, went back to Europe, then returned permanently to Jerusalem in 1747.

FIRST GENERATION OF DISCIPLES OF THE BAAL SHEM TOV

▸ **Rabbi Dov Ber, the Maggid of Mezeritch**, born 1704, died 1773. Primary disciple of the Baal Shem Tov and his successor as the leader of world Chassidus; became the most influential leader in the Chassidic world; spread Chassidus by sending his disciples to lead Jewish communities throughout Europe.

▸ **Rabbi Yaakov Yosef HaKohen of Polnoye**, died 1784. Known as the favorite disciple of the Baal Shem Tov, with whom he came to study as an established Rabbi. He developed a close friendship with the Maggid. His primary work, *Toldos Yaakov Yosef*, was the first to present the Baal Shem Tov's teachings in print.

▸ **Rabbi Nachum of Chernobyl**, born 1730, died 1798. Author of *Meor Einayim*; disciple of the Baal Shem Tov and the Maggid; founder of the Chernobyl Chassidic dynasty.

▸ **Rabbi Menachem Mendel of Vitebsk**, born 1730, died 1788. Disciple of the Baal Shem Tov and the Maggid. In 1777, led a group of 300 Chassidim to settle in *Eretz Yisrael*, first in Safed, later in Tiberias.

DISCIPLES OF THE MAGGID

▸ **Rabbi Aharon HaGadol of Karlin**, born 1736, died 1772. Spread Chassidus in Lithuania; founder of the Karlin-Stolin Chassidic dynasty.

▸ **Rabbi Shneur Zalman Schneerson of Liadi**, born 1745, died 1813. Founder of the *Chabad* approach to Chassidic thought. He authored many works, including *Likutei Amarim-Tanya*, on the basic philosophy of *Chabad*, and a halachic code which has come to be known as *Shulchan Aruch HaRav*.

▸ **Rabbi Elimelech of Lizhensk**, known as "the Rebbe Reb Meilech," died 1786. Author of *Noam Elimelech*; teacher of many of the next generation of Chassidic leaders.

▸ **Rabbi Meshulam Zusha of Hanipoli**, known as "the Rebbe Reb Zusha," died 1800. Brother of the Rebbe Reb Elimelech.

▸ **Rabbi Levi Yitzchak of Berditchev**, born 1740, died 1810. He was a prominent rabbi before becoming a Chassid. He authored *Kedushas Levi* on the Torah and was known as the great defender of the Jewish people with his loving prayers on their behalf.

▸ **Rabbi Pinchas HaLevi Horowitz** of Frankfurt, born 1730, died 1805. Author of many works on Talmud and *Shulchan Aruch*, including *Sefer Hafla'ah*, *Sefer HaMakneh*, and *Panim Meiros*. He was also a mentor of the *Chasam Sofer*.

▸ **Rabbi Shmelka HaLevi Horowitz** of Nicholsburg, died 1778. Brother of Rabbi Pinchas HaLevi; taught many of the Rebbes of his own generation.

▸ **Rabbi Yaakov Yitzchak Horowitz**, the Chozeh of Lublin, born 1745, died 1815. The one who brought Chassidus to Poland. Many of the next generation's Rebbes were his disciples.

▸ **Rabbi Yisrael Hopstein of Kozhnitz**, known as the Kozhnitzer Maggid, born 1726, died 1815. Author of *Avodas Yisrael*.

DISCIPLES OF RABBI ELIMELECH OF LIZHENSK

The Chozeh of Lublin and the Kozhnitzer Maggid were also disciples of the Rebbe Reb Elimelech.

They, together with Rabbi Avraham Yehoshua Heschel of Apta and Rabbi Menachem Mendel of Rimanov, spread Chassidus throughout Poland.

- **Rabbi Avraham Yehoshua Heschel of Apta**, born 1755, died 1825. Author of *Oheiv Yisrael*.
- **Rabbi Menachem Mendel of Rimanov**, died 1815. Author of many books, including *Menachem Tzion, Divrei Menachem,* and *Ateres Menachem*.
- **Rabbi Naftali Tzvi of Ropshitz**, born 1760, died 1827. Disciple of the Rebbe Reb Elimelech and the Chozeh; author of *Zera Kodesh*.

DISCIPLES OF THE CHOZEH OF LUBLIN

- **Rabbi Yaakov Yitzchak of Peshis'cha**, known as the "Yid HaKadosh," the Holy Jew, born 1766, died 1824. Served as a *rosh yeshivah* in Apta, where Rabbi Moshe Leib of Sassov attracted him to Chassidus. He ultimately settled in Peshis'cha.
- **Rabbi Simchah Bunim of Peshis'cha**, born 1767, died 1827. Although a student of the Chozeh, he was closest to the Yid HaKadosh and eventually assumed the leadership of Peshis'cha after his master's passing.
- **Rabbi Moshe Teitelbaum of Uhel**, born 1759, died 1841. Author of *Yismach Moshe* on the Torah. He was among those primarily responsible for the spread of Chassidus in Hungary.
- **Rabbi Sholom Rokeach of Belz**, born 1779, died 1855. Author of *Maaseh Rokeach* and founder of the Belzer Chassidic dynasty.
- **Rabbi Menachem Mendel of Kotzk**, born 1787, died 1859. Disciple of the Chozeh, the Yid HaKadosh and of Rabbi Simchah Bunim of Peshis'cha. He is known for his pursuit of truth, shunning of humor, and acute insights into human nature.
- **Rabbi Yitzchak Meir Rottenberg–Alter of Ger**, born 1799, died 1866. Student of the Kozhnitzer Maggid, Rabbi Simchah Bunim of Peshis'cha and the Kotzker Rebbe; founder of the Gerrer Chassidic dynasty; author of *Chiddushei HaRim*.
- **Rabbi Zvi Elimelech of Dinov**, born 1783, died 1841. Wrote several *sefarim*, including *Bnei Yissas'char, Agra D'Kallah, Derech Pikudecha,* and *Maayan Ganim*.

OTHER MAJOR REBBES OF THE PERIOD

- **Rabbi Moshe Leib of Sassov**, born 1745, died 1807. A disciple of Rabbi Shmelka of Nicholsburg; known for his boundless love for every Jew.
- **Rabbi Yehudah Leib Eiger** of Lublin, born 1815, died 1888. Grandson of Rabbi Akiva Eiger; disciple of the Kotzker Rebbe. Though the scion of a family of *misnagdim* — opponents of Chassidus — he was attracted to the movement. Known as Rabbi Leibele, he was the Rebbe in Lublin. Among his many works are *Toras Emes* and *Imrei Emes*.
- **Rabbi Avraham Borenstein of Sochatchov**, born 1838, died 1910. Son-in-law of the Kotzker Rebbe, his halachic works include *Eglei Tal* and *Avnei Nezer*.
- **Rabbi Tzadok HaKohen of Lublin**, born 1824, died 1900. A student of Rabbi Leibele Eiger; author of many profound works on Jewish thought based on Kabbalah and Chassidic teachings.
- **Rabbi Chaim Halberstam of Sanz**. Born 1793, died 1876. Founder of the Sanz dynasty of Chassidus; he was an acknowledged halachic authority and the author of *Divrei Chaim*.
- **Rabbi Menachem Mendel Hager of Kosov**, born 1768, died 1826. Disciple of Rabbi Moshe Leib of Sassov; author of *Ahavas Shalom*. He is the forerunner of the Vizhnitz dynasty.
- **Rabbi Yisrael of Ruzhin**, born 1797, died 1851. Great-grandson of the Maggid of Mezeritch; founder of the Ruzhin dynasty. Considered by many to be the leader of his generation.

It is impossible in a work of this scope to include comprehensive information about all the Chassidic dynasties. The following summarizes the genealogy of some of the best-known dynasties:

- Zlotshov—Zhvil
- Chernobyl—Tolna—Skvera—Rachmistrivka
- Karlin—Stolin
- Chabad—Lubavitch
- Mezibozh—Apta
- Uhel—Sighet—Satmar
- Ropshitz—Dzikov—Melitz
- Ziditchov—Komarna
- Kosov—Vizhnitz
- Premishlan—Kalish—Nadvorna
- Belz
- Dinov—Munkatch
- Peshish'cha—Kotzk—Alexander—Worka—Ger—Amshinov
- Sanz—Shiniva—Gorlitz—Tchechoiva—Tarna—Bobov—Klausenburg
- Ruzhin—Sadigora—Tchortkova—Husiatin—Bohosh—Boyan—Kopichinitz

People of the Book:
More Famous Commentators of the 1700's

Torah Commentators

ME'AM LOEZ

This compilation was written in Ladino, the language of Sephardic Jews. It is an encyclopedic commentary on the Books of the Bible, written in a style that brings the narrative to life and explains the halachos discussed in the Torah. *Me'am Loez* became particularly popular among those Sephardic Jews who found Hebrew-language commentaries difficult. It had a great impact on the Sephardic community, strengthening their Judaism. In the 1970's it was translated into both Hebrew and English versions, which immediately became popular. The commentary on the Book of Genesis and a portion of the Book of Exodus was written by Rabbi Yaakov Kuli. After his death, others completed the writing, following Rabbi Kuli's style.

SIFSEI CHACHAMIM

Of the hundreds of commentaries that explain Rashi on *Chumash*, the one that has achieved the greatest popularity is *Sifsei Chachamim*. It was written by Rabbi Shabsai Bass, a very learned printer of Jewish books who was also a noted bibliographer and cantor. At the age of 71 he was imprisoned for a short time by Christian authorities for printing Hebrew books which, they claimed, disparaged the Church. He was later vindicated and released.

Halachah Commentators

CHACHAM TZVI

A collection of responsa — letters answering halachic inquiries — by Rabbi Tzvi Ashkenazi. Though born to an Ashkenazic family, after studying in Budapest he pursued his studies in Sephardic lands. He settled in Constantinople, where the title "Chacham" — the Sephardic term for "Rabbi" — was bestowed upon him. He served as Rabbi in numerous cities, most famously as Rabbi of the Ashkenazic community of Amsterdam, where there were both Ashkenazic and Sephardic commu-

1760
First *Siddur* is
published in America.

nities. While there, he fought against the influence of the followers of Shabsai Tzvi, as his son, Rabbi Yaakov of Emden, did later.

NODA B'YEHUDAH

The author of Noda B'Yehudah, Rabbi Yechezkel Landau, was Chief Rabbi of Prague. He was recognized as a leading halachic authority of his generation. Questions were sent to him from communities all over the world. Many of his responsa were published as *She'eilos U'Teshuvos Noda B'Yehudah*. The first volume was published in 1776, at the dawn of the Emancipation movement, and it is one of the first books to deal with Jewish law at a time when traditional Jews began to confront the challenges of greater cultural freedom and exposure. Rabbi Landau addresses such questions as whether Jews are permitted to wear Western-style clothing and the permissibility of autopsies. It is a classic text which is often referred to by rabbis even today. The *Noda B'Yehudah,* as Rabbi Landau became known, was a valiant defender of traditional Judaism, battling the "Enlightenment," a movement which promoted the abandonment of elements of traditional practice in an effort to embrace Western culture. He had a close relationship with Emperor Franz Joseph II of Austria.

CHAYEI ADAM / CHOCHMAS ADAM

These are definitive summaries of the *Orach Chaim* and *Yoreh De'ah* sections of the *Shulchan Aruch*. Their concise format and straightforward style made these works easier to use by the masses than the comprehensive *Shulchan Aruch* and its commentaries. They were written by Rabbi Avraham Danzig, who was a rabbinical judge in the Vilna court during the lifetime of the Vilna Gaon, under whom he studied.

KETZOS HACHOSHEN

This classic example of Talmudic scholarship is studied intensively in yeshivos, and is the basis of many advanced Talmudic lectures. Its author, Rabbi Aryeh Leib HaKohen Heller, taught Talmud in Lemberg, and later became Rabbi of Stry, Poland. *Ketzos HaChoshen* is a commentary on *Choshen Mishpat,* the section of *Shulchan Aruch* which deals with business and monetary matters. Rabbi Aryeh Leib also wrote *Avnei Miluim,* a commentary on *Even HaEzer,* the section of *Shulchan Aruch* which deals with matters of marriage and divorce; and *Shev She'maitsa,* a collection of brilliant lengthy essays on the principles of possession and proof in Jewish law.

Did you know that?

Rabbi Yechezkel Landau once added an additional day to Passover, saving the Jews of Prague. This is what transpired: Over the Passover holiday, the Jews had no flour or *chametz*, so the day after Passover they would buy their bread from a bakery owned by gentiles. One year, a group of anti-Semites plotted to kill the Jews by poisoning the bread baked after Passover.

A gentile whom Rabbi Landau had once helped learned of the plot and told Rabbi Landau about it.

On the final day of Passover, Rabbi Landau told the Jews of Prague that an error had been made in the calendar, and they had started the Passover observance a day early. Passover, he said, would actually be celebrated for another full day. The murderous baker waited for his Jewish customers, but they did not come.

In the interim, the Rabbi reported the scheme to the authorities, who arrested the perpetrators.

SHULCHAN ARUCH HARAV

Rabbi Shneur Zalman of Liadi, founder of Chabad Chassidus, was also one of the great halachic authorities of his time. His *Shulchan Aruch HaRav,* a four-volume treatment of the entire *Shulchan Aruch,* remains a basic source book of Torah law to this day. In addition, he was the author of *Tanya,* a highly profound and influential work of Jewish theology. Rabbi Levi Yitzchak of Berditchev was quoted as saying of *Tanya,* "How could someone compress the wisdom of such a great G-d into such a small work!" *Tanya* is the basic text of Chabad, and is also studied universally.

NESIVOS HAMISHPAT

Nesivos HaMishpat, by Rabbi Yaakov Lorberbaum of Lisa, is an integral part of advanced yeshivah studies. It is a commentary on the *Choshen Mishpat* section of the *Shulchan Aruch.* This commentary often challenges the premises found in *Ketzos HaChoshen,* and the author of that work responds to these challenges in his *Meshoveiv Nesivos.* Together, these works provide scholars and students with in-depth knowledge and analysis of Jewish monetary and legal matters as set forth in the *Shulchan Aruch.* Rabbi Lorberbaum, a great-grandson of the *Chacham Tzvi,* also produced many other halachic and homiletic works.

Title page of the 1830 printing of *Nesivos HaMishpat*

5528 1768

TREACHERY IN UMAN

Did you know that?

$\wp$ Today Uman is a backward, sleepy Ukrainian village. However, one week a year it becomes a bustling place. Thousands of Breslover Chassidim, from America and Israel, fly to Uman to stay there for Rosh Hashanah. They come to pray and celebrate the holiday at the grave of Rabbi Nachman, who had expressed the wish that his Chassidim spend Rosh Hashanah together at his resting place.

The Haidamaks, a murderous Cossack band, had attacked the Ukrainian city of Uman which was then part of Poland. Thousands of Jews fought alongside their gentile neighbors and together they beat back the Cossacks. The Poles were told that they would be unharmed if they allowed the Cossacks to kill the Jews. Seeing this as an opportunity to buy their safety, the Poles agreed. That day thousands of Jews died in Uman *al kiddush Hashem,* sanctifying God's Name. Then the treacherous Cossacks proceeded to massacre all the Poles in Uman. Over half a century later, the great Chassidic Rebbe, Rabbi Nachman of Breslov, requested to be buried in the city which was the final resting place of so many Jewish martyrs.

5536 1776

THE AMERICAN REVOLUTION

Did you know that?

$\wp$ The American Revolution broke out on July 4, 1776. That day was the fast of the 17th of Tammuz.

$\wp$ A war costs money. An army has to pay its soldiers, buy them supplies, and purchase arms. The American Revolution was almost lost because the colonists had run out of money. A Jew by the name of Hayim Salomon came to the rescue and provided the financial assistance necessary to keep the Revolution going.

$\wp$ Francis Salvador was the first Jew to die in the American Revolution. He was a South Carolina plantation owner.

The founding of the United States of America established what would become, in later years, a safe haven for Jews, and created a government that protected the Jews' right to practice their religion freely. There were three Jewish majors and six Jewish captains in the Revolutionary Army.

At the time of the American Revolution, the Vilna Gaon was 46 years old. To read more about the Vilna Gaon see 5481/1720.

When George Washington was commanding the rebel forces, the Chasam Sofer had just passed his bar mitzvah. For more on the Chasam Sofer see 5566/1806.

A monument in Chicago, Illinois, honoring (left to right) Hayim Salomon, George Washington, and Robert Morris

5537 1777

1783

First man to fly — lifted
by a helium balloon!

5547 1787

Did you know that?

🔖 Centuries before Ashkenazic Jews took last names, Sephardic Jews had adopted last names such as de Castro, Toledano — names taken from the places in which they lived.

🔖 In later years many Jews had their last names changed when they arrived in America in the last decades of the 1800's. American immigration officials on Ellis Island, who couldn't understand the language of the foreigners or pronounce their last names, registered shortened or wrong versions of the names they were given. Sometimes the immigrants themselves chose to shorten or Anglicize their names.

DISCIPLES OF THE BAAL SHEM TOV AND THE VILNA GAON SETTLE IN *ERETZ YISRAEL*

The Baal Shem Tov's teachings about the unique place *Eretz Yisrael* occupies in Jewish life and thought, inspired his Chassidim. Rabbi Menachem Mendel of Vitebsk, a student of the Maggid of Mezeritch, together with 300 Chassidim, left Europe to live in *Eretz Yisrael*. Together with the *aliyah* of the Vilna Gaon's students in 1809, this was the beginning of a continuous Ashkenazic Jewish immigration from the Diaspora to *Eretz Yisrael* that is still happening today. Many thousands of Jews from countries all over the world immigrate to Israel each year.

ASHKENAZIC JEWS GET FAMILY NAMES

Traditionally, Jews identified themselves by their first names and their father's first name. For example, someone might be known as Moshe *ben* Yitzchak or Sarah *bas* Aaron. The Jews in Austria were ordered by Joseph II to pick a surname from a list of certified names. Wealthy Jews often bribed the clerks in order to choose their own names; otherwise, the bureaucrat would choose the name. Some examples of names that Jews wanted to take: Edelstein, which means precious stone; Safir, which means sapphire; and Kluger, which means wise. Sometimes the Jews took the name of the city they lived in as a last name, such as Brody, Hamburger, and Shapiro (which comes from the city of Speyer). In 1808 Napoleon Bonaparte ordered the Jews in his empire to adopt family names. Soon all Jews had family names.

Focus: Jerusalem Rabbis

In the 1700's many illustrious rabbis of great wisdom and scholarship lived in Jerusalem. Here are two of the most famous:

Chida: Rabbi Chaim Yosef David Azulai, a Sephardic sage, wrote scores of works on topics ranging from halachah and Kabbalah to Rabbinic biography and bibliography. When he was 29 years old, he was sent to the Diaspora to raise funds for the Hebron Jewish community. For five years he traveled to distant European lands such as Germany, Italy, and even England, where he toured the Tower of London. He returned to Jerusalem for a short time and once again set out, finally settling in Italy. While on his travels, he served as Rabbi in various communities, met with the leading Torah scholars of his day, and researched manuscripts found in libraries and collections throughout Europe. In addition to their own significance, Chida's works serve as a valuable source for the material in these manuscripts, many of which were never published. His opinions on Jewish law and customs are accepted by numerous Sephardic communities, and inform the decisions of many Ashkenazic rabbis.

The Or HaChaim HaKadosh: Rabbi Chaim ben Attar was born in Morocco and spent the last years of his life in Jerusalem, where he opened a yeshivah. He is the author of the *Or HaChaim* commentary on the Torah, a profound work which often draws on Kabbalah to explain the basic ideas of the verses and to resolve difficulties. *Or HaChaim* is recognized as one of the basic Torah commentaries. Rabbi Chaim ben Attar was also a great halachic authority and *rosh yeshivah*. He is generally referred to as the "Or HaChaim HaKadosh" — the Holy Or HaChaim, in tribute to his greatness and piety.

Did you know that?

§ Zionist Jews returning to *Eretz Yisrael* in the 1900's often had their Yiddish-sounding names changed to Hebrew or adopted new Hebrew names. David Green became David Ben-Gurion; Golda Meyerson became Golda Meir.

§ Two and a half centuries after the death of the Or HaChaim HaKadosh, the Jordanians, who had captured the Mt. of Olives in Israel's 1948 War of Independence, decided to build a road right through the ancient Jewish cemetery, desecrating many graves. When the roadwork reached the grave of Rabbi Chaim ben Attar the tractor miraculously flipped over. The driver was killed and the project subsequently abandoned.

§ The Or HaChaim's grave on the Mt. of Olives is visited, especially on his *yarhtzeit* (the anniversary of his death), by thousands of Jews praying that their requests be answered.

FRENCH REVOLUTION

5549 1789

The French Revolution brought an end to the monarchy and brought to power people who believed in the rights of man. Logic forced the revolutionaries to admit that "all men" included Jews. After lacking basic civil rights

1789

The radioactive element uranium is discovered.

1789

George Washington becomes first president of the United States.

5555
1795

for hundreds of years, the Jews were granted equal rights by the French National Assembly. Over the next century this concept would spread throughout Western Europe. After hundreds of years of living in ghettoes and being denied the rights of citizenship and equal economic opportunities, the Jews were freed of many such restrictions in France, Germany, England, and other Western countries. Unfortunately, this freedom led to many Jews leaving their traditions and beliefs. Some even converted or intermarried. What centuries of persecution had failed to do, the French Revolution accomplished in a century.

THE PALE OF SETTLEMENT

The Russian Czars had a long tradition of anti-Semitism which is why, up until the late 18th century, Russia had very few Jews living within its borders. When Poland was partitioned by its neighbors, the parts of Poland taken by Russia were populated by many Jews. By 1795 the Czars suddenly found themselves the rulers of about 400,000 Jews they did not want.

Czar Paul I decreed that all Jews must live in a special area called "the Pale of Settlement." It was illegal for a Jew to travel or spend the night outside this area without special government permission. Russia's Jews were allowed to live in only four percent of the country, although their population swelled to millions. Even within the Pale there were places where the Jews were not allowed to live. The law also restricted where they could conduct business and in which businesses they could engage. These regulations were part of a larger government plan which, in the words of a government official, sought to eliminate one-third of the Jews, convert one-third, and create conditions that would force one-third to emigrate. These regulations remained in effect until the Russian Revolution in 1917.

The oppressive conditions in the Pale of Settlement resulted in hundreds of thousands of Jews leaving Russia to settle in the land of freedom and economic opportunity: America.

Jews from the Caucasus region, during Czarist rule.
These photographs won honorable mention at the Paris Exposition, 1878.

5557 1797

Did you know that?

❧ "Ghetto" means iron foundry in Italian. In 16th century Venice, the Jews were restricted to living in an area that had previously been an iron foundry. Over time, the word "ghetto" came to refer to any location where Jews were forced to live. It is now used in connection with an area predominantly populated by a particular ethnic group.

VENICE JEWRY CELEBRATES BURNING OF GHETTO GATES

French soldiers, led by Napoleon Bonaparte, ripped down the gates that had shut in Venice's Jews for nearly 300 years. As the ghetto gates were publicly burned, the Jews and the soldiers danced together around the fires. Two years later, the old rulers were restored and the Jews were once again confined to the ghetto.

5559 1799

Napoleon I

NAPOLEON INVADES *ERETZ YISRAEL*

Napoleon Bonaparte, Emperor of France, led his armies on a campaign to enlarge his empire and conquer *Eretz Yisrael* and the Middle East. Invading from the south, he succeeded in defeating the Turks and conquering most of *Eretz Yisrael*. Napoleon laid siege to the port city of Acre, but Turkish forces, with the help of British armies and supplies, defeated him, and the French were forced out of the Middle East.

The opening session of the Grand Sanhedrin, held on February 9, 1807 (from a contemporary etching formerly in the collection of the Jewish community of Berlin)

1799
Volta invents the battery.

Napoleon's prison is the place where Dov Groner, an Irgun fighter, was hanged in 1947. This is his grave.

Focus: Napoleon and the Jews

In the times of the Temple the Sanhedrin had been the highest Jewish court, making legal decisions that were binding on all the Jewish people. Napoleon attempted to reestablish the Jewish court. He set up a "Sanhedrin" and personally appointed its members. It was to rule on questions about Judaism that Napoleon had prepared for them. Its members included Orthodox rabbis as well as secular Jews. Though meeting with great fanfare, pomp and ceremony, its impact on the Jewish people was minimal and it ceased to exist after only three months.

When Napoleon invaded Russia with his huge armies, some of the Jewish leaders of Russia hoped that he would free them from the brutal tyranny of the Czars. However, other Jewish leaders were concerned that Napoleon's freedom would lead to Jews assimilating into gentile culture, giving up their identity and Jewish practices, as had actually happened to many Jews living under Napoleon. These leaders encouraged the Jews to support Russia in its war against Napoleon.

Legend has it that Napoleon, traveling late one evening, heard sounds of people crying in a certain building. Ordering his coach to stop, he went to investigate. He entered a synagogue where Jews were sitting on the ground, crying. They explained that they were mourning the destruction of their Temple that had taken place over 1800 years earlier, on that date (Tishah B'Av). Napoleon responded, "If they still mourn for their own Temple after so long, they will certainly return to Israel one day and rebuild it."

Did you know that?

- The Acre fortress that withstood Napoleon's attack was, more than a century later, turned into a prison by the British. It was used to incarcerate and execute Jews who were members of underground forces fighting to liberate *Eretz Yisrael* from British rule. The thick stone walls that had withstood Napoleon's siege made the prison virtually impregnable. Despite this, in a daring rescue operation, the Irgun Zeva'i Leumi, a Jewish underground organization, blew a hole in the fortress walls, allowing many prisoners to escape. The fortress that did not fall to Napoleon fell to the Jews. The incident made international headlines, with details of the escape being reported in *The New York Times*.

- Afraid that Napoleon would defeat him, the Pasha of *Eretz Yisrael* turned to the Jewish community in Jerusalem and requested that they say special prayers for the safety of the country.

113

A Century of Great Polish Chassidim 1750 - 1850

The 18th century was blessed with many great Polish Chassidic leaders. Here's a sampling:

REB ELIMELECH AND REB ZUSHA

These brothers who spread Chassidus in Poland and Galicia were disciples of the Maggid of Mezeritch. Reb Elimelech was known as "The Rebbe, Reb Meilech." Every night, before going to sleep, Reb Elimelech would take any money left in his house and give it away to charity. Among his works are *Tzetel Katan* ("*The Small List*"), a seventeen-point program on how to be a good Jew, and *Noam Elimelech*, a classic Chassidic work on Torah. Reb Zusha was a *tzaddik* whose kindness and modesty were legendary.

A LEGEND / A THOUGHT

Reb Elimelech said: I know I will go to Heaven, because when the Heavenly Court asks me, "Did you learn, pray, and do good as you should have?" I will say, "No, no, no." The Court will then pass judgment, saying that because I told the truth I deserve to enter Heaven.

When Reb Zusha lay on his deathbed, he told his disciples he was not afraid of being asked why he wasn't as great as Moshe Rabbeinu. The Heavenly Court, he said, doesn't expect him to be that great. Instead, they will ask him, "Zusha, why weren't you Zusha? — Why didn't you achieve everything that you, Zusha, could have?"

THE CHOZEH (SEER) OF LUBLIN

Rabbi Yaakov Yitzchak Horowitz was called the Chozeh. It was said about him that he could see (*chozeh*) anything he wished, anywhere in Poland. He could also see into the depths of a person's soul. He was one of the founders of Polish Chassidus, and a disciple of the Maggid and Reb Elimelech. He taught that a Rebbe should be concerned not only about the religious needs of his Chassidim but also about their livelihood and physical well-being.

A LEGEND / A THOUGHT

The Chozeh would personally serve food to the poor he had invited to his table. Afterwards, he would clear away the dishes. A beggar once asked the Chozeh: "Bringing the food to feed me is a *mitzvah*, but why do you personally take away the dishes?" The Chozeh answered that clearing away the dishes is as holy an activity as the High Priest's service on Yom Kippur, when he took the empty incense pan out of the Temple's Holy of Holies.

THE KOZHNITZER MAGGID

Rabbi Yisrael Hopstein's reputation as a Torah giant and wonder worker were legendary, and many called him "the second Baal Shem." Reb Yisrael, the Kozhnitzer Maggid, spread Chassidus throughout Poland. At times, he was so physically weak that he had to be carried to the synagogue. As he began to pray, however, his strength and vigor would return, and he would sing and dance as he prayed with great devotion.

The "Revolution" Within Chassidus:

In order to gain an understanding of the following Rebbes, it is of utmost importance to be aware of the "revolution" created by their approach to Chassidus. The Chozeh ("Seer") of Lublin promoted an approach that developed into a more rigorously intellectual form of Chassidus. His disciples focused their energies on relentless Torah study, the shunning of material comforts and, above all else, the endless pursuit of truth. It was a philosophy that attracted many, yet was viewed by others as too radical a departure from traditional Chassidus. The many great Chassidic leaders who emerged from this school of thought stressed the ideals mentioned above. Among them were Rabbi Yaakov Yitzchak Rabinowitz, who was called the Yid HaKadosh ("the Holy Jew"), and was the teacher of Reb Simchah Bunim of Peshis'cha; as well as Reb Simchah Bunim's disciples.

REB SIMCHAH BUNIM OF PESHIS'CHA

A disciple of the Chozeh, Reb Simchah Bunim, known as the Rebbe Reb Bunim, refocused Polish Chassidus to stress Talmud study and scholarship. Before assuming the reins of Polish Chassidus, Reb Simchah Bunim had lived in Danzig, Germany where he was variously a lumber merchant and a pharmacist, and where he was active in "reaching out" to non-observant Jews in that cosmopolitan city. Among his outstanding disciples were Rabbi Menachem Mendel Morgenstern of Kotzk; Rabbi Yitzchak Meir Alter, the "Chiddushei HaRim," founder of the great Chassidic dynasty of Ger; and Reb Yitzchak of Worka.

A LEGEND / A THOUGHT

Reb Simchah Bunim would say: Every man has a treasure in his own backyard. It is foolish to search for happiness in other people's backyards. All we want we have inside of ourselves.

THE KOTZKER

Rabbi Menachem Mendel Morgenstern of Kotzk, Rabbi Simchah Bunim's disciple, despised wealth and searched for absolute truth and honesty. He demanded perfection and self-discipline from himself — and from his Chassidim. Rabbi Yitzchak Meir Rottenberg, the founder of the Gerrer dynasty of Chassidim, was a close colleague and disciple. His family name was later changed to Alter. It was Reb Yitzchak

Did you know that?

- Rabbi Simchah Bunim loved music, and was an accomplished chess player. In Danzig he convinced the Jewish stevedores to stop working on Shabbos. First he asked them not to record their work in writing, then to stop working on Friday night. Step by step, he made them Sabbath observers.

Meir who primarily succeeded the Kotzker as the leader of Polish Chassidus. The Kotzker's son-in-law was Rabbi Avraham Borenstein of Sochatchov, author of *Avnei Nezer*, a compendium of halachic responsa. After close to a decade of being Rebbe, the Kotzker mysteriously shut himself up in his room and for twenty years, until his death, rarely left his room or met with anyone.

A LEGEND / A THOUGHT

The Kotzker would say:

Where is God? Wherever man lets Him in.

It is a great thing to bring the dead back to life. But it is even greater to bring the living back to life.

5558 1798

JEWISH SLAVES IN MALTA FREED

Jew Stats:

In **1800**, there were **2,000** Jews living in the United States and **two million** in Europe. The number of Jews living in Europe had jumped to **seven million** by **1880**.

The island of Malta was given to the Knights of St. John by Charles V in 1530. The knights ruled this Mediterranean island and eventually became pirates. Over the years many Jewish travelers were captured and forced to live on the island as slaves. This Jewish community of slaves was finally freed after Napoleon conquered the island.

5562 1802

VOLOZHIN – THE MOTHER OF YESHIVOS – OPENS

Yeshivah Eitz Chaim of Volozhin

The greatest student of the Vilna Gaon, Rabbi Chaim Itzkovitz, known as Rabbi Chaim Volozhiner (of Volozhin), founded a yeshivah in Volozhin, Lithuania. The Volozhin Yeshivah, a central house of advanced learning for young men, altered forever the educational system of the Jewish people. Until then, Jewish boys would attend *cheder* (primary school) and go on to study with a private tutor, or in their community's study hall, usually led by the local rabbi. Volozhin changed all that. It was a yeshivah designed to attract outstanding students from cities and towns throughout Europe, and it was devoted to intensive Torah study. It attracted the brightest minds of Lithuanian Jewry. The yeshivah had lectures by different *roshei yeshivah* and a set schedule of study. Yeshivos of present times are all patterned, more or less, after the Volozhin Yeshivah.

As the first *Rosh Yeshivah* of Volozhin, Reb Chaim himself molded Volozhin, and through it, the entire yeshivah world.

In addition to his fame as being the founder of the Volozhin Yeshivah, Reb Chaim Volozhiner is the renowned author of the classic work, *Nefesh HaChaim*, which was published posthumously in 1824. It is a seminal work on Jewish thought which in many instances is based on Kabbalah. In the view of many, *Nefesh HaChaim* was meant to present the philosophy of the *misnagdim* (the opponents of the Chassidic movement at its outset), and indirectly address some Chassidic approaches that the *misnagdim* found troubling.

Reb Chaim was succeeded by his son, Reb Yitzchak Volozhiner, who, in addition to serving as *Rosh Yeshivah* of Volozhin, was active in many attempts to abolish Czarist decrees against Russian Jewry. Upon his passing, he was succeeded by his son-in-law, Rabbi Eliezer Yitzchak Fried. Upon his untimely passing, his brother-in-law, Rabbi Naftali Tzvi Yehudah Berlin (known as Netziv – both an acronym of his name and a Hebrew term for "prince" or "leader"), succeeded him.

(For more on Netziv, see Famous Commentators of the 1800's — Ha'amek Davar.)

The Netziv was joined at the helm of the yeshivah by a grandson of Reb Chaim Volozhiner, the legendary Rabbi Yosef Dov Ber HaLevi Soloveitchick, who served as associate Rosh Yeshivah. Rabbi Yosef Dov, who later became the Rabbi of Brisk, is known as the "Beis HaLevi," after his Torah works.

Rabbi Yosef Dov's son, Rabbi Chaim HaLevi Soloveitchik, who was married to a granddaughter of the Netziv, later became a member of the yeshivah's faculty, and eventually became an associate Rosh Yeshivah. He literally revolutionized Talmudic study through his method of analysis. (For more on Reb Chaim, see People of the Book: Famous Torah Works of the 1900's – Chiddushei Rabbi Chaim.)

The yeshivah remained open for almost ninety years, until the Czar's government demanded the authority to set the yeshivah's schedule and include secular studies in the curriculum. The Netziv refused to submit to Russian anti-Semitism and closed down the yeshivah.

5566
1806

THE CHASAM SOFER APPOINTED RABBI OF PRESSBURG

At the dawn of the 19th century, Jews who had been oppressed for centuries suddenly found themselves confronted with the challenges of greater freedoms and opportunities in secular society. In an effort to take advantage of these opportunities, many Jews in Western Europe abandoned *mitzvah* observance and Torah study.

This tide of cultural assimilation would have overtaken Hungary as well, had it not been for the efforts of Rabbi Moshe Sofer, known as the "Chasam Sofer," who defended traditional observance against change. He established the Pressburg Yeshivah, and his students became the inspired leaders who led the Jewish communities of Austria, Hungary and Slovakia and kept them loyal to Torah. An exceptional Torah scholar and a strong rabbinic leader, he was the leading halachic decisor of his generation. Thousands of questions on halachah were sent to him, and his responses are collected in the multi-volume *She'eilos U'Teshuvos Chasam Sofer*. His Talmudic novellae, Torah insights, and sermons have also been published and are popular even today. His *Sefer HaZikaron* describes the 1809 siege of Pressburg by Napoleon's troops.

The Chasam Sofer's legacy continued long after his death. His yeshivah in Pressburg flourished until World War II. Many of his descendants were great Torah scholars who led communities and headed yeshivos.

Rabbi Akiva Sofer, a great-grandson of the Chasam Sofer who was Rabbi of Pressburg before World War II, settled in Jerusalem, where he reestablished the Pressburg Yeshivah.

Did you know that?

- The Chasam Sofer was a descendant of Rashi.

- By the age of 15, he had completed the study of the entire Talmud.

- He was a *mohel* who performed more than 700 circumcisions.

- The Chasam Sofer was Rabbi Akiva Eiger's son-in-law.

- He was knowledgeable in mathematics, biology and astronomy.

- His son and successor, Rabbi Shimon Sofer, was a member of Parliament in a country that later would be known for its intense anti-Semitism — Austria.

- The Nazis desecrated the Pressburg graveyard, building a railroad through it. Yet miraculously the Chasam Sofer's grave was untouched.

Rabbi Moshe Sofer, the Chasam Sofer

5569 1808

FIRST JEW ELECTED TO CANADIAN PARLIAMENT

Ezekiel Hart was the first Jew elected to the Canadian parliament, but he refused to take the Christian oath and was not allowed to take his seat. As a result of this denial of Mr. Hart's rights, the parliament was dissolved. He was reelected, but again was denied his seat.

5570 1810

FIRST REFORM TEMPLE

A group of Jews in Seesen, Germany became the first to change the way Jews pray in a synagogue, breaking a millennium-old tradition. For the first time Jewish prayers were not said in Hebrew, but in a foreign language, German. German songs were sung as part of the services. Changes were made so that the temple would more closely resemble a church, including the introduction of an organ. Eventually, more Reform temples were opened throughout Germany, and Reform spread to America as well as to other Western countries.

Reform leaders continued to introduce changes in Jewish practice. The early Reform leaders attempted to do away with *bris milah*, the Sabbath (celebrating Sunday instead), and wearing *tefillin*. Today's Reform rabbis have gone so far as to even change the definition of a Jew, accepting patrilineal descent — recognizing a person born of a non-Jewish mother as Jewish.

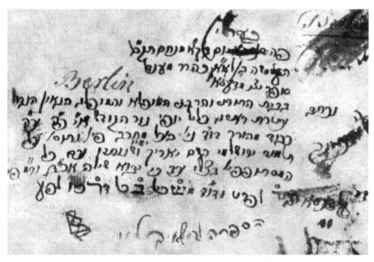
Moses Mendelssohn's Hebrew handwriting at the age of 13

Focus: Moses Mendelssohn

The emergence of the Reform movement is largely due to the "father of Reform," Moses Mendelssohn. Born in Dessau in 1729, Moses ben Menachem Mendel was raised as a traditional Jew. He was bright and very successful in his Torah studies. At the age of 14 he moved to Berlin, where Frederick the Great had passed laws giving the Jews greater civil rights. Thus, the atmosphere at the time was more accepting of the Jews than it had been in the Middle Ages. Mendelssohn applied his genius to secular studies, and was soon recognized by German gentiles as a great writer and philosopher. Despite his Judaism, he was accepted as an equal in intellectual circles. Though it seems that he was personally *mitzvah* observant, his desire to be accepted by the gentiles greatly influenced his outlook and teachings. These teachings became the basis for assimilation and the Reform movement. His philosophy succeeded in leading vast segments of Jewry away from their precious heritage of Torah study and *mitzvah* observance.

Did you know that?

- Moses Mendelssohn translated the Torah into literary German, and published it using Latin characters, rather than transliterating the translation in Hebrew letters as had been done until then. Mendelssohn's goal was to introduce even observant Jews to the German language, so that they, too, would be open to secular culture and influence.

- Mendelssohn won an academic competition against the famous German philosopher, Kant, even though Mendelssohn never had any formal university training.

- Mendelssohn had six children. Four of them converted to Christianity.

Moses Mendelssohn
(from the Mendelssohn family collection)

5570 1810 BIRTH OF REB YISRAEL SALANTER — THE *MUSSAR* MOVEMENT

The *mussar* revolution started with a single sentence. Reb Yisrael Salanter's mentor, Reb Zundel of Salant, told him, "Yisrael, learn *mussar* and you will learn to fear God." That sentence made him a changed man, and he went on to transform the Torah world.

Rabbi Yisrael Lipkin of Salant, known as Reb Yisrael Salanter, was a young disciple of Reb Zundel. From the time he heard that charge, he began to focus on *mussar*, the study of ethics and values, and to teach his students how to find weaknesses in their character and perfect themselves. He showed them how to control selfish urges and improve themselves spiritually. Though these goals were always part of the Torah way of life, Reb Yisrael's methods were new. He established "houses" of *mussar,* where *mussar* would be taught and studied by laymen as well as by yeshivah students. He also arranged for the printing of many classic works of *mussar*.

Later on, many yeshivos integrated *mussar* into their curricula. While the *Rosh Yeshivah* focused on teaching Talmud, the *mashgiach* would teach *mussar* to the students and guide their character development.

Reb Zundel, who had been one of Reb Chaim Volozhiner's closest students, moved from Salant to *Eretz Yisrael.* With his teacher gone, Reb Yisrael moved to Vilna, where he was appointed a *rosh yeshivah* and a member of the rabbinate. In Vilna, he was soon recognized as a great scholar, but was forced to leave the city

Did you know that?

◈ During a cholera epidemic in 1848, Reb Yisrael led relief efforts in Vilna. He ruled that Jews must eat on Yom Kippur so that their resistance would not be weakened. He set an example by going from synagogue to synagogue, reciting *Kiddush* and eating.

◈ In Reb Yisrael's passport were written the words, *"Immer Im Philosophish Gedanken Versunken"* — which means, "always immersed in philosophical thought." This was the government's way of telling the border guards and other authorities that this man had to be given special treatment.

◈ Reb Yisrael said: When faced with a decision, ask yourself: "What would I do if today were Yom Kippur?"

◈ He was once asked by a very busy businessman, "I have only an hour a day to study. Should I learn *mussar* or Talmud?" Reb Yisrael answered, "Study *mussar*, and as a result you'll find the extra time you need to study Talmud."

when he refused to accept a position in a government-controlled rabbinical seminary. He moved to Kovno, where he established a yeshivah and taught *mussar*.

When Reb Yisrael had to go to Germany for medical treatment, he saw the damage Reform had done to Jewish observance there and he decided to stay and strengthen Judaism. He worked with Jewish university students, helping them return to observance. He also traveled to Paris, where he sought to combat the forces of assimilation. His last years were spent in Germany.

Reb Yisrael's *mussar* gave many yeshivos and communities the strength to withstand the challenges of assimilation into Western culture. Many of today's yeshivos in America and Israel were founded by students of *mussar* yeshivos.

A YESHIVAH IS BORN:
MIR, 5575 / 1815

Rabbi Chaim Volozhiner was 66, and the Chasam Sofer was 53, in the year Napoleon was defeated at Waterloo. For more on Reb Chaim see 5562/1802. For more on the Chasam Sofer see 5566/1806.

The State of Israel boasts hundreds of yeshivos. The largest of all is Yeshivas Mir in Jerusalem. Inside its many study halls are thousands of students from all over the world. Some of them have been studying there for more than twenty years. The thunderous roar of their study fills the great halls.

The yeshivah was founded in 1815 in the small town of Mir, Lithuania. Its *roshei yeshivah* were noted scholars and its alumni served in posts throughout Eastern Europe. Rabbi Eliezer Yehudah Finkel, the famed Mirrer *Rosh Yeshivah,* and Rabbi Yerucham Levovitz, the Mirrer *Mashgiach,* were its dynamic leaders during the turbulent years after World War I.

More than a century after the yeshivah was founded, the Nazis put an end to Jewish life in Mir. Through a miraculous set of circumstances, 300 of the Mirrer yeshivah students escaped to Kobe, Japan. From there the Japanese relocated the yeshivah to Shanghai, China, where it remained until the War was

Did you know that?

⇨ The Japanese consul in Kovno, Lithuania, Chiune Sugihara, issued visas that saved the Mirrer students. He did so against the specific orders he had received from Japan, because he wanted to save Jewish lives. He issued a total of 6,000 visas to Jews escaping the Nazis.

1815

Napoleon is
defeated at Waterloo.

1819

Stethoscope
is invented.

over. Many Mirrer students who escaped the Holocaust and came to America became rabbis, *roshei yeshivah,* and teachers in yeshivos and day schools. They played an important role in developing America's flourishing Torah community.

After the War, Rabbi Finkel established the Mirrer Yeshivah in Jerusalem, which today has more than 3,000 students and is the largest yeshivah in the world, and Rabbi Avraham Kalmanowitz established it in Brooklyn.

Town of Mir

THE CANTONISTS

5587
1827

In Russia, Jewish boys were forcibly drafted into the army to serve for twenty-five to thirty years. Some as young as 9 or 10 were marched to military outposts hundreds of miles away from family and friends. There, all alone in a hostile environment, these boys, called "Cantonists," had to face Russian officers who did their best to convert them — using physical and mental torture. Nevertheless, many of these children were able to withstand the beatings and pressure and remained Jews. The Russian army did not need these boy soldiers; the draft was Czar Nicholas I's attempt to forcibly convert the Jews to Christianity. This episode in Jewish history was a double tragedy. Unfortunately, rich and influential individuals sometimes cooperated with the Russian authorities, allowing them to take orphans and children of widows — those who did not have the money or political power to protect themselves.

People of the Book: Famous Commentators of the 1800's

Torah Commentators

MALBIM

Malbim is an acronym for Rabbi Meir Leibush ben Yechiel Michel. When the Malbim's commentary was written, there were Reform Jews who taught that the Oral Torah was created by the rabbis and not part of the Torah given at Sinai. The Malbim showed where and how the laws in the Oral Torah are connected to the verses of the Written Torah. He also wrote a commentary on the entire *Tanach*. Through his commentary, and as Rabbi of Bucharest, the Malbim defended traditional Judaism. Afraid of him, Reform Jews in Bucharest arranged to have him arrested and put on trial for espionage! He was sentenced to death. Only through the efforts and intervention of Sir Moses Montefiore, who contacted officials of the Rumanian government, was his sentence changed to exile.

Rabbi Meir Leibush Malbim

Did you know that?

❧ Toward the end of the Malbin's life, the New York Jewish community offered him the position of Chief Rabbi, which would be created for him. His family persuaded him that at his age he was not strong enough for the post.

Did you know that?

🐌 Netziv's son, Rabbi Chaim Berlin, was the Chief Rabbi of Jerusalem's Ashkenazic community.

Rabbi Naftali Tzvi Yehudah Berlin of Volozhin, who had the courage to close down the greatest yeshivah in the world

Ben Ish Chai

HA'AMEK DAVAR

The author of *Ha'amek Davar*, Rabbi Naftali Tzvi Yehudah Berlin (known as Netziv), was born in the small village of Mir, Lithuania in 1817. Young Naftali Tzvi Yehudah was accepted to the famous Volozhin Yeshivah at only 11 years of age, and at age 36 he became *Rosh Yeshivah*, the position he held for forty years. The Netziv was in the forefront of the struggle against the Czar's anti-Semitic decrees. Late in the Netziv's career, the government ordered that the yeshivah cut its enrollment in half, reduce the hours of Torah study, and introduce secular studies. Refusing to submit, the Netziv closed down the yeshivah.

The Netziv was an outstanding Torah scholar, and halachic questions came to him from all over the Jewish world. Many of his responsa are published in *Meishiv Davar*, and his Talmud lectures are published as *Meromei Sadeh*. He also wrote *Ha'amek She'eilah,* a classic commentary on the *She'iltos d'Rabbi Achai Gaon,* and other works. *Ha'amek Davar* is his insightful Torah commentary.

His greatness as a Torah leader was achieved in great measure through his diligence and sacrifice for Torah study; for many years he studied at least 16 hours a day.

Halachah

KITZUR SHULCHAN ARUCH

The *Kitzur*, as it is often called, is a simplified, shortened form of the *Shulchan Aruch*. It clearly and simply explains a Jew's obligations over the course of his life. The author, Rabbi Shlomo Ganzfried, was Rabbi of the city of his birth, Ungvar, Hungary. The *Kitzur,* first published in 1835, achieved unprecedented popularity; 250,000 copies of it were sold within twenty-two years of its publication. Even today, it is the book used to teach and study Jewish law in many elementary yeshivos and high schools; most traditional Jewish homes have a copy.

BEN ISH CHAI

Chacham Yosef Chaim of Baghdad was one of the great Torah scholars of Sephardic Jewry. He was a genius, and upon the passing of his father, he became the de facto leader of Baghdad Jewry at the age of 25. He was a respected expert in Talmud, halachah, Kabbalah, and *Aggadah* (the non-halachic portion of the Talmud). He was particularly known for his talents as an orator. On the Sabbath, he gave three-hour speeches that captivated his audiences. On special Sabbaths he would address an audience of thousands of men, women, and children for four hours straight.

He would begin his sermons by explaining the week's Torah portion. Then he would discuss topics in halachah. These lectures form the basis of his *Ben Ish Chai*. He wrote many other works on halachah, *Aggadah*, Talmud, and Kabbalah. The halachic portions of *Ben Ish Chai* are used to teach halachah in many Sephardic communities, and are referred to by Ashkenazic as well as Sephardic scholars.

BE'ER YITZCHAK

This is a book of responsa written by Rabbi Yitzchak Elchanan Spektor, the Rabbi of Kovno, one of the greatest rabbis and Jewish leaders of the late 19th century. He was recognized as the preeminent halachic authority of his generation and was very involved in helping Jews in peril.

Rabbi Yitzchak Elchanan Spektor

Focus: Rabbi Yitzchak Elchanan Spektor

Rabbi Yitzchak Elchanan Spektor was one of the most revered halachic authorities of his generation. Born in 1816 in Grodno, Russia, he spent much of his youth assisting his father, a prominent rabbi. In 1863, he was appointed the Rabbi of Kovno, a position he held for thirty-two years until his death at the age of 79. He established a yeshivah in Kovno and his community service knew no bounds. There was not an area of halachah in which he was not expert and with which he did not deal to some extent. He was approached by all — layman and scholar, Ashkenazic and Sephardic Jew alike — for his rulings, and he responded to halachic inquiries both day and night. Together with Reb Yisrael Salanter, he formed a committee dedicated to fighting the harsh decrees of the Russian government, and they achieved much for the sake of the Jews in Russia. Reb Yitzchak Elchanan's piety and his concern for the welfare of each and every Jew are stuff of legend.

Toward the end of his life, he was very weak. It was the Sabbath before Yom Kippur, *Shabbos Shuvah*. Despite his feeble physical condition, Reb Yitzchak Elchanan was helped up to the podium and he prepared to address the congregation, as had been his custom for so many years. As he approached the podium he screamed, "People of Israel, repent! Woe, Jews of Kovno! What will be with the Sabbath observance in our city?" With that he fainted. He was revived, and as he took to the podium again, he screamed, "Woe, Jews of Kovno! What will be with the laws of family purity?" Again he fainted. The members of his congregation tried to revive him, but to no avail — his soul had departed.

His works, *Be'er Yitzchak* and *Ein Yitzchak* (responsa), and his work on *Choshen Mishpat* entitled *Nachal Yitzchak*, live on to inspire students and scholars alike.

Title page of Reb Yitzchak Elchanan's *Ein Yitzchak*, published in Vilna, 1889

5596 1836

RABBI S. R. HIRSCH AND *THE NINETEEN LETTERS*

The Reform movement had become very strong in Germany and had taken control of most of the Jewish institutions. Reform leaders portrayed Orthodox Judaism as something ancient and useless. *The Nineteen Letters of Ben Uziel*, written by Rabbi Samson Raphael Hirsch, was the first successful defense of Orthodox Jewry against Reform teachings. After the warm reception given *The Nineteen Letters*, he published *Horeb*, a book that elucidates the *mitzvos* and presents their philosophical underpinnings.

German youth were astounded when they read about the values of traditional Judaism. For the first time, they learned how relevant these values were to their own lives. Rabbi Hirsch, a great scholar and outstanding leader, spent much of his life successfully strengthening Torah life in Germany — through his many articles and essays, and through his many books, including monumental commentaries *on Chumash*, the *Siddur*, and *Tehillim*. Though he was Chief Rabbi of the large province of Moravia and an influential member of the Austro-Hungarian parliament, he left his position to become the Rabbi of a small group of Orthodox Jews in Frankfurt, Germany. This group became the living example of Rabbi Hirsch's philosophy, called *Torah im Derech Eretz* — Torah living while engaged in worldly pursuits. He began in Frankfurt with only eleven families, but became the leader and teacher of many thousands.

His followers never compromised Jewish law, however they accepted Western dress and language, received a secular education and took part in the modern gentile world. Their children were given a full Torah education and were fiercely proud of their Orthodoxy.

Did you know that?

§ Rabbi Dr. Joseph Breuer, Rabbi Hirsch's grandson, left Frankfurt as a refugee from Nazi Germany. Arriving in the United States in 1939, he transplanted the Frankfurt Jewish community to Manhattan's Washington Heights, where he built a German-Jewish community that continues to teach and practice Rabbi Hirsch's *Torah im Derech Eretz.*

§ Rav Hirsch wrote *Horeb* before *The Nineteen Letters*, but his publisher was afraid to invest in such a large book. Rav Hirsch then wrote the shorter *Nineteen Letters,* which is a series of letters by Ben Uziel, a rabbi, explaining the beauty and logic of Orthodox Judaism to his boyhood friend. *The Nineteen Letters* became so popular that the publisher accepted *Horeb.*

Rabbiner Hirsch had a magnificent German writing style, which helped him spread his message to well-educated Jews. His books, now available in English and Hebrew, are as popular as ever.

EARTHQUAKE IN *ERETZ YISRAEL*

5597 1837

One Sunday afternoon a powerful earthquake shook *Eretz Yisrael*. Within moments, the northern cities of Safed and Tiberias were turned into rubble. In Safed, 2,000 Jews died, buried under fallen buildings. After the earthquake, Jerusalem became the city where most religious immigrants settled.

Did you know that?

According to legend, moments before the earthquake struck, Rabbi Avraham Dov of Avritch, the Rabbi of a synagogue in Safed, ordered the people in his synagogue to stand with him next to the holy Torah ark in the synagogue. When the earthquake struck, the ceiling caved in, but the ark protected the Rabbi and his congregation. Today many people visit the site, which has been rebuilt, to see the wall that miraculously did not collapse.

Jew Stats:

In **1841,** there were **500** Jews living in Jerusalem. Sixty years later, there were **30,000**. By **1880,** there were more Jews than Arabs living in Jerusalem.

1840
The bicycle is invented.

REFORM MOVEMENT OFFICIALLY CHANGES THE *SIDDUR*

5605 1845

At a conference of Reform rabbis in Germany, the delegates decided to update the *Siddur*. Passages praying for the Jews' return to *Eretz Yisrael* and the restoration of Jewish independence under a descendant of King David were removed.

5608
1848

AMERICAN CONSUL CONVERTS TO JUDAISM

Warder Cresson, a Quaker born in Philadelphia, was the first United States consul in Palestine. While living in *Eretz Yisrael*, he decided to become a *ger tzedek* (a convert). He changed his name to Michael Boaz Israel. He passed away twelve years later and is buried in the ancient Jewish cemetery on the Mt. of Olives.

Warder Cresson — Michael Boaz Israel

Lord George Gordon

Focus: *Gerim* (converts)

Throughout history there have been gentiles who have converted to Judaism.

THE HIGH PRIEST: Jethro, father-in-law of Moses, was the High Priest of Midian. After the Exodus from Egypt he joined the Jews in the desert and became the first *ger* in history. A section in the Torah is named for him.

THE ROMAN: Onkelos was the nephew of the Roman general who destroyed the Second Temple. He converted, and wrote *Targum Onkelos*, recognized by the sages of the Mishnah as the definitive translation of the Torah into Aramaic.

Targum Onkelos is printed alongside the standard *Chumash* text.

THE NOBLEMAN: Valentin Potocki was the son of a Polish count. Upon converting he took the name Avraham ben Avraham, and became a Torah scholar and *tzaddik*. The church had him burned at the stake in the city of Vilna. He lived during the lifetime of the Vilna Gaon, and the Gaon visited him in prison.

THE BRITISH LORD: Lord George Gordon, son of a duke, was born in 1750. Lord Gordon converted to Judaism and changed his name to Israel ben Avraham Gordon.

WISSOTZKY FOUNDS TEA COMPANY

5609
1849

An alumnus of the Volozhin Yeshivah, Ze'ev Wolf Kelonymous Wissotzky became a millionaire selling tea. The company he founded became the largest tea company in Russia, selling 40 million pounds of tea a year. The company also sold tea in America, Europe, and *Eretz Yisrael*. Wissotzky was a philanthropist who gave large sums of money to charity. Today Wissotzky is the largest tea company in Israel.

Jew Stats:

In **1850,** Britain had **30,000** Jews. Sixty years later, the population was ten times as large: **300,000.**

Then and Now: A modern box of Wissotzky Tea

A Century of Great Chassidim
1750 - 1850

The 18th century saw the rise of many great Chassidic leaders, men of lofty spiritual achievements. Here is a sampling:

RABBI LEVI YITZCHAK OF BERDITCHEV

Rabbi Levi Yitzchak always found a way to point out the best in the Jewish people before God. He was a disciple of the Maggid of Mezeritch and became Rabbi of Berditchev, from where he spread the teachings of Chassidus throughout the Ukraine.

RABBI NACHMAN OF BRESLOV

Rabbi Nachman was a great-grandson of the Baal Shem Tov. His grandmother was the Baal Shem Tov's only daughter, Udel. Rabbi Nachman lived in Breslov, where he taught Chassidus. His student, Rabbi Nosson, recorded many of his teachings in a book called *Likutei Moharan*. Rabbi Nachman taught some of his most profound ideas through parables about kings, generals, and poor people. These seemingly simple stories contained great Torah wisdom. After his death, Rabbi Nachman's Chassidim decided that no one could replace him, and to this day, two centuries after his passing, Breslover Chassidim refer to Rabbi Nachman as their Rebbe. (To read more about Breslov, see the entry on Uman, 5528/1768.)

A LEGEND / A THOUGHT

Rabbi Nachman taught:

The whole world is a narrow bridge; the main thing is not to be afraid.

It's a great *mitzvah* to always be happy.

Wherever I travel, I'm on my way to *Eretz Yisrael*.

RABBI YISRAEL FRIEDMAN OF RUZHIN

The Rebbe known as the Admor of Ruzhin was a grandson of the Maggid of Mezeritch. The Rizhiner was considered by many to be the greatest Rebbe of his time, and even great Rebbes many years his senior traveled to seek his counsel. Although he avoided pleasure for himself, he put on an outward display of royal opulence, to lend glory to Judaism and Chassidus. Despite his greatness and high status, he was a victim of much persecution. The Czarist government imprisoned him and he eventually was forced to leave Russia. Thanks to his exile, he spread Chassidus through much of the Austo-Hungarian Empire. Nearly all of his sons and sons-in-law were great leaders in their own right.

Part of the Rizhiner's dynasty survived the Holocaust, through his descendants, the Rebbes of Sadigora, Boyan, and Kopichinitz.

A LEGEND / A THOUGHT

Rabbi Yisrael said: The holy letters of the Hebrew alphabet need vowels to give the letters the proper sound. The Rebbe is the letters, his Chassidim are the vowels.

A Rebbe needs his Chassidim as much as the Chassid needs his Rebbe.

JERUSALEM GROWS BEYOND THE CITY WALLS

5615
1855

Today Jerusalem is a city of about fifty neighborhoods built on the mountains that surround the ancient walled city. For centuries before, though, Jerusalem was just a small walled village. As more Jews began to immigrate to *Eretz Yisrael,* Jerusalem's Old City became overcrowded. In addition, many houses were owned by Arab landlords who charged the Jews exhorbitant rent. Sir Moses Montefiore, a wealthy and influential English Jew, built the first neighborhood outside the city walls, Mishkenot Sha'ananim. In 1890, this neighborhood was absorbed into the Yemin Moshe neighborhood, which is named after Sir Moses Montefiore and is identified with the landmark windmill that Montefiore built. Mishkenot Sha'ananim was the first of many Jewish neighborhoods such as Nachalat Shivah, Meah Shearim, Beit Yisrael, and Batei Varsha that were built in the 1800's. Some of these were established by members of the "Old *Yishuv*" — the traditional Jewish community that had lived in Jerusalem for decades. These neighborhoods ultimately led to the expansion of Jerusalem into the large metropolis that it is today.

The Montefiore Windmill

Did you know that?

- Moses Montefiore was elected Sheriff of London.

- The small domed building that until recently housed *Kever Rachel* (Rachel's Tomb) was built with Montefiore's support.

Jew Stats:

In **1855,** there were **100,000** Jews in America. Over the next 45 years, **900,000** more Jews would immigrate to America, for a total population of **one million** by **1900.**

Focus: Moses Montefiore

Having made an incredible fortune by the age of 40, Sir Moses Montefiore decided to devote the rest of his life to helping the Jewish people. His wealth and influence gave him audiences with czars and sultans in his endeavors to protect the Jews. Through his efforts, Jews in Damascus who were imprisoned and tortured, falsely accused in a blood libel, were released. In another incident the famous Bible commentator, Malbim, was also released from prison as a result of his intervention. A Sephardic English Jew, Montefiore's greatest desire was to help rebuild *Eretz Yisrael*. He visited *Eretz Yisrael* seven times, his last trip there at the age of 90 — not an easy journey in an age when there were no airplanes! Montefiore lived to celebrate his 100th birthday. Sir Moses was a Jew who practiced *mitzvos* and remained humble. He gave away fortunes of money to help the poor and support Torah.

A typical street in Meah Shearim

Coat of arms of Sir Moses Montefiore

AMERICAN CIVIL WAR BREAKS OUT

5622
1861

In the Civil War, 6,000 Jews fought for the Union, and the Confederate army claimed 10,000 Jewish soldiers. Six Jews were awarded the Congressional Medal of Honor for their bravery in Civil War battles.

Judah P. Benjamin, a Jew, served the Confederacy first as secretary of war, then as secretary of state. Before the war, Mr. Benjamin was the first Jewish member of the United States Senate, representing Louisiana from 1853-1861. Following the war, he moved to London where he was a successful attorney.

Rabbi Yisrael Salanter was 52, and Rabbi Samson Raphael Hirsch was 53, in the year the Civil War broke out. For more about Rabbi Salanter see 5570/1810; for more about Rabbi Hirsch see 5596/1836.

Memorial at Cypress Hill Cemetery in Brooklyn, New York, for Jewish soldiers killed during the Civil War

Judah P. Benjamin

Captain Abraham Cohen, who served in the Civil War

Bellechase, Judah P. Benjamin's Louisiana estate

5622 1862

GENERAL GRANT'S ORDER #11

Abraham Lincoln

Believing anti-Semitic accusations that Jewish traders and businessmen were using illegal business practices to make large profits from the war, General Ulysses S. Grant ordered the U.S. Army to expel all Jews from the states of Kentucky, Tennessee, and Mississippi within twenty-four hours. The American Jewish community protested to President Abraham Lincoln, who ordered the expulsion order canceled.

A YESHIVAH IS BORN: SLABODKA, 5623 / 1863

Did you know that?

- The Alter was a devoted *rebbi* to his students. For thirty years he studied and lived with his students in Slabodka. He would visit his family, who lived in another village, only on holidays.

In 1863, a small yeshivah was founded by Rabbi Tzvi Levitan in Slabodka. In 1877, Rabbi Levitan was joined by Rabbi Nosson Tzvi Finkel. Concurrently, Rabbi Finkel joined Rabbi Yitzchak Blaser — a primary disciple of Rabbi Yisrael Salanter — in establishing a *kollel* in nearby Kovno for the advanced study of Torah and *mussar*. With time, Rabbi Finkel began what became the first *mussar* yeshivah, Knesses Yisrael in Slabodka. Rabbi Finkel, known as "the Alter of Slabodka," stressed not only scholarship but also character development.

"The Alter" was a master educator, and many of his students became leading rabbis. Several of them went on to found and lead many of the great American yeshivos: Rabbi Aharon Kotler of Beth Medrash Govoha, Lakewood; Rabbi Reuven Grozovsky and Rabbi Yaakov Kamenetsky of Yeshivah Torah Vodaath; Rabbi Yaakov Yitzchak Ruderman of Yeshivas Ner Israel in Baltimore; Rabbi David Leibowitz of Yeshivas Chafetz Chaim; and Rabbi Yitzchak Hutner of Mesivta Chaim Berlin in Brooklyn were all his students. In 1924 the Alter of Slabodka moved to *Eretz Yisrael*, with the *Rosh Yeshivah* Rabbi Moshe Mordechai Epstein. They opened a branch of the yeshivah in the city of Hebron. After the Arab massacre in Hebron (see 5689/1929), the yeshivah relocated to Jerusalem, where it flourishes today.

Rabbi Nosson Tzvi Finkel, the Alter

5628 1868

1869
Suez Canal
is opened.

5633 1873

Did you know that?

🐚 The Chafetz Chaim lists fourteen positive Torah commandments and seventeen Torah prohibitions associated with improper speech.

🐚 The Chafetz Chaim died in 1933. After World War II, the gentiles of Radin refused to release his body for reburial in Israel. They believed that because of him their town was the only one in the area to escape destruction during the War, and they did not want to give up this protection.

JEW MURDERED IN TENNESSEE

S.A. Bierfield, a Russian Jewish immigrant, was a store owner in Franklin, Tennessee. On August 15, 1868 a Ku Klux Klan mob riding on horseback shot him to death, together with his African-American clerk, Lawrence Bowman. Mr. Bierfield's crime? He had befriended — and even employed — members of the town's African-American community.

THE *SHEMIRAS HALASHON* REVOLUTION

The Torah commands us to guard our tongue from evil speech such as gossip, falsehood and slander.

To make Jews aware of these laws, Rabbi Yisrael Meir HaKohen Kagan wrote *Sefer Chafetz Chaim,* a handbook of the laws and guidelines of proper speech. The title is taken from a verse in Psalms (34:13-14): "Who is the man who desires life (*chafetz chaim*) …? Guard your tongue from evil and your lips from speaking falsehood …" Published in 1873, it became very popular, and quickly had an impact on the way people spoke. The author became known by the book's title, Chafetz Chaim.

The Chafetz Chaim wrote a second book, called *Shemiras HaLashon* ("Guarding the Tongue"), on the same topic. *Chafetz Chaim* is a halachic work, while *Shemiras HaLashon* is an ethical tract. Today, both books are studied by many people. Each summer, thousands of women attend a convention in Jerusalem on the topic of *shemiras halashon*. Similar conferences are held throughout the world.

There are *shemiras halashon* groups, where people take upon themselves to be particularly careful not to engage in forbidden speech during certain hours of the day. People sometimes join these groups as a source of merit for someone who is ill or who has some other special need.

Rabbi Yisrael Meir Kagan,
the Chafetz Chaim

Focus: The Chafetz Chaim

One of the most revered Jews of the 20th century, Rabbi Yisrael Meir HaKohen Kagan was an unusually humble man. He was born in 1839, in the town of Zhetel, near Grodno, Poland. He lost his father at the age of 10, and studied in Vilna during his teens. He lived simply in the small Polish village of Radin, where he founded a yeshivah. He wrote his *Chafetz Chaim* anonymously, and traveled from town to town acting as the book's salesman. By doing so he hoped to escape the honor that would be given to the author. The impact of his books and his great love for the Jewish nation made him famous all over the Jewish world.

To help Jews properly observe the *mitzvos* he wrote *Mishnah Berurah*, a six-volume masterpiece on Jewish law. It took him over twenty years to write this comprehensive treatment of the *Orach Chaim* section of the *Shulchan Aruch* — the section that deals with daily living, the Sabbath, and the Festivals. The volumes show the great genius of the Chafetz Chaim and his vast Torah knowledge and scholarship. *Mishnah Berurah* is a reference work for Jews who want to know how to perform the *mitzvos*. For rabbis and scholars, it is an important resource for deciding Jewish law.

Rabbi Yisrael Meir was concerned about all Jews and wrote *sefarim* to help them. For the Jewish immigrant to America or South Africa, all alone in a strange new country, he wrote *Nidchei Yisrael*. For Jewish soldiers drafted into gentile armies he wrote *Machaneh Yisrael*. He also wrote books specifically for Jewish women. In all, he authored some thirty-five volumes.

The Chafetz Chaim was considered one of the most pious Jews of his generation. He passed away at the age of 95, leaving a legacy of books, traditions, and stories that continue to inspire us today.

▸ An unknown customer in his wife's grocery store once forgot to take the herring for which he had paid. The Chafetz Chaim went door to door in an effort to locate the man, but it was to no avail. To ensure that he not be guilty of having money that was not rightfully his, Rabbi Yisrael Meir undertook to do a project for the public good.

▸ The Chafetz Chaim had his wife close the grocery early, so that she would not take away business from his competitors.

▸ So as not to cheat people, the Chafetz Chaim checked every one of the books he sold to make sure no pages were missing.

▸ When he was in his 80's, he traveled to collect funds to help people whose homes had burned to the ground in a fire in Radin.

▸ He personally shoveled the snow in front of his yeshivah so that the students would not slip.

▸ When the government issued an edict that threatened Torah education, the Chafetz Chaim, then 90-years-old, led a delegation to Warsaw to meet with the Polish prime minister. Rabbi Yisrael Meir spoke in Yiddish, which the prime minister did not understand. A Jewish senator stepped forward to translate, but the prime minister waved him away, saying, "He spoke from the heart and hearts understand each other." He rescinded the edict.

▸ When he heard that one of his students had been sentenced by the Czar's military court to ten years imprisonment, the Chafetz Chaim said, "Ten years? The government may not even last ten weeks!" Less than ten weeks later, the Russian Revolution toppled the Czar.

▸ In the last years of his life, he predicted that great dark clouds would loom on the horizon, and that the Jews would be in grave danger. The Holocaust began six years after he died.

A YESHIVAH IS BORN: TELSHE, 5635 / 1875

In 1875, a yeshivah opened in the city of Telshe, Lithuania. Its goal was to educate the young men from Telshe and the surrounding villages. The great Torah scholar, Rabbi Eliezer Gordon, became *Rosh Yeshivah* in 1885, and under his guidance the yeshivah became one of the noted Torah institutions of Europe.

In 1940, the Communists occupied Lithuania. They evicted the students of the Telshe Yeshivah and turned the building into a military hospital. Due to both the takeover by the Communists, who worked hard to destroy religious practice, and the impending attack by the Nazi war machine, it was decided to move the yeshivah. Rabbi Elya Meir Bloch and Rabbi Chaim Mordechai Katz went to America to arrange for the yeshivah to be transferred to the United States. Meanwhile, the Nazis invaded. The families of Rabbi Bloch and Rabbi Katz, and the yeshivah, were caught in the burning inferno of Nazi Europe. In America, out of touch with their families and not knowing what was happening to them, Rabbi Bloch and Rabbi Katz decided there was no choice — they would work to rebuild Torah in America, while praying for their loved ones on the other side of the ocean. In Cleveland, they opened a new Telshe Yeshivah. The yeshivah began with several American boys and three refugees. The legacy of Telshe Europe was transplanted onto American soil, first in Cleveland, Ohio and then in the Chicago, Illinois branch of the yeshivah, and later in Riverdale, New York.

After the passing of Rabbis Bloch and Katz, the Cleveland yeshivah was guided by two great leaders of American Orthodox Jewry: Rabbi Baruch Sorotzkin and Rabbi Mordechai Gifter.

1876

Custer makes his last stand and is defeated by the Sioux Indians.

1876

Alexander Graham Bell invents the telephone.

Did you know that?

🐝 The Telshe Yeshivah became the hub of Orthodox life in the Cleveland area. Under its influence and with its personnel, the Hebrew Academy and Yavneh High School for girls set standards for American Torah schools.

🐝 Rabbi Mordechai Gifter was the first American-born major *rosh yeshivah.* He studied in the original Telshe before the War. A powerful, eloquent orator and a brilliant scholar, he became a leading figure on the Orthodox scene.

Rabbi Eliyahu Meir Bloch

Rabbi Chaim Mordechai Katz

Rabbi Baruch Sorotzkin

Rabbi Mordechai Gifter

The yeshivah building in Telshe, Lithuania

5639 1879

1879
Edison invents
the electric light bulb.

In the year the electric light bulb was invented the Chafetz Chaim was 41 years old. Rabbi Chaim of Brisk was 26. For more on the Chafetz Chaim see 5633/1873. For more on Rabbi Chaim of Brisk see People of the Book: Famous Commentators of the 1800's.

FIRST "ANTI-SEMITE"

Wilhelm Mark was a German who wrote a number of booklets against Jews. He coined the term "anti-Semite," and went on to found the League of Anti-Semites.

JEWISH EMIGRATION

5640 1880

Russian anti-Semitism left many Jews with only one choice — to leave Mother Russia. Between 1880 and 1914, 60,000 Russian Jews moved to *Eretz Yisrael* and two million left for America. Arriving at Ellis Island, most of the Jews settled in New York's Lower East Side. Jewish organizations helped these refugees get settled.

Did you know that?

Engraved on the plaque on the base of the Statue of Liberty is the poem "The New Colossus," written by Emma Lazarus, a fourth-generation American Jew. Its memorable lines are: "Give me your tired, your poor, Your huddled masses yearning to breathe free, The wretched refuse of your teeming shore. Send these, the homeless, tempest-tost to me, I lift my lamp beside the golden door!"

The Statue of Liberty greeted generations of people immigrating to the United States. To many it became a symbol of freedom and hope.

143

Al Jolson, a Jewish actor, in "The Jazz Singer,"
the first commercial motion picture
to feature people speaking

Focus: American Jewish immigrants

Freedom and economic opportunity were waiting for the Jewish immigrant arriving from his European *shtetl*. Many Jews quickly became financially successful and made a great impact on America. The Jewish American immigrant played a prominent role in the growth and development of the garment industry, Hollywood, labor unions, music, advances in medicine, and the great American department stores. Unfortunately, Torah and *mitzvah* observance in America at that time was both difficult and unpopular. It was almost impossible for a Sabbath observer to find a job. With few yeshivos available, Jewish children were sent to public schools where they learned to become "good Americans" but drifted away from Judaism.

The price many Jews paid for American freedom and opportunity was the abandonment of Judaism and their children's resulting ignorance of their rich heritage. Today's assimilation and intermarriage were the almost inevitable fruits of such seeds.

The Downtown Talmud Torah on New York's Lower East Side in the early 20th century

ROTHSCHILD BEGINS TO SUPPORT NEW SETTLEMENTS IN *ERETZ YISRAEL*

5641 1881

In the second half of the 1800's, as a result of pogroms in Russia as well as the efforts of groups that encouraged the settlement of *Eretz Yisrael*, both secular and religious Jews began to make their way there in increasing numbers.

They built farm villages and small towns all over the land, in places like Zichron Yaakov, Gederah, Metulah and others. The conditions in *Eretz Yisrael* were so difficult that people were unable to make a living. The new settlements were in danger of being abandoned.

Edmond Rothschild, a wealthy French Jew, opened his heart and his pocketbook to these settlements. Over a six-year period he spent $6 million to buy land, build homes, support immigrants, and establish synagogues. Many of the small settlements he supported are today large Israeli cities.

Nathan Mayer Rothschild, third son of Mayer Amshel, scion of the Rothschild dynasty

Focus: The Rothschilds

A popular Yiddish saying in the 1900's to describe a wealthy Jew was, "He's as rich as Rothschild." The Rothschilds were the first Jewish millionaires of the modern world. There are many legends as to how Mayer Amshel Rothschild became rich. Though differing in details, all of them agree that Mayer had received a rabbi's blessing for wealth in return for his hav- ing done an exceptional good deed with his money. Mayer himself was a devout Orthodox German Jew. He and his five sons, whom he sent to the financial capitals of Europe, created a banking empire that was influential with European govern- ments. Mayer was an example of the great philanthropists who used their wealth to help the Jewish people.

Did you know that?

❧ The city of London elected Mayer Amshel's grandson, Lionel, to Parliament. However, in order to serve, he was required to take a Christian oath. He refused to do so, and was not allowed to enter Parliament. He was reelected three times before the British Parliament finally agreed to allow him to take a Jewish oath.

Jew Stats:

In **1881, 60 percent** of the doctors in Vienna were Jews, including the emperor's per- sonal physician.

Right to left:
Nathan Mayer Rothschild and his sons: Mayer, Lionel and Anthony

The Rothschild mansion at Tring Park, London, which was presented to the British government during World War II

ELIEZER PERLMAN MOVES TO *ERETZ YISRAEL*

5641
1881

As the "father of modern Hebrew," Eliezer Perlman, boarded the ship to Palestine, he made a solemn promise: He would not speak any language but Hebrew.

Though his parents were Orthodox Jews, Eliezer was a secular Zionist who spoke out stridently against the traditional Jewish way of life. He took a Hebrew name, Eliezer Ben-Yehudah, and spent his life convincing the secular Jews in Palestine to speak Hebrew rather than Yiddish, German, or French.

In 1919 the British recognized Hebrew as an official language of Palestine.

Ben-Yehudah published the first modern Hebrew dictionary, in which he traces the usage of Hebrew words and phrases since the time of the Bible. In addition, Ben-Yehudah and his colleagues coined new Hebrew words and phrases to describe things that did not exist when Hebrew was a spoken language.

Hebrew was eventually adopted by the secular Zionists living in Palestine and became the official language of the State of Israel.

Focus: Jewish Languages

LESHON HAKODESH: The first man and woman, Adam and Eve, spoke *leshon hakodesh* (the holy language), the Hebrew used in the Torah. It was the universal language of all the people in the world until the Tower of Babel was built 1996 years later. It is the primary language of prayer, the Bible, and the Mishnah. It was the main language spoken by Jews until the destruction of the First Temple, and it was used by many until after the destruction of the Second Temple. Modern Hebrew, though similar, contains many words, expressions and syntax not found in *leshon hakodesh*.

ARAMAIC: Aramaic was the language of the Babylonians. The Jews, during the Babylonian exile, spoke this language. They wrote in Aramaic, using Hebrew letters. The Talmud is written in Aramaic.

YIDDISH: In the early Middle Ages, the German Jews began speaking Yiddish. Though many of its words come from German, it is written in Hebrew letters. It became the language of Ashkenazic Jewry. By the 1930's it was spoken by 11 million Jews. Yiddish includes many words and phrases that come from the Bible, Midrash, and Talmud. The language captures the feelings of the Jews over their long European exile. Ashkenazic Jews the world over called it *"mama loshon,"* mother tongue.

LADINO: Spoken by Sephardic Jews from Morocco, North Africa, and the former Turkish Empire, Ladino is a dialect of Old Spanish, and is written using Hebrew letters. Many traditional Sephardic songs are written in Ladino, and are sung even today.

5641 1881

A JEW HELPS ORGANIZE AMERICAN RED CROSS

Did you know that?

🐚 The first Red Cross nurses' uniforms were designed by a Jew, Henry Dix. He also designed uniforms for army and navy nurses.

The decision to organize the American Red Cross was made in Washington, in the home of Adolphus Simeon Solomons, a traditional Jew of Sephardic descent. Together with Clara Barton, Solomons worked to build the organization.

HATIKVAH — THE ZIONIST ANTHEM

At the Eighth Zionist Congress the song *Hatikvah* was chosen as the Zionist movement's anthem. With the declaration of the State of Israel, it came to be considered the anthem of the independent state. The words of *Hatikvah* were written by Naftali Herz Imber as a poem which he published in 1886. The words were set to the music of a Moldavian-Rumanian folk song by Samuel Cohen, a resident of Rishon LeTzion.

After years of battling addiction to alcohol, Imber, a Galician-born poet, died a pauper in the United States.

ARRIVAL OF FIRST — AND LAST — CHIEF RABBI OF NEW YORK CITY

When Rabbi Jacob Joseph arrived at the port in Hoboken, New Jersey, throngs of Jews turned out to greet New York City's first Chief Rabbi. He had been selected by the great rabbis of Europe, at the request of New York City's Orthodox synagogues. They had asked that someone of outstanding ability be sent to lead New York City's Orthodox Jews. Before coming to the United States, Rabbi Jacob Joseph had studied in Volozhin, and had been a disciple of Rabbi Yisrael Salanter. He was a rabbinic judge in Vilna, and was famous for his eloquent sermons.

Unfortunately, because of the nature of American Jewry at that time, the Chief Rabbi of New York City

5646 1886

Did you know that?

🐾 The Israeli government never officially recognized *Hatikvah* as Israel's national anthem.

5648 1888

Rabbi Jacob Joseph

1888

Ballpoint pen is invented, and it replaces messy fountain pens.

149

Yeshiva University

was not accepted by many of the most powerful elements of the city. Secularists and assimilationists opposed him. When he tried to establish reliable kashruth supervision, the butchers and matzah bakers came out against him. In the end he was reduced to a figurehead without any real power. With the passing of Rabbi Jacob Joseph, the Orthodox congregations of New York never again attempted to unite under a Chief Rabbi. Rabbi Jacob Joseph was the first, and last, Chief Rabbi of New York. After his passing a yeshivah was established bearing his name. Yeshivah Rabbi Jacob Joseph became a major institution.

One of Rabbi Jacob Joseph's lasting influences on New York Jews was his involvement in Yeshivah Eitz Chaim. Eitz Chaim, on the Lower East Side, the earliest yeshivah in America, later developed into a major institution of American-Jewish education — Yeshiva University, which has been named as one of the top fifty universities in the country.

Focus: Yeshiva University

Yeshivah Eitz Chaim was the first American yeshivah elementary school. In 1915 it merged with Yeshivas Rabbeinu Yitzchak Elchanan [Rabbi Isaac Elchanan Theological Seminary (RIETS)], New York's only European-style advanced yeshivah, which had been established for European immigrants and was named for the recently deceased Rabbi of Kovno.

By the mid-1920's the merged school had become a "yeshivah college," combining yeshivah studies with an undergraduate degree program. Yeshiva College was led by Rabbi Dr. Bernard Revel, a pioneer of Torah education in America. He was succeeded by Rabbi Dr. Samuel Belkin and then Rabbi Dr. Norman Lamm.

Over the years, additional undergraduate and graduate divisions were added, forming Yeshiva University. Among the new divisions were Stern College for Women and the Albert Einstein College of Medicine, the only medical school in the world under Orthodox Jewish auspices.

In addition to its Judaic Studies programs — the yeshivah and postgraduate *kollel* divisions — Yeshiva University enables its students to pursue liberal arts and professional training in an Orthodox environment.

RIETS has provided thousands of rabbis and educators to serve the Jewish community. The medical school has graduated hundreds of Orthodox doctors, who are knowledgeable of and sensitive to the needs of Orthodox patients.

1893
The zipper
is invented.

ALFRED DREYFUS SENTENCED TO DEVIL'S ISLAND

5655
1895

Alfred Dreyfus was an assimilated Jew who considered himself first and foremost a patriotic Frenchman. He rose through the ranks in the army to become a member of the French General Staff. When there was suspicion that a member of the General Staff was a traitor who had sold military secrets to Germany, Dreyfus was accused. To protect the guilty parties, forged documents were created to prove his guilt. The court sentenced Dreyfus to life imprisonment on Devil's Island, a dreaded prison off the northern coast of South America. To humiliate him publicly, the badges and decorations were cut off his uniform and his sword was broken in two. As he was marched through the streets of Paris, the crowds shouted, "Death to Dreyfus! Death to the Jews!"

Alfred Dreyfus

Theodor Herzl was an Austrian journalist who covered the event for his paper. The crowd's anti-Semitism led to Herzl's working for the establishment of a Jewish state, and the Zionist movement was born.

Later, largely due to the efforts of Emile Zola, the conspiracy against Dreyfus was uncovered. Zola, a non-Jewish writer, revealed the truth to the public under the banner headline "J'Accuse!" (I accuse!). Eventually Dreyfus was pardoned by the French president and freed from Devil's Island. He rejoined the army and rose to the rank of general.

Emile Zola

Did you know that?

- Herzl once presented a plan for Jews to build their homeland in ... Uganda, Africa!

- Herzl's grandfather was an Orthodox rabbi.

- The word "Zionism" was coined by an assimilated Jew, Nathan Birnbaum. Birnbaum later became a *baal teshuvah* and an anti-Zionist. He joined Agudath Israel and was one of its leaders.

Theodor Herzl

Nathan Birnbaum

Focus: Theodor Herzl

Herzl, considered the founding father of the Zionist movement, was born in 1860 in Budapest, Hungary to non-observant Jewish parents. Herzl himself was so assimilated that he knew no Hebrew, was not connected to any synagogue, and did not even circumcise his son. At one time he considered solving the problem of anti-Semitism by proposing that all Jews convert to Christianity. He studied law in Vienna and became a journalist. After the Dreyfus trial he wrote a book called *Judenstaat* (The Jewish State), which was published in 1896. In this book he proposed the establishment of a secular Jewish state. Until he died, he worked tirelessly for the realization of this dream, and even suggested that it be created in Uganda. He met the Kaiser of Germany and other important European figures, trying to convince them to support his plan. He also organized Zionist congresses to undertake the task of creating a Jewish homeland. His idea inspired many young, assimilated Jews to come to *Eretz Yisrael* and build what eventually became the State of Israel.

5656 1896

KOSHER MEAT FRAUD

The butcher license of Nicholas Smart, a non-Jewish New York City butcher, was canceled by the New York City Common Council. He was caught putting kosher seals on non-kosher meat.

New York State was the first state to make it illegal to sell non-kosher meat as kosher. The law was passed in 1915.

A YESHIVAH IS BORN: NOVARDOK, 5657 / 1896

With a combined student body of 4,000 students in eight branches, Novardok was the largest *"mussar"* yeshivah in Europe. The force behind the yeshivah, and its founder, was the "Alter of Novardok," Rabbi Yosef Yoizel Horowitz. He had been a businessman until he met the founder of the *mussar* movement, Rabbi Yisrael Salanter. As a result of this meeting the Alter abandoned his business and built a yeshivah that taught Torah and stressed intense dedication to studying *mussar* and living by its ideals. Novardok taught its students to pursue a simple life and reject luxuries. Students would spend hours and days in self-criticism, trying to correct their faults.

Novardok students also undertook to spread Torah, and they established a network of yeshivos called Beis Yosef.

Though these yeshivos were destroyed during World War II, Rabbi Avraham Yoffen, a son-in-law of the Alter, and a number of students miraculously made their way to America. They established yeshivos in New York and Israel.

BUND FOUNDED

5658 1897

The "Bund" (formally: *Algemeiner Yiddisher Arbeiter Bund in Lita, Poilin, un Russland —* The Jewish Workers' Union of Lithuania, Poland and Russia) was a radically socialist labor organization that opposed Jewish tradition, observance, study, and nationalism. Instead, it encouraged "Yiddish culture," and empowerment of the working class.

Did you know that?

❧ The largest Yiddish newspaper in America was "The Jewish Daily Forward." It was read by hundreds of thousands of Jewish immigrants in America. Like the Bundists, the paper was strongly anti-religious. In fact, the Forward annually sponsored grand balls on Yom Kippur!

❧ Shalom Aleichem was the pen name of Solomon Rabinowitz.

❧ Today the overwhelming majority of Jews who speak and read Yiddish are Orthodox. The grandchildren of the Bundists, by and large, are totally assimilated.

❧ Jews played an important role in establishing the American labor movement. The principles of the movement were similar to the socialist aspects of the Bund ideology. Many leaders of the American movement were immigrants who had been active in the Bund.

Shalom Aleichem
(Solomon Rabinowitz)

To further their aims, the Bundists published newspapers and translated classics such as Shakespeare into Yiddish. Yiddish novels were published and Yiddish plays were staged.

The Bund wielded great political influence. Virtually every town in Poland, Lithuania, and Russia that had Jews also had a local branch of the Bund, which was active in promoting the party's secular ideals. The Bundist philosophy attracted many brilliant young people, who thought it would be a salvation for the laboring class.

Yiddish-language literature was important to the Bundists. The most famous Yiddish writer was Shalom Aleichem, often referred to as "the Jewish Mark Twain." He and his colleagues wrote stories about life in the European *shtetl* (small village) and generally portrayed traditional Judaism in the most unflattering of ways. Another famous Yiddish writer, Isaac Bashevis Singer, won the Nobel Prize for Literature.

5658 1897 THE FIRST ZIONIST CONGRESS

Theodor Herzl gathered Jews from sixteen countries in Basel, Switzerland, to discuss establishing a homeland for the Jews in *Eretz Yisrael*, or Palestine as it was then called. This first of many congresses met to plan the rebuilding of the land. After the first congress Herzl wrote in his diary: "At Basel, I founded the Jewish state. In fifty years everyone will know it."

A ZIONIST CONFERENCE.

Sir,—I am desired to announce that preparations are being made for the holding of a representative Zionist Congress at Munich, on August 25th next

The preliminaries have been settled by well-known Continental Zionists prominent among whom is Dr. Th. Herzl, who, as many others, has been struck with the necessity for combining the several Zionistic movements, and for giving shape and direction to their ideas.

The details so far settled are that representatives of all countries in which Jews reside shall meet at Munich on the above-mentioned date, and during a session lasting three days shall discuss the all-important questions that so deeply affect Jewish interests, the Zionist ideals to which the masses of Israel so zealously—and so persistently cling.

Everything will be done to render this Congress, the first to be held by Jews, as imposing, as its discussions will be of importance to Israel. In order to give the Conference a thoroughly representative character delegates will be invited from all Zionist movements, political or philanthropic, local or general, in their aims.

As the Agenda has, of course, not been definitely fixed, I shall be glad to receive suggestions and convey them to the proper quarters. The following topics will be deliberated upon:

(a) The position of the Jews in all the countries in which they reside (one representative to report on each country), with statistical information on the economical, social and political situation.

(b) Reports on colonisation movements.

(c) The Chaluka.

(d) The Emigration Question.

(e) Agitation, Funds, &c.

It will be seen that this world congress has unde the scheme of organisation will, I am sure, prove equ

My object in making public this proposal, is to g it needs, and at the same time to obtain as general an possible on the issues involved.

To this end, I shall be glad if the Secretaries of as well as the administrators of colonisation societies, kindred organisations, will communicate to me at the

I shall, with your permission, give further deta Congress at an early date.

Yours obedi

8, South Street, Finsbury, E.C.,
London, March 16th, 1897.

A notice about the Zionist Congress

The Second Zionist Congress in Basel, Switzerland

5658 1897

ZIONISTS CHOOSE THE *MAGEN DAVID*

The *Magen David* (Star of David) was chosen to be the symbol of the Zionist movement. Years later, this symbol was incorporated into the Israeli flag.

Did you know that?

- The Second Zionist Congress chose the colors blue and white for the Zionist flag, which became the Israeli flag.

- The Eighth Zionist Congress adopted *Hatikvah* as the national anthem.

- It wasn't until the Tenth Zionist Congress that meetings were conducted in Hebrew.

Focus: American Orthodoxy begins to organize

Orthodox Union

By 1898 it was clear that American Orthodox Jews needed to unify their efforts to retain Jewish observances and culture. Rabbi Henry Pereira Mendes, of the prestigious Spanish-Portuguese Synagogue in New York City, attempted to do so by establishing the Union of Orthodox Jewish Congregations of America. Its goal was to create a network of Orthodox synagogues. With unified action, they could accomplish a great deal more than they could individually. Moreover, just knowing that other congregations faced the same difficulties would bolster morale and lead to more effective efforts.

Chief among Rabbi Mendes' many prominent successors was Rabbi Herbert S. Goldstein, an American-born rabbi who did much to improve the situation of Orthodox Jews in the United States and in Israel.

The UOJCA (which later shortened its name to Orthodox Union) undertook numerous activities on behalf of Orthodox congregations and individuals. Many of the rights for which it fought were taken for granted by Jews in later years.

The Orthodox Union also saw as its mission the preservation of Orthodox congregational practices, such as retaining the *mechitzah* and banning the use of microphones on the Sabbath. This effort was especially important as the wave of Conservative Judaism swept over most American communities.

Perhaps the Union's most notable innovation was the Kashruth Division, with its now famous OU symbol. Aided by its rabbinical arm, the Rabbinical Council of America, the OU devised the infrastructure for kashruth supervision used by agencies worldwide. Eventually it certified thousands of different food items from manufacturers all around the world.

Its youth organization, the National Conference of Synagogue Youth, started as a small effort with little hope of influencing the vast majority of secularized Jews. Yet over the years, NCSY became an important force in keeping Orthodox youth loyal to Orthodoxy and in introducing Orthodox Judaism to countless teens who did not grow up in Sabbath-observant homes.

To bring pressure on the administration to engage in rescue efforts during the Holocaust, over 300 rabbis, mostly members of the Agudath HaRabbonim marched in Washington a few days before Yom Kippur, 1943. They met with leaders of Congress, but President Roosevelt, acting on the counsel of his non-Orthodox advisers, was "too busy" to see them.

Agudath HaRabbonim

The Agudath HaRabbonim, the Union of Orthodox Rabbis of the United States and Canada, was founded in 1902 as the first official organization of Orthodox rabbis in America. Comprised of illustrious rabbis with European Torah learning and background, it was very influential in Orthodox society for a number of decades. It prominent leaders were scholars who had studied in the rigorous yeshivos of Eastern Europe; many had held prestigious rabbinic positions before immigrating to the United States.

The rabbinical organization responded to the religious and social problems of new Jewish immigrants in America. As emerging technologies and modern culture created new halachic questions, the rabbis of Agudath HaRabbonim applied Jewish law with the knowledge and expertise they had perfected in their earlier years. In addition, since most Jewish children were anxious to belong to the secular culture of their new American friends — even if this meant discarding traditional Jewish life — the Agudath HaRabbonim worked hard to strengthen the faith and religious observances of these Jews who desperately needed their leadership.

At the behest of Rabbi Chaim Ozer Grodzenski (see p. 173), in 1914 the Agudath HaRabbonim founded the Central Relief Committee to aid institutions that had suffered the devastating effects of war, pogroms and mass starvation. One year later, it established Ezras Torah to support needy scholars and their families worldwide. These relief agencies eventually became organizations in their own right, providing substantial aid and encouragement to many people.

The Agudath HaRabbonim spared no effort or expense to save as many Jews as possible from the physical destruction of the Holocaust. During World War II, the organization was highly active in relentless rescue efforts and was instrumental in the formation of the Vaad Hatzalah.

Young Israel

Founded in 1912 by young Orthodox Jews on the Lower East Side of New York, the Young Israel sought to encourage Orthodox belief and practices among a rapidly assimilating generation of young Jews. Seeing that young people were anxious to leave behind the religious commitment of their immigrant parents, Young Israel founders responded by using English language and modern culture, but ensuring that Orthodox ideals and halachic standards would be upheld. In addition to youth-oriented prayer services, the synagogue provided classes on Jewish topics as well as English language.

The Young Israel's insistence on English language, as opposed to Yiddish, and its stress on social and communal activities attracted many young people. It gave them an Orthodox framework and social setting at a time when many of their acquaintances were shedding Orthodox practices and attempting to fit into secular American culture.

Synagogues emulating the original Young Israel were established across the United States. In the 1920's the National Council of Young Israel was established to coordinate these various congregations. Today the National Council of Young Israel is active in communal affairs and serves as the hub of hundreds of congregations in America and Israel.

Rabbinical Council of America

Founded in 1923 as the Rabbinical Council of the UOJCA, the Council functioned as the halachic authority of the congregational organization. It took on a broader scope in 1935 when it merged with the Rabbinical Association of the Rabbi Isaac Elchanan Theological Seminary and was reconstituted as the Rabbinical Council of America (Histadrut HaRabbanim). Although it was now an independent organization, it remains affiliated with the UOJCA.

The RCA represented American-born and educated young rabbis who sought to lead the newly emerging Orthodox Jewish community. Most of its early membership was ordained through Yeshiva University's RIETS division or by the Hebrew Theological College in Chicago. Today it includes rabbis ordained by numerous yeshivos in the United States and Israel. Its members serve as pulpit rabbis and in Jewish education.

In addition to these organizations, Agudath Israel, founded in Europe in 1912, began to take root in America; see 5672/1912.

5662
1902

MIZRACHI FOUNDED

Many Orthodox Jews supported the Zionist goal of settling and building *Eretz Yisrael*, but they opposed the secular orientation of the new movement. In response, they created the Mizrachi, an organization that would join the Zionists, but fight within the movement for allegiance to the Torah while building the land.

The founder of Mizrachi was Rabbi Jacob Reines, the Rabbi and *Rosh Yeshivah* of Lida, Lithuania, and an alumnus of Volozhin. He had the support of some leading rabbis. The Mizrachi was anxious to work with the Zionists, but insisted that Zionism be strictly a *political* movement and not involve itself in cultural activities, because so-called cultural work would be devoid of Torah values and would undermine religious observance. At first, the Zionists agreed, but in 1914 they voted to include cultural activities, which angered Mizrachi, but the organization decided to remain affiliated with Zionism and to work from within. Also in 1914, Rabbi Meir Berlin (later Bar-Ilan) became the leader of Mizrachi.

The organization labored tirelessly to develop *Eretz Yisrael* and worked closely with the secular Zionists to do so. The organization opened its own bank, Bank Mizrachi. After the establishment of the State of Israel, Mizrachi formed a political party, known today as the NRP, National Religious Party. Its representatives are members of the Knesset and have served in important positions in most of Israel's governments.

A Jewish settler works the land of *Eretz Yisrael*

Mizrachi created a youth movement called Bnei Akiva and after the creation of the State, it built a network of yeshivos, including "hesder yeshivos," that combine Torah study with army service.

Early Zionist settlement
efforts in *Eretz Yisrael*

The Wright brothers' airplane

Jew Stats:

IN THE YEAR 1900, the world had **10,600,000** Jews.

8.6 million Jews lived in Europe, **78,000** in *Eretz Yisrael*; **1,000,000** in the United States.

7 percent of world Jewry was Sephardic.

In **1939**, there were **17 million** Jews — a population sharply reduced by the Holocaust.

ONE HUNDRED YEARS LATER, IN 2000, the world had **13 million** Jews.

Eretz Yisrael has a population of **4.8 million** Jews — over 60 times as many as in 1900; the United States has a population of **5.7 million** Jews — nearly 6 times as many as in 1900; and all of Europe has only **1.5 million Jews** — less than 20 percent of the Jewish population in 1900.

25 percent of world Jewry is estimated to be Sephardic.

1903

The Wright brothers
take to the skies!
The first airplane flight
is at Kitty Hawk,
North Carolina.

5666 1906

Rabbi Chaim Berlin

Did you know that?

🐝 The first Nobel Prize awarded to an American was presented to Albert Abraham Michelson, a Jew, in 1907 for his work on measuring the speed of light.

5669 1909

RABBI CHAIM BERLIN ARRIVES IN *ERETZ YISRAEL*

Among the many famous rabbinic personalities to immigrate to *Eretz Yisrael* in the 1800's and early 1900's was the famed Rabbi Chaim Berlin, son of the Netziv of Volozhin. Rabbi Chaim was appointed Rabbi of Moscow in 1871, and seven years later left Moscow to assist his father in Volozhin. He delivered lectures at the yeshivah, but when the yeshivah closed, he left Volozhin. He eventually settled in Jerusalem, where he served as a rabbinic leader of the Ashkenazic community. This great man's name is memorialized by Yeshivah and Mesivta Rabbi Chaim Berlin in Brooklyn.

TEL AVIV FOUNDED

Today a busy, modern metropolis full of glass and steel skyscrapers, Israel's largest city and its financial center began as sand dunes outside the Arab city of Jaffa. After the War of Independence, Tel Aviv absorbed Jaffa. Tel Aviv is now the secular, cultural, and business hub of the country, the center of an unbroken "urban sprawl" of growing suburban cities.

THE FIRST KIBBUTZ, DEGANIA

5669
1909

Many of the secular Zionists who arrived in Israel settled on kibbutzim. These were agricultural communes — farm villages dedicated to building a socialist community. On these kibbutzim, manual labor was valued over all else, and, for the most part, the Jewish religion was not practiced.

Following socialist doctrine, everyone worked together to produce goods and provide the services needed by the community. The responsibilities for farming, cooking, and educating the children were all shared. The kibbutz, in turn, provided everyone with housing and food. These belonged to the kibbutz and were supposed to be divided equally among all the members. Individuals could not have private property. If a kibbutz member received a gift, it was to be shared by everyone on the kibbutz. In many of them, the children were brought up communally, with parents spending time with them during the day.

The first kibbutz was Degania, built along the shores of Lake Kinneret. Soon, other kibbutzim were founded throughout *Eretz Yisrael*. Some religious *kibbutzim* were established as well. In these kibbutzim, each family lived together as a unit, and religion played an integral role in kibbutz life.

"Kibbutzniks" — the members of the kibbutzim — played the most prominent roles in the creation of the State of Israel, and they took their places as military and political leaders of the nascent State of Israel.

Israel's government reflected the values of the secular kibbutzim, and was socialistic and anti-religious in character. In recent decades, the size and influence of the kibbutzim have declined precipitously, as has their radical socialist orientation.

Did you know that?

- On most kibbutzim, children did not sleep at home. They also did not eat with their parents. They were raised by kibbutz staff in "children's houses."

161

5671
1911

Mendel Beilis

THE BEILIS TRIAL

In 1911, the canard "blood libel" was once again renewed against the Jewish people. Apparently angered by the large number of Jews involved in left wing, anti-government causes, the Russian government hoped to force the Jews to leave Russia by reviving the blood libel. The Russian police arrested a Jew named Mendel Beilis from Kiev on "charges" that he slaughtered a Christian child and used his blood for Jewish rituals. Beilis was jailed for two years before finally coming to trial in 1913 (even though the police had already found the child's true murderer). He was released, as there was not enough evidence to convict him. The Beilis trial sent shock waves throughout the Jewish world and shattered much of the stability felt by the Jews of Russia and Eastern Europe. The case was the basis for a best-selling novel, "The Fixer," by Bernard Malamud.

5672
1912

AGUDATH ISRAEL FOUNDED

The turn of the 20th century was a time of raging ideological debate. Socialism, secular Zionism, and other irreligious movements were attracting observant Jews at an alarming rate. These groups used their political influence to undermine traditional practice and to do away with the communal structure.

In response, many of the greatest rabbinic leaders of European Orthodox Jewry gathered together in Kattowitz, Poland, and formed Agudath Israel. Giants of Torah Jewry — the Gerrer Rebbe, the Chafetz Chaim, Rabbi Chaim Ozer Grodzenski and Rabbi Chaim Soloveitchik — were there. The many different types of Orthodox Jewish communities — Chassidim, Hirschian Germans, Lithuanian

The first *Knessia Gedolah* of Agudath Israel

yeshivah students — would unite in Agudath Israel. The organization's stated principle was to deal with all problems in the spirit of the Torah. Its activists would protect the interests of the Orthodox communities — Torah education and Torah life — while strengthening observance within the community and protecting Torah living from outside attack.

The uniqueness of Agudath Israel lies in the fact that its policies are decided not by the organization's lay leadership, but by the great Torah scholars who comprise the group's highest policy-making body, the *Moetzes Gedolei HaTorah* — Council of Torah Sages.

In the United States, an idealistic young group of Orthodox Jews joined their European counterparts and founded an American Agudah in 1923. Its educational programs, youth groups, and summer camps played an important role in inspiring young Jews and keeping them loyal to their heritage. During the Holocaust, the American Agudah worked to rescue Jews from Europe and helped provide for survivors. Agudath Israel continues to advocate on behalf of Jews in need and presents the Orthodox viewpoint to the media and United States lawmakers. Over the years, Agudath Israel has become an important voice for Orthodoxy in America.

In Israel, Agudath Israel does its work as a political party, with Knesset representation and a role in many governments.

5674
1914

Did you know that?

✍ During World War I Jews fought on both sides, in opposing armies. There were 140,000 Austrian and German Jewish soldiers, and 250,000 Jews served in the American army. 12,000 German Jewish soldiers were killed in action, and 10,000 Jews died while serving in the British army.

WORLD WAR I BREAKS OUT

On Tishah B'Av, the First World War broke out. It began an era of terrible suffering for the Jews, which would end with the Holocaust thirty years later. As a result of the War, many Jewish communities were destroyed and yeshivos forced into exile.

Legend has it that two soldiers were battling to the death. As one soldier raised his bayonet high in the air to stab his opponent, the intended victim began to recite "*Shema Yisrael.*" The soldier suddenly lowered his bayonet and completed the sentence, "*Hashem echad.*" The two soldiers, who just moments before had been locked in mortal combat, turned and walked away from one another.

Jewish refugees driven from their homes by the Czar's armies during the collapse of the Russian front

Memorial tablet in commemoration of the Jewish soldiers killed in World War I

Rabbi Moshe Feinstein was 19 years old when World War I broke out. The Chafetz Chaim and Rabbi Chaim of Brisk were still alive.

A YESHIVAH IS BORN: PORAT YOSEF, 5674 / 1914

A rich Jew from Calcutta, India wanted to help the Jews in Jerusalem. He was advised by the Ben Ish Chai to build a yeshivah in the holy city. The famous Porat Yosef Yeshivah, under its first *Rosh Yeshivah*, Rabbi Ezra Attiyah, became a great center for Sephardic Talmud students. Its most famous graduate, a student of Rabbi Attiyah, is Rabbi Ovadiah Yosef, at one time the Sephardic Chief Rabbi of Israel, and today recognized by the large majority of Sephardic Jewry as their elder sage.

1914

The Atlantic and Pacific Oceans shake hands: The Panama Canal is opened, connecting the two largest bodies of water on earth.

Roshei Yeshivah - Early 1900's

RABBI ISSER ZALMAN MELTZER / SLUTZK

Originally a member of the faculty of Yeshivah Knesses Yisrael of Slabodka, Rabbi Isser Zalman was sent by the famed Alter of Slabodka to Slutzk, in order to lay the foundation of this up and coming yeshivah. In 1903, Rabbi Isser Zalman became the head of Slutzk, and proceeded to mold and strengthen it. After serving for many years as *Rosh Yeshivah,* he left for *Eretz Yisrael* in 1925, a refugee from Communist persecution. In Eretz Yisrael he was chosen to head the oldest Ashkenazic yeshivah in Jerusalem, Yeshivas Eitz Chaim. He became one of the most beloved personalities of Jerusalem, and was acknowledged as the *"z'kan roshei hayeshivah"* (senior *Rosh Yeshivah.*) He served at the helm of Eitz Chaim until his death in 1954.

Rabbi Isser Zalman, a brilliant Talmudic scholar, had been a student in Volozhin and was one of the primary disciples of the great Rabbi Chaim Soloveitchik of Brisk. He also studied in Radin, in the Chafetz Chaim's yeshivah. He authored the famous commentary on Rambam entitled *Even HaAzel*.

His son-in-law and student was the famed *Rosh Yeshivah* of Lakewood, Rabbi Aharon Kotler. His nephew was the venerable *Rosh Yeshivah* of Ponevezh, Rabbi Elazer Menachem Man Shach.

Rabbi Isser Zalman Meltzer in Jerusalem

Rabbi Shimon Shkop

RABBI SHIMON SHKOP / GRODNO

Rabbi Shimon Shkop was one of the great Talmudic geniuses of his day. His novel ideas and methods of Talmudic analysis have had a major influence on most present-day yeshivos. Rabbi Shimon was born in 1859 in Turtz, Lithuania. Despite their extreme poverty, his parents struggled to provide young Shimon with suitable *melamdim* (private instructors), and by the time he was 12, there was no one in the city capable of teaching him. He left Turtz to study in Mir and later in Volozhin. The effort that he put into Torah study was legendary. Day and night he toiled in the *beis midrash,* developing a clear understanding of the Talmud. At the age of 24 he was appointed to the faculty of the Telshe Yeshivah, where his fame spread far and wide.

In 1920, at the urging of Rabbi Chaim Ozer Grodzenski, Reb Shimon became *Rosh Yeshivah* of Yeshivah Sha'ar HaTorah in Grodno, which was founded in 1914. Under his leadership, the yeshivah's enrollment grew to over 300 students. It was in Grodno that he authored his classic work on the Talmud, *Sha'arei Yosher.* The name of the yeshivah is perpetuated at Sha'ar HaTorah in Queens, under the leadership of Reb Shimon's grandson-in-law, Rabbi Zelik Epstein.

RABBI ELCHANAN BUNIM WASSERMAN / BARANOVITZ

The influence of Rabbi Elchanan Bunim Wasserman, *Rosh Yeshivah* of Yeshivah Ohel Torah Baranovitz, reached far beyond those he taught as *Rosh Yeshivah.* He literally shaped the outlook and perspective of the Torah world.

Whether it was from a podium of a gathering of Agudath Israel or through his many articles and publications, Reb Elchanan espoused Torah values that have molded the minds of generations of Torah-observant Jews.

He was born in 1871 and in his youth studied in Telshe. He benefited greatly from the tutelage of Rabbi Eliezer Gordon and Rabbi Shimon Shkop. From Telshe he traveled to study under Rabbi Chaim Soloveitchik, who shaped Reb Elchanan's learning method.

From Brisk, Reb Elchanan traveled to Radin, to learn at the feet of the saintly scholar, the Chafetz Chaim, who became his primary mentor. He gained immeasurably in both piety and Talmudic knowledge from his years of learning with the

Rabbi Elchanan Bunim Wasserman

Chafetz Chaim. Reb Elchanan eventually established the yeshivah of Baranovitz.

In 1939, just before Germany's invasion of Poland, Reb Elchanan was in America raising funds for his yeshivah. Despite the danger of traveling back to Europe, and the protests of his American hosts, his dedication to his students did not allow him to remain in America, and he returned to Europe to be with them. He died *al kiddush Hashem,* sanctifying God's Name, in Kovno, murdered by Lithuanian allies of the Nazis.

His great legacy lives on through his students and his published works, which include *Kovetz He'aros* and *Kovetz Shiurim,* based on his Talmudic lectures, and *Kovetz Maamarin* and *Ikvesa D'Meshicha,* works of Jewish thought.

Yeshivah Ohel Torah in Baranovitz

RABBI BARUCH BER LEIBOWITZ / KAMINETZ

When the name "Reb Baruch Ber" is mentioned, one immediately associates it with deep analytical thought, piercing accuracy in textual understanding, and the utmost piety. He was born in 1870, studied in Volozhin, and was the primary disciple of the great Rabbi Chaim Soloveitchik. Indeed, repeatedly throughout his classic Talmudic work, *Birkas Shmuel,* Reb Baruch Ber quotes the teachings of Reb Chaim. In 1904, Reb Baruch Ber became the head of Knesses Beis Yitzchak, a yeshivah named after the great Rabbi of Kovno, Rabbi Yitzchak Elchanan Spektor. Knesses Beis Yitzchak stressed intensive Talmud study, and did not include *mussar* in its program.

The yeshivah disbanded upon the outbreak of World War I, and was later reestablished in Kaminetz, Poland. When Kaminetz was occupied during World War II, the yeshivah fled to Vilna. There, Reb Baruch Ber passed away and was buried.

RABBI YECHIEL MORDECHAI GORDON / LOMZA

Despite a life marred by personal tragedy, Rabbi Yechiel Mordechai Gordon stands out as a towering figure of faith and perseverance. Born in 1883, he studied in Slabodka, where his reputation as a prodigy spread. He became the

Rabbi Baruch Ber Leibowitz

Did you know that?

New York City Mayor Jimmy Walker presented Reb Baruch Ber with the keys to the city when he arrived in America on a fund-raising mission for the yeshivah! The mayor said, "Rabbi Leibowitz disproves Darwin's theory of evolution. A holy person like him could have been created only by God."

son-in-law of Rabbi Lazer Shulevitz, the founder of the Lomza Yeshivah, but his bride died within their first year of marriage. He then married Rabbi Shulevitz's second daughter, and, at the age of 24, assumed the position of *Rosh Yeshivah* in Lomza. With great difficulty he arranged for his students not to be drafted into the anti-Semitic Polish army. In 1926, Rabbi Gordon, with forty students, traveled to *Eretz Yisrael* and established a branch of the yeshivah in Petach Tikvah. To support his two yeshivos he traveled the world over collecting funds. When Poland was invaded at the outbreak of World War II he was in America, where he spent the war years working to save European Jewry by helping create the Vaad Hatzalah, a rescue organization. Most of his family, his yeshivah and his students perished in the War. After the War he returned to the yeshivah he had established in Petach Tikvah. Rabbi Gordon passed away in 1966, leaving behind his scholarly work, *Nesiv Yam*, as well as hundreds of students.

Lomza Yeshivah in Poland

COMMUNIST REVOLUTION

5677 1917

A bloody revolution brought the Communists to power in Russia, with the help of many Jewish Communists. The commander-in-chief and minister of war in the Communist government was a Jew named Leib Davidovich Bronstein, better known as Leon Trotsky. Unfortunately, most of the Jewish Communists were self-hating Jews who helped persecute religious Jews and Zionists. The wars between the "red" Soviet and "white" anti-Soviet armies in the early years of the Russian Revolution caught the Jews in the middle. Each army saw the Jews as its enemy, resulting in terrible, brutal pogroms — over 2,000 of them — that left more than 100,000 Jews dead.

The rise of Communism led to the spiritual exile of three generations of Jews, who would grow up under the Communist regime, cut off from Torah knowledge and prevented from practicing Judaism. When Stalin rose to power, he had most of the Jewish Communists, who had brought about the revolution, exiled to Siberia or executed. Trotsky went into exile in Mexico, where he was eventually axed to death.

Leon Trotsky

5678
1917

BALFOUR DECLARATION

Lord Arthur James Balfour, the British foreign minister, addressed a letter to Lord Rothschild, a leader of the Jewish community. In it, he declared the British support for a Jewish homeland in Israel, where the Jews could live and build their own country. However, after Arab pogroms against the Jews in the 1920's, and a revolt against the British in the 1930's, the British issued a "White Paper," severely limiting Jewish immigration to Palestine to a total of 75,000, spread out over five years. This policy doomed many Jews in Europe to death at the hands of the Nazis.

Did you know that?

◆ Chaim Weizmann was a Jewish scientist who made important contributions to the British war effort during World War I. Through his work, he came to know Prime Minister Lloyd George and Lord Balfour, and his influence helped persuade them to issue the Balfour Declaration.

> Foreign Office,
> November 2nd, 1917
>
> Dear Lord Rothschild,
>
> I have much pleasure in conveying to you, on behalf of His Majesty's Government, the following declaration of sympathy with Jewish Zionist aspirations which has been submitted to, and approved by, the Cabinet.
>
> 'His Majesty's Government view with favour the establishment in Palestine of a national home for the Jewish people, and will use their best endeavours to facilitate the achievement of this object, it being clearly understood that nothing shall be done which may prejudice the civil and religious rights of existing non-Jewish communities in Palestine, or the rights and political status enjoyed by Jews in any other country"
>
> I should be grateful if you would bring this declaration to the knowledge of the Zionist Federation.

The Balfour Declaration

ALLENBY CONQUERS JERUSALEM

5678
1917

On the 24th of Kislev, 1917, the Turkish mayor of Jerusalem symbolically surrendered the keys of the city to General Edmund Allenby, commander of the British forces. On Chanukah, General Allenby and his army actually entered the walls of Jerusalem. This was the beginning of the British Mandate over Palestine. The British governed until 1948, when they left and the State of Israel declared its independence.

Sir Edmund Allenby outside the gates of Jerusalem

Did you know that?

The conquering General Allenby, out of respect for the holy city, entered the city on foot and not on horseback.

1918
Treaty of Versailles ends World War I.

171

5678 1918

LAST RUSSIAN CZAR EXECUTED

The Russians Czars had a long history of terrorizing the Jewish people in their empire. The last Czar, Nicholas II, and his wife and children, were executed in a field by revolutionaries. Buried in an unmarked grave, their fate ultimately resembled that of thousands of victims of the Czars' own anti-Semitic policies.

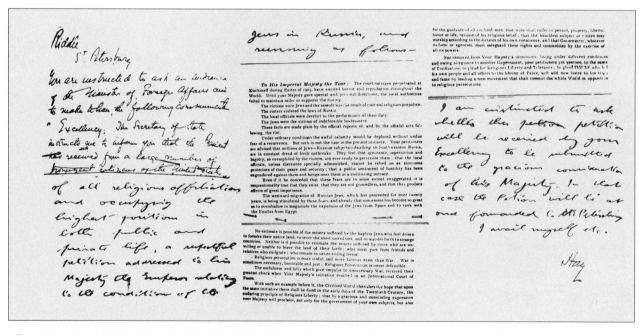

Facsimile of an official petition by John Hay, United States Secretary of State, transmitted to the Czar of Russia, protesting the pogrom at Kischineff. It reads in part: "The cruel outrages perpetrated at Kischineff during Easter of 1903 have excited horror and reprobation throughout the World. ... The Jews were the victims of indefensible lawlessness."

Jew Stats:

From the 1870's onward the population of the city of Jerusalem kept growing.
Over 50 percent of the people living there were now Jewish.

- In **1870** there were **10,000** Jews out of a total city population of **20,000.**
- In **1939** there were **80,000** Jews out of a total city population of **110,000.**
- in **1948** there were **100,000** Jews out of a total city population of **165,000.**

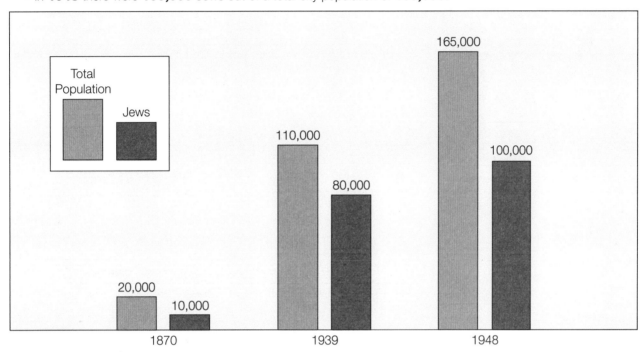

People of the Book: Famous Torah Works of the 1900's

ACHIEZER

Achiezer contains a selection of Rabbi Chaim Ozer Grodzenski's halachic responsa. Reb Chaim Ozer was recognized as the outstanding leader of European Jewry between the two World Wars. He was known as a person of boundless energy, who had the ability to concentrate on several tasks at once: He wrote, studied, and listened to people all at the same time.

In addition to being a leading scholar, he was responsible for helping the poor, and he founded and supported many charitable organizations. His efforts were vital in rebuilding the Torah education infrastructure that had been destroyed during World War I.

Rabbi Chaim Ozer Grodzenski

Rabbi Eliezer Silver

His Vaad HaYeshivos organization helped fund the yeshivos in Poland and Lithuania, provided for needy students, and represented the interests of the yeshivos. He was influential in founding Ezras Torah, an American based relief agency which provided funds for destitute scholars in Europe.

Through his disciple, Rabbi Eliezer Silver, one of the leading Orthodox rabbis in the United States at the time, Rabbi Grodzenski had a profound influence on American Jewry as well. It was at the behest of R' Chaim Ozer that Rabbi Silver took a leading role in establishing the Vaad Hatzalah (see 5740/1939).

He spent the last year of his life working tirelessly to support the thousands of refugee yeshivah students, rabbis, and ordinary Jews who had fled to Vilna in an attempt to escape from the Nazis and the Russians. Though he was in excruciating pain from the cancer that eventually killed him, he refused to use scarce funds for his painkillers. He used the money to help the refugees.

KAF HACHAIM

Kaf HaChaim, a comprehensive, multi-volume commentary on the *Orach Chaim* section of Jewish law, was compiled by Chacham Yaakov Chaim Sofer of Baghdad. Chacham Yaakov moved to Jerusalem at the turn of the 20th century, to study in the famous Beit El Yeshivah for Kabbalah study. He wrote the *Kaf HaChaim* while quietly studying and writing day and night in a small upstairs room of the yeshivah.

CHIDDUSHEI RABBI CHAIM

In today's yeshivos, the *Chiddushei Rabbi Chaim*, Rabbi Chaim Soloveitchik's essays on Rambam and topics in the Talmud, are considered the most challenging and exciting topics of study. Rabbi Chaim Soloveitchik developed the "Brisker derech," a unique approach to analyzing Talmudic principles. This approach defines and pinpoints the finest distinctions in Jewish laws. He is known as one of the most innovative Talmud scholars of the 19th and 20th centuries. A master teacher, his heart overflowed with compassion for the poor and he gave generously though he himself had very little. Sometimes infants were abandoned on his doorstep, and he would take care of these children until they were grown. When he was only 27, Rabbi Chaim began to lecture in the "mother of yeshivos," Volozhin. He remained at the yeshivah until the Russian authorities closed it. He then moved to Brisk. In 1892, he succeeded his father as Rabbi of Brisk, a post he held until the end of his life in 1918.

Rabbi Chaim Soloveitchik

Focus: Rabbi Chaim Brisker's wit & compassion

Rabbi Chaim used to say: If you can't explain it, you don't understand it.

When a fire destroyed much of the Jewish Quarter in Brisk, he didn't rest for days on end, working tirelessly to help the homeless and destitute.

One Sabbath, Rabbi Chaim hosted forty Jewish soldiers who had arrived on Friday and had no place to stay.

When asked why he was lenient in allowing the sick to eat on Yom Kippur, he answered, "I'm not lenient about Yom Kippur; I'm strict about the commandment to preserve life."

A non-religious Jewish youth from Brisk was condemned to death by firing squad for throwing a bomb at a Russian general in Warsaw. The general happened to be the nephew of the Czar! The news of the boy's pending execution arrived on Yom Kippur eve, as the Jews of Brisk were about to begin *Kol Nidrei*. Rabbi Chaim stopped the prayers in his synagogue, and had the other synagogues in Brisk do the same. He would not allow *Kol Nidrei* to be said until 10,000 rubles were collected. He then used the money to bribe the police commissioner, who testified on behalf of the Jewish boy. The boy was freed.

Focus: The Soloveitchik family

The Soloveitchik family was known for the many great rabbinical leaders it had produced. Rabbi Yosef Dov ("Yosheh Ber") was one of the great Torah luminaries of his day. For a period of time he was the associate *Rosh Yeshivah* of the famous Volozhin Yeshivah (the Netziv was *Rosh Yeshivah*). After leaving his post, he served as Rabbi in Slutsk and then in Brisk. Rabbi Yosef Dov published *sefarim* of responsa and a commentary on the first two books of the Torah, *Bereishis* and *Shemos*. He entitled these *Beis HaLevi*, and that is the name by which he has became known.

Both his son, Rabbi Chaim (known as Rabbi Chaim Brisker, see above) and grandson, Rabbi Yitzchak Zev (Velvel) served as Rabbis of Brisk. During the Second World War, the Germans destroyed Brisk, but Reb Velvel (commonly referred to simply as "the Brisker Rav") miraculously escaped to *Eretz Yisrael* where he established a house of advanced Torah study. Another son of Reb Chaim, Rabbi Moshe Soloveitchik, ultimately came to the United States, where he became a *Rosh Yeshivah* at Yeshivas Rabbeinu Yitzchak Elchanan.

Rabbi Yosef Dov Soloveitchik

S'FAS EMES

Rabbi Yehudah Aryeh Alter was the second Gerrer Rebbe, succeeding his illustrious grandfather, who was known by the title of his multi-volume commentary on the Talmud, "Chiddushei HaRim." All of the Chiddushei HaRim's children died in his lifetime, so his grandson Yehudah Aryeh became the leader of tens of thousands of Chassidim when he was in his 20's.

Reb Yehudah Aryeh was equal to the task, not only as a spiritual guide, but also as a scholar and teacher who inspired his followers to strive for greatness in learning. The ranks of his Chassidim grew to well over 100,000.

His three-volume commentary on the Talmud is regarded as a standard text in advanced academies, especially the parts that deal with *Kodashim*, the Temple service. His five-volume work on the Torah and Festivals contains the Sabbath discourses he delivered over a period of thirty-three years. Both works are called *S'fas Emes*, and both are distinguished for their intellectual brilliance, breadth of knowledge, and piercing insights.

S'fas Emes is a Chassidic work that is popular across the spectrum of Torah scholars – among Chassidim and non-Chassidim alike. One distinguished 20th century *Rosh Yeshivah* said, "I go through the *S'fas Emes* every week, and every year I find new insights."

DARCHEI TESHUVAH

Rabbi Zvi Hirsh Shapira was both the Rabbi and Chassidic Rebbe of Munkatch, which belonged to Hungary before World War I and to Czechoslovakia after the War. He was a man of strong character, who would not compromise where truth and principle were involved.

The Hungarian government forced all children to attend secular schools, even on the Sabbath and Jewish festivals. In most communities this decree was reluctantly accepted, but not in Munkatch. Reb Zvi Hirsh worked tirelessly, and ultimately successfully, to have Jewish children in his community excused on such days.

Darchei Teshuvah, his most famous work, was accepted throughout Europe as a basic commentary on the *Yoreh Deah* section of the *Shulchan Aruch*. In it he compiled the rulings and opinions of the major halachic works up to his time, and added his own comments. It is amazing that he was able to produce such a work while he was deeply involved with the affairs of the community and his many Chassidim. One of his greatest rabbinic contemporaries said that he kept *Darchei Teshuvah* on his desk always, because, "without it I cannot rule ... on the various questions that come before me in this great city."

The Darchei Teshuvah

TORAH TEMIMAH

The author of the *Torah Temimah,* Rabbi Baruch HaLevi Epstein, collected the Talmud's halachic statements on the Torah and explains in an engaging style how the Sages deduced them. The name *Torah Temimah* means "the complete Torah," because his commentary highlights the direct relationship between the Written Torah and the Oral Torah. The son of Rabbi Yechiel Michel Epstein, Rabbi of Novardok and author of the halachic classic *Aruch HaShulchan*, Reb Baruch was among the youngest students of the Volozhin Yeshivah, which he entered at the age of 13.

The Netziv, *Rosh Yeshivah* of Volozhin, was his uncle. After leaving Volozhin, Reb Baruch earned his living as an accountant, and became a prominent banker in Pinsk. He then moved to New York, but after a short time, returned to Pinsk. His memoirs are published under the title *Mekor Baruch*.

He was murdered two days after the Nazis invaded his city.

OR SAMEI'ACH

In the city of Dvinsk lived Rabbi Meir Simchah HaKohen, the man Rabbi Chaim Soloveitchik called "The Prince of Torah." The Jewish world today knows him by the title of his commentary on Rambam's *Mishneh Torah*, "Or Samei'ach," a work that presents brilliant and original approaches in understanding passages of Rambam and Talmud. It is a classic text, treasured by yeshivah students and accomplished scholars alike.

The Or Samei'ach was Rabbi of Dvinsk and was respected as a holy man even by the gentiles of the town. When he was arrested by Communist police, the gentiles of the town — at great personal risk — helped arrange to have him released. During World War I, despite great danger, he refused to leave his city, staying on to help those Jews who could not flee the war zone.

He also authored a classic work on *Chumash*, *Meshech Chochmah*, a work that combines textual analysis, halachic commentary and profound philosophical perspective. Amazingly, Reb Meir Simchah authored *Meshech Chochmah* when still a young man, though it was not published until after his death.

Rabbi Meir Simchah HaKohen
of Dvinsk

CHOVAS HATALMIDIM

Rabbi Klonimos Kalmish Shapira was the Chassidic Rebbe of Piesechna, Poland. He was a charismatic leader and teacher, who felt very strongly that he must concentrate on guiding and educating children and young men. To do this he wrote two books that became very popular. The first was *Chovas HaTalmidim* (Obligations of the Students). It was written in a style that would appeal to serious boys in their teens, and it sets forth how they should strive to develop themselves. He also wrote *Hach'sharas HaAvreichim* (Preparation of Young Men), in which he guided young married men in religious development and introduced them to the world of Kabbalah.

During World War II, he was interned in the Warsaw Ghetto. Even there he kept up his work as an inspirational teacher and leader. He maintained a secret synagogue, even though this was forbidden by the Germans, and discovery could have meant instant death. On the Sabbath, he delivered discourses in which he called upon his followers not to despair and inspired them to serve God with joy, despite the starvation, persecution, deportation and murder that surrounded them. His written copies of these discourses were discovered in the ruins of the Ghetto after the War. They were published with the very apt title, *Aish Kodesh* (Holy Fire).

Rabbi Klonimos Kalmish risked his life to save people in the Ghetto, but it was there that, in 1944, he became one of the Six Million.

MANUSCRIPTS THAT WERE NEVER PUBLISHED

When we think of the Holocaust, we automatically think of the loss of the Six Million and the destruction of Jewish life in most of Europe. There was another aspect of the loss. No one will ever know how many important Torah manuscripts were lost or destroyed both during the War and under the rule of the anti-Semites of Soviet Russia. Here are just a few examples:

The Gerrer Rebbe, Rabbi Avraham Mordechai Alter, had many boxes of handwritten commentaries, all of which were destroyed.

Rabbi Menachem Ziemba was regarded by many as the greatest Talmudic scholar in Poland. He was murdered in the Warsaw Ghetto, and all of his writings went up in flames.

When Rabbi Moshe Feinstein was in the Soviet Union, he completed a commentary on the entire Talmud Yerushalmi. In those days, before copying machines, he had only one copy, and he was taking it with him to show to his father. A Communist guard on the train took it from him and destroyed the precious manuscript before his eyes.

Focus: Torah pioneers in America

Before World War II numerous attempts had been made to establish yeshivos on the American continent. Notable among them is the yeshivah established by Rabbi Yehudah Levenberg in New Haven, Connecticut in 1922. This yeshivah was the first yeshivah for advanced Talmudic study outside New York City.

The brief profiles below are limited to those whose yeshivos continue to this day, and who are not treated elsewhere in this volume.

Before the arrival of tens of thousands of observant Jews on American soil in the aftermath of the Holocaust, there were already great Jewish leaders who were determined to raise American-born Jews committed to Torah study and *mitzvah* observance. To achieve that goal they established – or headed — yeshivos. Here are a few of them:

Rabbi Dr. Dov Revel — Yeshivas Rabbeinu
Yitzchak Elchanan

Rabbi Revel was born in Kovno, Lithuania, in 1885. He studied at the Telshe Yeshivah before immigrating to the United States in 1906. In America, he attended Yeshivas Rabbeinu Yitzchak Elchanan.

After his marriage, he joined his in-laws' oil business, first in Marietta, Ohio and then in Tulsa, Oklahoma.

Several years later, Rabbi Revel returned to New York to become *rosh yeshivah* at Yeshivas Rabbeinu Yitzchak Elchanan. His innovations at the yeshivah were designed to make it appeal to a broader segment of the American Jewish public. In 1916, he established the first yeshivah high school with both religious and secular studies programs.

Under Rabbi Revel's leadership, Yeshivas Rabbeinu Yitzchak Elchanan became Yeshiva College, combining religious and secular education, the forerunner of Yeshiva University (see Focus: Yeshiva University).

Reb Shraga Feivel Mendlowitz —
Torah Vodaath and Torah Umesorah

Largely due to the efforts of one man's vision and determination, Jewish children all across America, observant and non-observant, were given the opportunity to be taught about God, His Torah, and their Jewish heritage. The organization he founded, Torah Umesorah, helped build schools in Allentown, Pennsylvania; Atlanta, Georgia; Dallas, Texas, and in hundreds of other cities across America. In these schools children learn about the Jewish holidays and how to read Hebrew. They study *Chumash*, Mishnah and the Talmud as well.

Rabbi Shraga Feivel Mendlowitz was an intensely modest chassidic Jew who came to the United States as a young man.

The parade celebrating Mesivta Torah Vodaath's move to a new building on South 3rd Street in the Williamsburg section of Brooklyn

Reb Shraga Feivel in 1913

He would correct anyone who called him "Rabbi" and request that he be called "Mr. Mendlowitz." He made the point that Jewish education and practice is everyone's concern — for the "misters," not just the rabbis. In truth, Rabbi Shraga Feivel Mendlowitz had received rabbinical ordination when he was only 17, but it was a fact he tried to conceal from the public. He was a master educator who arrived in America from Europe in 1913, at the age of 27. Rabbi Shraga Feivel began his teaching career as a teacher and principal in the Scranton Talmud Torah and afterward moved on to head Yeshivah Torah Vodaath in Brooklyn. As a result of his leadership Torah Vodaath became a major yeshivah. He quickly grasped the needs of American Jewish youth and was responsible for the establishment of a high school that would teach Torah subjects.

He also founded the first Torah-oriented summer camp. The high school and the camp were innovations that inspired Jewish youth to be committed to Torah values even in America. Reb Shraga Feivel is forever remembered by his students for the very close relationships he nurtured with them, by teaching them and inspiring them with his melodious *niggunim*. During his lifetime of accomplishments he always remained first and foremost a teacher.

Rabbi David Leibowitz —

As a teenager, David Leibowitz, a great-nephew of Rabbi Yisrael Meir HaKohen Kagan – the Chafetz Chaim – studied under the great sage at the yeshivah in Radin. In fact, he was his great-uncle's *chavrusah* (study partner) when the Chafetz

Reb Shraga Feivel Mendlowitz (seated, right) discusses education with Rabbi Aharon Kotler (seated, left) at a conference in Cleveland, Ohio, 1947 (photo courtesy of Torah Umesorah)

179

Teaching about Rosh Hashanah
in a Jewish day school

Chaim was compiling the section of *Mishnah Berurah* that deals with the laws of *succah*.

From Radin, he went to study under "The Alter," Rabbi Nosson Tzvi Finkel, in Slabodka. He left Slabodka to succeed his father-in-law as Rabbi of Selechnik, but after six years in that post, the Alter called him back to become a pioneering member of the advanced Kovno-Slabodka *kollel*.

Members of the *kollel* routinely went out to raise funds for the institution. In 1926, Rabbi Leibowitz was in the United States raising funds when he was offered the position of *rosh yeshivah* of Mesivta Torah Vodaath.

During his seven years at Torah Vodaath, he inspired the students and developed close relationships with them.

In 1933, he left Torah Vodaath to pursue his vision of creating a yeshivah on the Slabodka model. He founded Yeshivas Rabbeinu Yisrael Meir Hakohen, named after the Chafetz Chaim, who had just passed away. Rabbi Leibowitz's goal was to create Torah scholars unfailingly diligent in both their Torah study and their personal character development.

Today, his yeshivah, known as Yeshivas Chafetz Chaim, and led by his son, Rabbi Alter Henach Leibowitz, has hundreds of students in its Queens campus and in branches around the globe.

Rabbi Yaakov Yitzchak Ruderman —
Yeshivas Ner Israel

Rabbi Ruderman arrived in America in 1931, after studying in the Slabodka Yeshivah. In 1933, Rabbi Ruderman founded Yeshivas Ner Israel in Baltimore, with only five students. When the *rosh yeshivah* passed away in 1987, the yeshivah — which consisted of a *mechinah* (high school), *beis midrash*, and *kollel* for married students — had grown to 600 students. Over the years, thousands of American-born and foreign young men have studied in the yeshivah.

Rabbi Ruderman was known for the care and concern he had for his students. He encouraged them to become *talmidei chachamim* and insured that they remain committed Torah Jews. The *rosh yeshivah* became one of the leaders of Orthodox Jewry, providing guidance to nationwide Orthodox organizations such as Torah Umesorah. He was a member of the *Moetzes Gedolei HaTorah* of Agudath Israel.

Rabbi Ruderman was a great Torah scholar. Even as a young yeshivah student he managed to review the entire Talmud in only six months!

When he founded Ner Israel, Rabbi Ruderman faced opposition from some elements of Baltimore's Jewish community. But his dream became a reality, and today Baltimore boasts a large and vibrant Torah community — a direct result of Rabbi Ruderman and his yeshivah.

Rabbi Yitzchak Hutner — Mesivta Chaim Berlin
Rabbi Hutner's name is synonymous with the great American yeshivah he built from modest beginnings: Mesivta Chaim Berlin. Starting with a handful of students, it became a major Torah institution that today spreads over almost an entire square block in Brooklyn.

Before coming to America in the early 1930's, Rabbi Hutner had studied in the famed Slabodka Yeshivah. He then traveled to *Eretz Yisrael*, learning in the Slabodka branch in Hebron. In America he provided guidance and leadership to the national organizations of American Orthodox Jewry — Agudath Israel and Torah Umesorah. His deep thoughts on Jewish *hashkafah* and ethics are recorded in his classic work, *Pachad Yitzchak*.

As *rosh yeshivah* of Chaim Berlin, he exhibited an extraordinary ability to mold students, each according to his own character and talent. He would plumb the depths of a student and guide him as an individual.

Rabbi Yaakov Yitzchak Ruderman

Rabbi Yaakov Kamenetsky

Rabbi Yitzchak Hutner

Thanks to him, Mesivta Chaim Berlin survived neighborhood changes and, under his disciples is enjoying unprecedented success. Yeshivah Pachad Yitzchak in Jerusalem is named for him.

Rabbi Yaakov Kamenetsky — Yeshivah Torah Vodaath

Rabbi Yaakov's unusual sensitivity and brilliance in providing advice to the thousands of Jews who came to him with their problems prompted Rabbi Mordechai Gifter (*rosh yeshivah* of Telshe, Cleveland) to call him the "*pike'ach*" (wise man) of the generation. His face radiated warmth, love and wisdom to all who came to meet him.

Reb Yaakov arrived in America in 1937, first serving as a Rabbi in Seattle. He moved on to become a Rabbi in Toronto. After several years there, he came to Yeshivah Torah Vodaath, in Brooklyn, where he became one of its *roshei yeshivah*. Reb Yaakov was one of the great builders of Orthodox Jewry in America, guiding many students and offering wise advice to Torah leaders. He was involved in the communal activities of organizations such as Agudath Israel and Torah Umesorah, and was particularly influential in *chinuch*, educating Jewish youth. When Soviet Jews were finally allowed the freedom to immigrate to America, Rabbi Yaakov used all his energies and influence to insure that their children would receive a proper Jewish education. He remained actively involved serving the Jewish people into his 90's! He addressed a gathering of over 5,000 at the eighth *Siyum HaShas* (completion of the Talmud) when he was 91.

Reb Yaakov was born in Russia and studied in Yeshivah Knesses Yisrael, the famous Slabodka Yeshivah, and became one of the great Talmudic scholars of his generation. He was blessed with a wonderful memory, and was quoted as saying, "I did not experience forgetfulness until I was in my 80's."

Reb Yaakov lived to the age of 95. His advice to people who wanted to reach a ripe old age was to live as he did all his life — avoiding hurting others and never speaking falsely.

Did you know that?

- On September 6, 1970 a TWA flight leaving *Eretz Yisrael* was hijacked by Palestinian terrorists. The hijackers forced the plane to land in Jordan; there, the passengers were taken off and their plane was blown up. Rabbi Hutner was one of the passengers on the plane. Rabbi Hutner's ordeal as a captive of Palestinian terrorists lasted three weeks. Upon his arrival back in America, a large crowd of people waited at the airport to greet him.

- Rabbi Yaakov Yitzchak Ruderman and Rabbi Yaakov Kamenetsky were first cousins.

181

Rebbetzin Vichna Kaplan — Bais Yaakov Vichna Eisen, who was born in Slonim, Russia about 1913, was orphaned of both her parents by the time she was 11. She and her brother were then raised in the home of their uncle, Rabbi Yisrael Yaakov Lubchansky, *mashgiach* of Yeshivah Ohel Torah in Baranovitz.

At the age of 16, Vichna enrolled in Sarah Schenirer's Beth Jacob Seminary in Cracow, and over her two-year course of study she developed a close personal association with Frau Schenirer. Upon graduating, she began her over half-century career as an educator, spending five years as the only Hebrew teacher in the Beth Jacob school in Brisk.

She followed her future husband, Rabbi Baruch Kaplan, to America in 1937.

Numerous attempts had been made to found elementary schools for Orthodox girls, and 1937 saw the establishment of the first successful girls' day school, in Brooklyn's Williamsburg section.

Concurrently, Rebbetzin Kaplan was laying the foundations for a Beth Jacob high school and seminary, teaching a group of girls who gathered, after public school hours, around her dining-room table. The Kaplans finally succeeded in opening a full-day high school in January 1944, followed by a teachers' seminary.

Today, a Jewish high school education for Orthodox girls in the United States and in other Jewish communities around the world is a matter of course. There are hundreds of schools serving many thousands of students. And it was Rebbetzin Vichna Kaplan who was at the forefront of that revolution.

5680 1920

1920
Women given right to vote in the United States.

HAGANAH ESTABLISHED

In a meeting in Kibbutz Kinneret in Palestine, it was decided to establish a Jewish underground defense organization called the Haganah. Its establishment was precipitated by the failure of the British Mandatory Government to adequately protect the Jews and their property from Arab attacks. With the establishment of the State of Israel, the Haganah formed the basis of the Israeli army.

5683 1923

1923
First Ford Model-T rolls off the assembly line.

REVOLUTION IN GIRLS' EDUCATION — BETH JACOB

A remarkable woman, Sarah Schenirer of Cracow, single-handedly started the first school for Jewish girls in Poland. At the time, it was unheard of for Jewish girls to study Torah subjects in school. Sarah

Schenirer's little school started a revolution. With the approval of the Gerrer Rebbe and the Chafetz Chaim, her school of twenty-five children grew into hundreds of Beth Jacobs all over Europe. Today, every major and even most small Jewish communities have at least one Beth Jacob. The Cracow teachers' seminary she founded trained women to be role models and teachers for the many schools in the Beth Jacob network. Her students were dedicated to Torah and *mitzvos*, unlike many of their Jewish sisters, who, unfortunately, had become assimilated. Sarah Schenirer never had children of her own. Her children were her students, then and now.

Did you know that?

- A work that Sarah Schenirer loved to teach her students was Rabbi Samson Raphael Hirsch's *Nineteen Letters*.

- Sarah Schenirer passed away shortly after lighting her *Shabbos* candles.

Stanislawa 10 — The building of the Beth Jacob Seminary in Cracow as it neared completion. The building survived the War and is now the Polish national dental school.

5684 1924

Did you know that?

🐚 In 1926 the National Broadcasting Company was formed by a Jew, David Sarnoff. Sarnoff recognized the potential of radio because in 1912 he was the man on duty at a wireless telegraph in New York who heard the frantic distress call of the sinking Titanic. It was through him that, over the next 72 hours, America learned the news of the tragedy.

BNEI BRAK FOUNDED

In 1924, Rabbi Yitzchak Gershtenkorn, a Polish Jewish immigrant to *Eretz Yisrael,* founded Bnei Brak. It is the only large city in the world that has all of its streets closed on the Sabbath. Known as the "Torah city," after Jerusalem it is the city that boasts the most yeshivos, synagogues, and Beth Jacob schools in *Eretz Yisrael.* Because the crime rate is so low, Bnei Brak has no police station! A large part of the city studies Torah either full or half-time, and its mayor is a rabbi.

5687 1927

FIRST ASHKENAZIC CHIEF RABBI IN PALESTINE APPOINTED

Rabbi Abraham Isaac HaKohen Kook was appointed by the British government in Palestine to be the first Ashkenazic Chief Rabbi of the country.

Focus: Rabbi Kook

A brilliant student at the Volozhin Yeshivah, Rabbi Kook served as a Rabbi in Lithuania and eventually made *aliyah.* In *Eretz Yisrael* he became Chief Rabbi of the city of Jaffa. In 1914, Rabbi Kook left *Eretz Yisrael* to attend the Agudah conference in Europe; the outbreak of World War I made it impossible for him to return. Trapped in Europe, he became Rabbi of the Machzikei Hadas Synagogue in London.

He was recognized as one of the great Jewish minds of his time. For religious Zionists, he was their greatest rabbi and teacher. Rabbi Kook was known for his overwhelming love for the Jewish people, religious and non-religious alike. The yeshivah he started, now called Merkaz HaRav Kook, was a model for Zionist yeshivos in *Eretz Yisrael.*

Upon Rabbi Kook's return to Palestine, he was appointed Chief Rabbi. There were many leading rabbis, and particularly rabbis of Jerusalem's "Old *Yishuv*" community, who opposed the idea of a gentile government appointing a Chief Rabbi. They also disagreed with Rabbi Kook's pro-Zionist ideas. (The "Old *Yishuv*" was comprised of pious Jews of Eastern European origin. Many were from families that had been in Israel for generations, since the 18th century. Others had endured much self-sacrifice in order to immigrate to *Eretz Yisrael* in the 19th century.)

Focus: Rabbi Yosef Chaim Sonnenfeld

As a youth in Hungary, Yosef Chaim was one of the prized students of Rabbi Avraham Shmuel Binyamin Sofer, otherwise known as the K'sav Sofer, son of the Chasam Sofer.

His humility was legendary. Shortly before Reb Yosef Chaim was married, he approached the K'sav Sofer, who wrote him a letter of ordination containing lofty praises and adulation. Knowing that the letter contained praises, Rabbi Yosef Chaim put it away and did not read it for twenty years! Upon immigrating to *Eretz Yisrael*, Reb Yosef Chaim, despite his Torah greatness, considered himself a disciple of the great Torah leaders of the Old *Yishuv* of Jerusalem. Upon the death of Rabbi Shmuel Salant in 1909, Rabbi Sonnenfeld became the *de facto* Rabbi of the Ashkenazic community of Jerusalem. He agreed to formally accept the position only in 1920.

In the tradition of other great leaders of the Old *Yishuv*, such as Rabbi Shmuel Salant, Reb Yosef Chaim did his utmost to preserve Jewish tradition in the land of Israel.

It is interesting to note that while Rabbi Sonnenfeld was opposed to many of the views of Rabbi Kook, the two of them had a warm personal relationship, and they admired and respected each other. In fact, in 1913-1914 they traveled together around the north of *Eretz Yisrael* trying to inspire Jews to *teshuvah* (repentance).

Rabbi Abraham Isaac Kook

Rabbi Yosef Chaim Sonnenfeld

Did you know that?

- Shaarei Zedek Hospital was established in Jerusalem by Dr. Moshe Wallach, an Orthodox Jew from Cologne, Germany. It operates strictly according to halachah.

Shaarei Zedek Hospital during the time of the Old *Yishuv*

1927
Charles Lindbergh takes first solo flight across the Atlantic.

5689 1929

1929
Wall Street takes a dive. Stock market crash brings on Great Depression.

1930
Discovery of the last planet in our solar system: Pluto.

MASSACRE IN HEBRON

The Arab population of Hebron, on the holy Sabbath, marched on the Jewish neighborhood with knives and hatchets. In a brutal attack they tortured, terrorized and killed the Jews of Hebron. Fifty-nine Jews were murdered. The first to be killed were students of the Hebron Yeshivah, including twelve who had come from America to learn there. The British police did nothing to stop the killing. After the pogrom all the Jews living in Hebron left, and the Hebron Yeshivah moved to Jerusalem. The Jews returned to Hebron only after the Six Day War in 1967.

A Century of Great Polish Chassidim 1850 - Holocaust

In many ways, the century before the Holocaust was the Golden Age of Chassidus. By then, Chassidus had spread throughout Eastern Europe, inspiring Jews and helping stem the tide of assimilation. Scores of great Rebbes attracted hundreds of thousands of Chassidim. These four profiles present leaders from different countries and with diverse approaches in the service of God. Of course, this is but a minute sampling of the many prominent Rebbes who formed the fabric of pre-War Jewish life.

RABBI CHAIM OF SANZ

Rabbi Chaim Halberstam was a towering figure in Torah scholarship, in his influence on the Chassidic movement in his own and future generations, in his incredible generosity, and in his personal humility.

He was not born to a Chassidic family, and did not become an adherent of the movement until — already an accomplished and respected scholar – he became a disciple of Rabbi Naftali of Ropshitz. In 1830, at the age of 37, he became Rabbi of Sanz, in Galicia, where he remained for the rest of his life. The Sanzer Rav was one of the most revered Rebbes of his generation. Even a man as great as the Darchei Teshuvah of Munkatch used to come to him for blessings. Chassidim of the time related that it was thanks to the Sanzer Rav's blessing that the Darchei Teshuvah had children who survived infancy.

He was so highly regarded as an expert in halachah that hundreds of rabbis sent him their knotty questions, and he responded. His responsa are collected in the several volumes of *Divrei Chaim*, and are still regarded as classics of the genre.

His love of fellow Jews was extraordinary. He himself lived in poverty because he gave away everything he received from the countless people who came to him for advice and blessings. He even borrowed money to give to the poor. In response to his children who complained that he should not go into debt to give charity, he said, "Who *ever* heard of children who would deny their father the only *mitzvah* that he has?"

The Divrei Chaim spawned many prominent Chassidic dynasties, which spread his teachings. Most of them tragically were victims of the Holocaust, but his legacy still lives on brightly, since his surviving descendants reestablished their movements from scratch. Among them are Bobov, Klausenburg, and many others that are not as well known.

THE YENUKA OF STOLIN

In 1870, when Rabbi Yisrael Perlov, the future Rebbe of Stolin-Karlin, was born, his grandfather, Rabbi Aharon, was the Rebbe, and his father, Rabbi Asher, was a young man with the promise of a bright future. When the infant Yisrael was only 3 years old, his grandfather and then his father died. Thousands of Stolin-Karlin Chassidim were orphaned of their leaders. It seemed as if an end had come to the Chassidic dynasty that had begun with Rabbi Aharon of Karlin, one of the illustrious disciples of the Maggid of Mezeritch.

The senior Chassidim then made a risky decision – they accepted the 3-year-old Yisrael as their leader. Not surprisingly, he was called the "Yenuka" (Child), a name that remained with him all his life.

Although he played like other children, he was different. He studied intensely and even then gained respect for his sage advice. The great Rabbi Yitzchak Elchanan Spektor once visited Stolin and, after spending two hours with the 12-year-old Yenuka, described him as a *gaon*.

When he was 52 years old, he traveled to Frankfurt for medical treatment and it was there that he died. He had left a will in which he stated that there should be no eulogies at his funeral and that he should be buried in the city where he died. Thus it was that he was buried in Frankfurt, and the Stolin-Karlin Chassidim refer to him as "the Frankfurter."

His six sons carried on his tradition of Torah and Chassidus. Four of them were killed in the Holocaust. His son Reb Yaakov Chaim settled in Brooklyn before the War. His son Reb Yochanan survived despite terrible deprivation and re-ignited the movement in Jerusalem and America.

It is now led by the Yenuka's great-grandson, Rabbi Baruch Shochet, the Stolin-Karlin Rebbe, who resides in Givat Ze'ev, near Jerusalem.

THE MODZHITZER

To a Chassid, the name Modzhitz brings to mind beautiful music, music as it may even be sung by the angels. Rabbi Yisrael Taub, the first Rebbe of Modzhitz, Poland, was famous for his complex classical Chassidic melodies.

It is said that Reb Yisrael once underwent surgery and refused anesthetic. He overcame the terrible pain of the operation by concentrating on composing and singing a very long and beautiful song known as "Ezkera," to the words of a stanza from the Yom Kippur *Ne'ilah* service.

Through his music and Torah teachings, he touched the souls of thousands, who were attracted to his court and to stronger religious observance. Many Jews who had abandoned Jewish practice were inspired by his melodies and returned to traditional Judaism.

His tradition of Talmudic scholarship, Chassidic discourses, and exceptional music was carried on by his successors. The Modzhitzer court and yeshivah moved to New York, Tel Aviv and finally Bnei Brak after the War.

RABBI CHAIM ELAZAR SHAPIRA OF MUNKATCH

Rabbi Chaim Elazar Shapira succeeded his father as Rabbi of Munkatch at the age of 41, in 1913, and led with a combination of strength and compassion.

He had been his father's student, as well as his companion and confidant. In addition, he edited and published the final volume of his father's monumental work, *Darchei Teshuvah*.

Once he assumed his father's mantle, he revealed extraordinary powers of leadership. He threw himself into community affairs and showed his mettle when World War I broke out. Thousands of refugees poured into Munkatch and, when the invading Russian army drew near to the city, the Rebbe stilled the panic of his followers by assuring them that the city would not become a battlefield. So it was; the advancing army stopped at the approach to the city, and never went further.

Despite his heavy responsibilities, the Munkatcher Rebbe wrote over twenty volumes, including the four-volume responsa *Minchas Elazar*, by which he became known. He established a yeshivah where he himself taught, and which attracted hundreds of students from several countries.

He loved *Eretz Yisrael* with a passion and had a special affection for people who lived there. Nevertheless, he was a strong and outspoken opponent of secular Zionism.

In 1930, he fulfilled a long-time goal when he traveled to *Eretz Yisrael* to visit Rabbi Shlomo Eliezer Alfandri, the Sephardic sage known as the Saba Kadisha (Holy Elder). At that time the Saba Kadisha was 112 years old, and his mind and memory were as sharp as ever. They discussed matters of halachah and Kabbalah, and at the end of their last meeting, the Saba Kadisha died. The Minchas Elazar tore his clothes and wept bitterly.

Did you know that?

A major goal of the Chassidic courts was to produce laymen whose lives exemplified the spiritual ideals of their mentors. R' Berish Teichman of Munkatch (1870-1940) exemplified this feature. A Chassid of Munkatch and Belz, he was a prosperous businessman whose generosity was legendary. His family never sat down to a Sabbath meal without at least twenty poor people as honored guests. Indeed, his epitaph compared his hospitality to that of Avraham Avinu. Today, the Teichman family carries on the legacy of their illustrious grandfather in Los Angeles, where they are respected community leaders.

Rabbi Chaim Elazar Shapira

He was sickly for much of his life and asked that on his tombstone should be inscribed, "He studied Torah despite suffering."

Munkatcher Chassidus continues to thrive today, under the leadership of the Minchas Elazar's grandson, Rabbi Moshe Leib Rabinovich of Brooklyn, New York.

5692
1932

RABBI JOSEPH B. SOLOVEITCHIK ARRIVES IN AMERICA

Born in Pruzhen, Poland, a grandchild of Rabbi Chaim of Brisk, Rabbi Joseph B. Soloveitchik became the spiritual leader of American Modern Orthodoxy, and was known to many thousands of his students and followers simply as "The Rav."

Rabbi Joseph B. Soloveitchik

As a child Rabbi Soloveitchik studied Torah in *cheder* and later with his father, Rabbi Moshe Soloveitchik, the son of Rabbi Chaim of Brisk. At the age of 23, he enrolled in the University of Berlin where he received a doctorate in philosophy.

When he arrived in the United States in 1932, he became the head of Boston's Council of Orthodox Synagogues *(Vaad Ha'ir)*. In Boston, he greatly improved the quality and standards of kashruth supervision and founded the Maimonides Day School.

He succeeded his father as the senior *Rosh Yeshivah* of Yeshivas Rabbeinu Yitzchak Elchanan in 1941.

Rabbi Soloveitchik's lectures stressed the Brisker approach. His classes — which could take three hours or more — were both absorbing and popular, often attracting more than 100 students. His annual public lectures in memory of his father and on repentance attracted over 1,000 people, who would listen to Rabbi Soloveitchik for over four hours.

Many of his students became rabbis and community leaders throughout the world.

Few of his works were published during his lifetime, but many of his writings — and books based on recordings and notes of his lectures — continue to be published, bringing Rabbi Soloveitchik's teachings to an ever-widening audience. He passed away on Chol HaMoed Pesach, 1993.

BABA SALI VISITS ISRAEL

Because some people visiting the ancient synagogue of the Arizal in Safed had died mysteriously, it was decided to close the site to visitors. The synagogue stayed closed for a number of years, until Baba Sali visited Israel. He insisted on praying and eating in the synagogue, and when he exited unharmed he let the people of Safed know that it was now safe to enter.

Rabbi Yisrael Abuchatzeira, known as the Baba Sali (which means "Honorable

Did you know that?

- In 1959, Rabbi Soloveitchik was offered the position of Chief Rabbi of Israel, but he did not accept.

- From 1946 onwards, Rabbi Soloveitchik was honorary president of Religious Zionists of America.

5681 1921

Did you know that?

- The hooded Moroccan robe worn by Baba Sali is called a jalabiya.

- Baba Sali was offered the position of Chief Sephardic Rabbi of Israel, but he refused it.

Rabbi Yisrael Abuchatzeira, Baba Sali

Grandfather"), was born in Morocco. He was a genius in Talmud and halachah. He was also a Kabbalist, deeply versed in the mystical secrets of the Torah, and a *mohel*, *shochet*, and *sofer*. He was a saintly man who slept only three hours a night and prayed at sunrise. He moved to *Eretz Yisrael* and in 1970 decided to live in Netivot, a small village in the Negev.

Thousands from around the world sought his guidance, prayers, and blessings.

Did you know that?

🔹 Baba Sali would study the *parashah* from a *Sefer Torah* he had written himself.

🔹 He once traveled 380 kilometers by railroad to get to a place where the moon was visible so that he could say *Kiddush Levanah*.

🔹 When Rabbi Yisrael Abuchatzeira visited the then 105-year-old Saba Kadisha (Holy Elder), Rabbi Shlomo Eliezer Alfandri, the great sage of Jerusalem stood up for him. Baba Sali was only 32 years old at the time.

Focus: Baba Sali's vision and blessings

▶ A childless couple came to Baba Sali asking for help. He told them to remove the impure books from their home. They went home, searched their bookshelves, and couldn't find anything that would be classified as impure. They returned to Baba Sali, who told them to look again. They finally found what Baba Sali had "seen": in an attic corner, the previous tenants had left a copy of the New Testament. They removed it and not long afterwards celebrated the birth of their child.

▶ In 1970 terrorists hijacked a planeload of travelers, holding them as hostages and threatening to blow up the plane. Baba Sali entered his room to pray for the hostages' safety. Some time later he came out and said, "Everything is all right; the hostages are safe." Soon, the radio announced that the hostages had been freed at the exact moment that Baba Sali had finished his prayers.

▶ Baba Sali once rejected a gift of fresh vegetables, claiming them unfit to be eaten. After investigation, it was discovered that the vegetables had been picked on the Sabbath.

▶ After four years of treatment the doctors told an invalid that there was no hope for her to ever walk again. She came to the Baba Sali for a blessing. Baba Sali gave her water to rub on her legs. She came to him not long afterwards for another visit. This time she was walking! Her doctors, amazed by the miracle, came with her to ask for the Baba's blessing as well.

5693 1933

HITLER COMES TO POWER

Adolf Hitler's appointment as chancellor of Germany marked the coming to power of a fiendish madman who would plunge the world into a world war. His ambitions resulted in the deaths of over 50 million people — the biggest bloodbath in history. Under Hitler's direction the German people, with the cooperation of Poles, Ukranians, Hungarians and others, systematically sought to destroy European Jewry with savage barbarism. Hitler and his partners in murder showed no mercy for any Jew; young children, women, the elderly, and the sick were all equally targeted.

Germany had been one of the first European countries to grant Jews civil rights and equality. It was a country where the great majority of Jews were assimilated, where intermarriage was rampant. It was home to the first Reform temple. And it became the country which brought about the most tragic event in modern Jewish history.

Did you know that?

The year Hitler came to power was the year the Chafetz Chaim passed away. It was also the year Franklin Delano Roosevelt became president of the United States.

Rabbi Aharon Kotler was 42 years old in the year that Hitler came to power.

5695 1935

Did you know that?

§∂ After World War II, some of the leading Nazis were sentenced to death for their part in murdering millions of people. Their trial took place in the city of Nuremberg.

5698 1938

Did you know that?

§∂ The United States Congress rejected a proposal to allow 20,000 German Jewish children to enter America. As a result, these children were all murdered by the Nazis.

§∂ The German ship St. Louis left Hamburg, Germany on May 13, 1939, with 937 passengers desperately fleeing the Nazis. The ship arrived at the Cuban port of Havana. However, their hopes of escape were dashed when the Cubans allowed only thirty passengers to land. The St. Louis sailed along the American coast, hoping that the United States would save them. Though so close to safety, after three days they were forced to sail back to Europe, condemned to the flames of the Holocaust. Only 287 survived.

NUREMBERG LAWS

The German government passed the Nuremberg Laws, which effectively revoked the basic rights of its Jewish population. Jews were declared non-citizens in the country of their birth, and were not entitled to the protection of the justice system.

These laws were applied to anyone of Jewish descent. Even a Jew who had been baptized, or a non-Jew with a single Jewish grandparent — was labeled by the Nazis as a Jew.

EVIAN CONFERENCE

Representatives from more than thirty countries gathered in Evian, France. The purpose of the conference was to discuss ways to help the tens of thousands of Jews trying to escape Nazi Germany. The Jews wanted to flee Germany to save their lives, and would accept haven in any country in the world.

Hardly any of the nations represented in Evian — not even such free countries as the United States, Canada, and Australia — were willing to open their doors wide for Jewish immigration!

No one wanted the Jews.

KRISTALLNACHT

5698 1938

On November 7, 1938, a young Jew Hershel Grynszpan, shot a German official in Paris. The German died soon after. Then one horrifying night, November 9-10, pogroms erupted in all the cities of Germany. The police were given orders to allow these pogroms to happen. Synagogues which had stood for centuries were burned, Torah scrolls and libraries desecrated. Jews were killed, beaten, and publicly humiliated. The windows of Jewish-owned businesses were shattered and their merchandise was looted. There were so many bits of broken glass in the street that the night became called Kristallnacht, the night of broken glass. One hundred and ninety-one synagogues were burned that night, countless Jewish homes and businesses were looted and destroyed, and 20,000 Jews were arrested and sent to concentration camps.

The German government said that Kristallnacht was a "spontaneous" response to the killing. That was not true. Kristallnacht took place on orders from Berlin.

Did you know that?

§ Signs saying "No Jews wanted" were placed at the entrance of some German towns and cities.

§ On a memorial to the heroes of World War I who had died for the "fatherland," the Jewish names were scratched out.

A synagogue in flames on Kristallnacht

5699 - 5705
1939 - 1945

WORLD WAR II: THE DEATH OF 6,000,001 JEWISH MARTYRS

In the month of Elul, Germany invaded Poland, beginning World War II.

No short passage in a book can do justice to the evil murder of 6,000,001 human beings, of whom about 1,500,000 were children.

The statistic of 6 million murdered in the Holocaust is too large a number for us to understand. It's a nice round number that is easy to remember, but impossible to comprehend.

Each individual of the six million who were killed was a world, a life. Someone's father or mother, brother or sister, son or daughter. Their loss was irreplaceable, the hurt of the loss — to those who knew them and loved them — eternal.

Remember that it wasn't just six million who died — it was six million and one. *That one was my wife's brother. His name was Shlomo Nachum, and he was murdered when he was just 15 months old.*

The horrible suffering of the Jews who survived the torture of the Nazis and the nations who helped them must be remembered as well. Millions of people who had been living normal, everyday lives were denied the privilege of getting up in their own bed and going to work or school, with food in their stomach, and the peace of mind of knowing that the next day would be the same. Suddenly, they were starving, homeless victims, never knowing if the next day would bring violent death or new suffering at the hands of their tormentors. The extermination camps named Auschwitz, Treblinka, Buchenwald, Chelmno, Sobibor, Bergen-Belsen and Majdanek will be forever remembered with horror. And the 6,000,001 will be forever remembered as martyrs dying *al kiddush Hashem, sanctifying God's Name.*

Focus: Jewish heroes of the Holocaust

Many people, in defiance of the Nazis, succeeded in keeping *mitzvos* and preserving their Jewish values. They were heroes of the Holocaust. This is a very small sampling:

▸ The dozen starving children of Buchenwald, who exchanged their tiny bread rations for watery soup on Pesach.

▸ The town thief who refused to spit at a Torah Scroll and was killed for his defiance.

▸ The starving young women at a slave labor site near Auschwitz who refused to eat on Yom Kippur, and were forced to feed their food to the pigs.

▸ The mother holding her young son, who circumcised him on her way to the gas chambers, to ensure that he enter the Covenant of Abraham before he died.

▸ The Slonimer Rebbe, who was determined to celebrate Purim and challenged a Nazi prison guard to a dance contest. He sang and danced with all his heart, though starving and emaciated, uplifting the spirit of the other Jews on that Purim day.

▸ The young Gerrer Chassid who defiantly shouted at his tormentors, "Shoot me, but I won't let you cut off my beard."

▸ The young Gerrer Chassidim in the Plashev slave labor camp who sang and danced with joy, moments before their execution, celebrating their opportunity to die *al kiddush Hashem*, sanctifying God's Name.

▸ The bar mitzvah boy who, hidden by a gentile for years, ate only bread and onions in order to keep kosher. For many years this boy pretended to be mute, never saying a word, in order to protect himself from having to participate in Christian rites.

▸ The 17-year-old girl who refused to save herself from sadistic medical experiments because that would have caused a different girl to be taken.

▸ The 19-year-old who, exhausted and starving after days of forced marches, refused to pluck food growing out of the ground because it would desecrate the Sabbath.

▸ The 18-year-old Beth Jacob girl who, under cover of darkness, brought lifesaving medicine to inmates at great personal risk. She was known as the White Angel of Auschwitz.

5740 1939 VAAD HATZALAH IS FOUNDED

In response to the news of the genocide that was taking place in Nazi Germany, groups of European-born rabbis, American businessmen and yeshivah students formed the Vaad Hatzalah. This was an American-based organization dedicated to rescuing Jews who were being mercilessly slaughtered by the Nazis. The organization was started by the Agudath HaRabbonim, the Union of Orthodox Rabbis, upon the urgent request of Rabbi Chaim Ozer Grodzenski. Over the years, the key leaders of the Vaad were Rabbi Eliezer Silver, Rabbi Avraham Kalmanowitz, and Rabbi Aharon Kotler, and it had the support of several other Jewish organizations, including Agudath Israel and the

Children brought from Poland by the Vaad Hatzalah and the Sternbuchs, arriving in Prague, 1946

Mizrachi. They worked around the clock and exerted all of their efforts in order to save Jewish lives.

There were other Jews who put forth heroic efforts in order to help save Jewish lives. Here are three such heroes:

ISSAC AND RECHA STERNBUCH

This Swiss couple's determination and courage in the face of danger enabled them to save thousands of Jews from destruction. They enlisted the aid of the Polish ambassador to Switzerland, Alexander Landos, as well as the Papal Nuncio, Monsignor Philippe Bernardini, to assist their rescue efforts. Their many activities included smuggling Jews across borders, obtaining illegal documents and illegally transferring money to Jewish refugees to save them from starvation.

Did you know that?

§∾ Recha Sternbuch once personally rescued twelve Jews from the hands of a Gestapo commander!

Mrs. Sternbuch (center) with a group of children saved from non-Jewish homes in France. The children were placed at a home in Ville Juif. This picture shows Dr. Isaac Lewin affixing a *mezuzah* to the doorway of this home. At the right is the lawyer, Mr. M. Soifer.

Rabbi Michael Ber Weissmandl

RABBI MICHAEL BER WEISSMANDL

Due to his efforts, the first eyewitness descriptions of the mass slaughters taking place in Auschwitz reached America, England and the rest of the free world. His negotiations and a bribe of $50,000 brought a temporary halt to the deportation of Slovakian Jews. Rabbi Weissmandl made a major effort to save Hungarian Jewry from the gas chambers, enlisting the influence of high-ranking Nazis, including Eichmann's lieutenant.

He was captured by the Nazis, but succeeded in escaping from the cattle car which was on its way to the death camps. In 1944, two Jewish prisoners escaped from Auschwitz with a map of the camp and the gas chambers, and a complete account of the extermination process. They brought these to Rabbi Weissmandl, who sent messages to the Allied forces and begged them to bomb those areas and the railroad tracks leading to Auschwitz, in order to help prevent the deaths of additional Jews. Unfortunately, his pleas were not heeded.

Prior to the War he was a Talmud lecturer in the Nitra Yeshivah, which was headed by his father-in-law. After the War, Rabbi Weissmandl reestablished the yeshivah in Mount Kisco, New York.

Nitra Yeshivah in the United States

TEL AVIV BOMBED

In an unusual raid, Nazi pilots hurled their deadly bombs on Tel Aviv, killing and wounding some Jews and damaging buildings.

RABBI AHARON KOTLER ARRIVES IN AMERICA

Rabbi Aharon Kotler, *Rosh Yeshivah* of Kletzk, Poland, arrived in America as a refugee from Hitler's Europe. He had two burning ambitions: to save Jews from the Nazis and to reestablish Torah study and Jewish life in America.

With dedication and courage he assisted the Vaad Hatzalah, a New York-based organization that worked tirelessly to save Jews from the Holocaust. At the same time, he planned on building a new kind of yeshivah in America — one where students pursued Torah study not in order to become professional rabbis or clergymen, but simply *lishmah,* for its own sake. It would be a yeshivah like those that had existed in Europe. Everyone told him it could not be done. "Rabbi, this is America," they said. "Money is valued, the dollar is king, not idealism or spiritual values. Your dreams are for Europe." These people underestimated Reb Aharon. He would not compromise. They also underestimated the potential of America's Jews.

Reb Aharon was a man of great personal warmth. He also had awe-inspiring charisma and

5700 1940

5701 1941

A letter confirming arrangements for Rabbi Aharon Kotler's passage to America

A newspaper reports that "A large crowd of Jews came to greet the *rosh yeshivah* of Kletzk, Rabbi Aharon Kotler"

unlimited perseverance. Rabbi Meir Simchah of Dvinsk, known as the Or Samei'ach, said that Reb Aharon was the greatest prodigy to be born in forty years. As Reb Aharon grew older, the Chafetz Chaim recognized his potential to become a *gadol hador*. Reb Aharon studied in Slabodka and founded a yeshivah in Kletzk, which had over 200 students before World War II.

He escaped the Holocaust by fleeing to Japan via Russia, and from there he came to the United States.

In America, Reb Aharon became the leading figure of many Torah organizations, including Torah Umesorah

— a national Jewish education network, and Agudath Israel — a Jewish community activist organization. He was chairman of the *Moetzes Gedolei HaTorah* (Council of Torah Sages) of Agudath Israel. In addition, he was very active in Chinuch Atzmai, the independent Orthodox school network in Israel. He also played an active role in guiding Jewish communities around the world.

Reb Aharon's crowning achievement was Beth Medrash Govoha, the yeshivah for advanced Torah study that he established in Lakewood, New Jersey. It was a yeshivah where students studied Torah exclusively. Over the years the yeshivah in Lakewood became by far the largest advanced yeshivah in America.

Lakewood's example inspired other institutions to emulate Rabbi Aharon's goals. After only two decades in America, his influence had transformed the American horizon. By then, the country was home to many yeshivos devoted to studying Torah *lishmah*. Rabbi Aharon had defied the predictions — he had done "the impossible."

Rabbi Aharon Kotler

Beis Medrash Govoha

5700
1940

THE LUBAVITCHER REBBE COMES TO AMERICA

Rabbi Yosef Yitzchak Schneerson, the Lubavitcher Rebbe, arrived in the United States and immediately began a new era of his movement's efforts to spread Orthodox Judaism. Behind him in the Soviet Union, he left a network of brave followers who continued to defy Communist persecution as they followed, taught, and spread Judaism. They were harassed constantly and faced threats of imprisonment, torture, and exile to Siberia. The Rebbe himself was sentenced to death in 1928, but was freed thanks to the intervention of foreign governments, including the United States.

The movement, also known as Chabad, founded its first major yeshivah in the town of Lubavitch, Belorussia, in 1898. Soviet Russia closed down all the yeshivos, but the Lubavitcher Rebbe began again in the New World, as one of his priorities was to send followers throughout the country to found yeshivos and afternoon schools, and community outreach centers.

This initiative was broadened extensively by his son-in-law and successor, Rabbi Menachem Mendel Schneerson, who became Rebbe in 1948. Under his leadership, Chabad centers and schools were established throughout the world, wherever there are Jews. The outreach movement continues to grow as more than 2,500 emissaries, known as *sh'lichim,* are active in scores of countries – including the former Soviet Union, where their predecessors once risked death to keep Judaism alive.

Rabbi Yosef Yitzchak Schneerson

5701
1941

THE "FINAL SOLUTION" ORDER

On July 31, 1941 — the 7th of Av — Reinhard Heydrich was ordered by Hermann Goering, Hitler's second-in-command, to coordinate the efforts to make Europe *Judenrein,* free of Jews.

On January 20, 1942 Heydrich met with sixteen men in Wannsee, a Berlin suburb. Each one was an important official in the Nazi government. Together they created a plan that coordinated German banks, factories, railroads, and military for the purpose of murdering millions of innocent people, guilty only of the crime of being Jewish.

Focus: The righteous gentiles

Without the cooperation of the gentile citizens of the countries the Nazis occupied, they could not have murdered as many as they did. There was a country, however, that did its utmost to save its Jews — Denmark. The Nazis wanted to transport the entire Danish Jewish population to concentration camps on Rosh Hashanah. The Danish people alerted the Jews, and they went into hiding. Over the next month, with the cooperation of schoolteachers, shopkeepers, taxi drivers and, most importantly, Danish fishermen, 7,400 Jews were smuggled out by boat to safety in Sweden. Almost the entire Jewish community was saved.

There were individual heroes too.

Raoul Wallenberg: A Swedish diplomat, he issued "protective passports" which would save Hungarian Jews who were waiting to be transported to the death factories of Auschwitz. As a result of this one man, tens of thousands of Jews were saved. Wallenberg was arrested by Soviet authorities after the War and was never heard from again. It is believed that he died in captivity or was killed by the Communists.

Oskar Schindler: Working under the noses of notorious Nazis in his factory that manufactured goods for the German army, Schindler protected hundreds of Jews who worked for him. He was memorialized in the book and movie *Schindler's List*.

Ho Fengshan: A Chinese diplomat in Austria who helped 4,000 Jews escape the Nazis by issuing them visas allowing them to leave Austria.

There were many other cases, not so well known, of gentiles hiding or sheltering Jews. These people risked their own lives for the sake of their Jewish neighbors or friends. Unfortunately, however, the overwhelming majority of housewives, farmers, scientists, doctors, professors, and shopkeepers cooperated and encouraged the Germans' destruction of their Jewish neighbors, or did nothing to stop it.

THE WARSAW GHETTO

When the Germans occupied Poland, they separated the Jews from the rest of the population. There were about twenty large ghettoes in Poland. The largest and best known was the Warsaw Ghetto, where 350,000 were crowded into a tiny part of the city. The trapped Jews were expected to die of starvation, disease, and exposure to the cold winters. Those who survived these conditions were taken to death camps or slave labor camps.

Focus: The Ghetto and Judenrat

The Germans supplied food to the ghettoes, but not very much. In the Warsaw Ghetto, the daily diet was 1200 calories, about half of what a person needs to be healthy. Even the food that *did* come in was often spoiled.

The Germans would appoint a *Judenrat* (Jewish Council) to run day-to-day affairs. Of course, the only power the *Judenrat* had was to carry out Nazi orders. Many Jewish leaders refused to serve on a *Judenrat,* because they would be forced to persecute their brethren; others agreed to serve because they thought that they would be able to help their fellow Jews, at least in some ways. In a few cases, the heads of the *Judenrats* were selfish people who took advantage of their position for personal gain. The latter thought that they could save their lives by doing everything to please the Germans, but they went to the same gas chambers as everyone else.

When the Germans had prepared their death camps and slave labor camps, and they were ready to murder all the Jews, they would order of the *Judenrat* to round up a specific number of Jews for deportation, usually several thousand. When the members of the *Judenrat* thought the deportees were being sent to work, they cooperated, thinking that this was a way to save lives. But when they realized that people were going to the gas chambers, many refused to carry out the order. Some even committed suicide. The institution of the *Judenrat* turned out to be just a cruel device to make the Jews suffer and help in their own extermination.

5701 1941

BABI YAR

They were marched out of Kiev, herded by Nazi soldiers. The long line of Jewish men, women, and children, the sick and the old, were taken to Babi Yar, a ravine outside the city. There, members of special German killing squads armed with machine-guns were waiting for their victims. Lined up, group after group was shot. Those waiting their turn were forced to see their friends, neighbors, and families killed.

Over two days, endless lines of Jews were killed at Babi Yar … 35,000 human beings in all. The mass murder was just one example of the crimes committed by the German special killing squads, the Einsatzgrupen, which followed the German army as it swept across the Soviet Union.

In town after town the Einsatzgrupen herded the Jews into the forests outside the cities and forced them to dig their own graves. They would then line their victims up at the edge of the mass grave and shoot them, causing them to fall into the large pits they had dug. Five months after the German invasion of Russia, the Einsatzgrupen had slaughtered 500,000 Jews. All told, they killed at least 1,250,000 Jews.

Did you know that?

❧ The commanders of these death squads were particularly well educated. The commander of Battalion "D" had degrees from three universities. A Battalion "C" commander was a Protestant clergyman and a church official.

THE FIRST DEATH CAMP

5702 1941

In December of 1941, Chelmno, a concentration camp in Poland, became the first place were Jews were gassed to death. The method was as primitive as it was cruel. A hundred Jews would be herded into the sealed cargo area of a truck. The motor would be turned on and exhaust fumes – with poisonous carbon monoxide – would be piped into the truck, until everyone was dead. The bodies would be removed by slave laborers and the next hundred people would be forced into the truck.

Did you know that?

🍂 On December 7, 1941, "a day that will live in infamy," Japanese pilots bombed the naval base at Pearl Harbor, Hawaii, destroying many warships and killing thousands of sailors. The United States did not enter World War II until after that attack. Until then, despite the fact that Hitler's intentions were clear, a very powerful and vocal group of Americans promoted an isolationist stance, trying to persuade the public that they were safe from the flames destroying Europe, and from Japan's conquests in Asia.

President Franklin Delano Roosevelt, fearing that he would be attacked for fighting "The Jews' War" kept America neutral.

The Japanese attack, however, brought the war home to America, and the United States was drawn into the conflict.

Entrance to the Auschwitz Concentration Camp

Focus: The killing factories

Once the decision had been made to carry out the Final Solution – Nazi Germany's delicate term for the genocide of the Jews – a way had to be found to do so quickly, economically and in huge numbers. The Chelmno method was too slow. The Germans devised two methods.

Since 1933, in Germany itself there had been concentration camps, where people were "concentrated" as if in a very large prison. When the war began, these camps were used mainly for Jews. They would die of starvation or disease. Many of them were slave labor camps, where the Jews did work for the German war effort, but they were fed so little and treated so harshly that nearly all of them would slowly die!

The second method was the gas chamber. A special gas, zyklon B, was developed, which could kill hundreds of people in less than half an hour. The bodies would be burned to ash in specially built crematoria. In these death camps, as many as 10,000 people could be murdered in a single day.

The biggest and most notorious of these, in southeastern Poland, was Auschwitz-Birkenau, which was both a death camp and a slave labor camp. In northwestern Poland, Treblinka was a place where the only industry was death. The Jews of the Warsaw Ghetto were gassed in Treblinka. All together, nearly a million people were murdered there.

A YESHIVAH IS BORN: PONEVEZH, 5702 / 1942

The German army was in Egypt and was poised to enter *Eretz Yisrael*. The people living in *Eretz Yisrael* were frightened. They knew by then that Germany was intent on ridding the world of Jews. Despite this, the Rabbi of pre-War Ponevezh, Lithuania, Rabbi Yosef Shlomo Kahaneman, was planning a future. He bought land on which to build a yeshivah in the small city of Bnei Brak. His faith made him certain that God would not allow the Nazis to conquer *Eretz Yisrael*. The Ponevezher Rav was a refugee from Nazi Europe, and had been a prominent rabbi and *rosh yeshivah* before being forced to flee. He devoted his life to building the world-famous Ponevezh Yeshivah. Although the yeshivah was started with only a handful of students, today the large study hall thunders with the sound of great numbers of students learning Torah.

5702 1942

GENERAL ROMMEL DEFEATED

German Field Marshall Erwin Rommel was leading his vaunted Afrika Corps in their conquest of North Africa. "The Desert Fox," as Rommel was known, was in Egypt. He was Germany's best general and it seemed inevitable that he would conquer *Eretz Yisrael*.

In October 1942, the British, under Field Marshal George Montgomery, defeated Rommel's armies in el-Alamein, Egypt. The Nazi juggernaut in North Africa had been halted and *Eretz Yisrael* was spared.

The railway tracks used to transport Jews to the Auschwitz-Birkenau Concentration Camp in Poland

5705
1945

AUSCHWITZ LIBERATED

When the Allies liberated Auschwitz, the most infamous of concentration camps, there were only 2,819 survivors left there. The Germans who operated Auschwitz were responsible for an estimated two and a half million murders. In the various extermination camps liberated by Allied soldiers, horrific evidence of Nazi atrocities was found. There were crate-loads of gold teeth that had been removed from the mouths of the dead, and mountains of children's shoes and clothing, taken from them before their murder.

5705 1945

WORLD WAR II ENDS

Eight-year-old Israel Meir Lau leaving the Buchenwald Concentration Camp after its liberation. The son of the Rabbi of Psheml, Poland, he became the Ashkenazic Chief Rabbi of Israel.

Close your eyes. Imagine what it would be like if, when you opened them, everyone in your neighborhood had, God forbid, disappeared. Neighbors, friends, storeowners — all gone. Parents, siblings, aunts, uncles, and cousins — taken away.

After the nightmare of the Holocaust, the survivors awoke and found nearly all the great synagogues of Europe destroyed. The Jewish population was decimated. The communities and their infrastructures, the Rabbis, the famous yeshivos, *roshei yeshivah* and Rebbes — gone. Their friends, murdered. Their families, killed without mercy. Their homes, destroyed or taken over by gentiles. The survivors were, by and large, alone.

But while the Nazis destroyed Jewish Europe, they could not destroy the Jewish spirit that was in every yeshivah. They could not destroy the legacy of Torah and faith in God that the Rabbis and Chassidic Rebbes had left behind them. This Jewish spirit eventually blossomed into the great yeshivos, synagogues, Chassidic centers and Jewish communities that now flourish all over the world.

The concentration camp panel at the Yad Vashem memorial exhibition

210

5705 1946

POGROM IN KIELCE

Ninety-seven percent of Polish Jewry had been wiped out in German gas chambers. Some of the survivors thought they could return to the Polish towns and cities where they had been born and raised, to rebuild their lives. Kielce was one of those cities. Before the War, its Jewish population was 25,000; after the war 200 survivors came back to rebuild their lives. But the Poles, their former neighbors, did not want them. One day, the police confiscated the few pistols owned by the Jews. The next day there was an organized pogrom, in which forty-two Jews were killed and many others injured. The horror of a pogrom immediately after the Holocaust came as a terrible shock. The message was clear to many Polish survivors: Don't come back!

NAZIS EXECUTED

At war crimes trials held in Nuremberg, Germany, eleven Nazi war criminals were sentenced to death because of the part they played in the mass murder of Jews. Ten were hanged. The eleventh, Field Marshall Goering, committed suicide.

1945

Two atomic bombs are dropped on Japan. World War II ends.

5707 1946

Did you know that?

§ In the Purim story, Haman had ten sons who were hanged, and his daughter committed suicide. At Nuremberg ten leading Nazis were hanged, while one more committed suicide. Strangely, as the last one was led to the gallows, he screamed "Purimfest (festival of Purim) 1946."

§ The sentences of the first Nazis were handed down on Yom Kippur — the Day of Judgment.

211

Focus: Post-Holocaust Chassidic Courts

Most of the great and lesser-known Chassidic courts were wiped out in the almost total destruction of Eastern European Jewry, but a handful of leaders survived and recreated the world that was. As a result, Chassidus, in its many forms, is flourishing in many countries, although most of the names of the past are being forgotten. Many of the surviving and growing movements, such as the dynasties of Munkatch and Stolin-Karlin, have been mentioned above, in connection with their forebears. A few of the others are mentioned here.

Belz

Rabbi Aharon Rokeach, the Belzer Rav, was so renowned as a righteous man far removed from the pleasures and mundane concerns of this world, that his vast knowledge of Torah was overshadowed. He succeeded his illustrious father, Rabbi Yissachar Dov, as Rabbi and Rebbe of Belz, Galicia, in 1927, and became the spiritual guide to tens of thousands of people.

During the Holocaust, the Belzer Rav was a prime target of the Nazis, but with the aid of his loyal Chassidim and many others who revered his greatness, he was able to elude his pursuers, moving from ghetto to ghetto. The Germans caught his son and heir apparent, however, and threw him into a crowded synagogue, which they set on fire. When the Rabbe heard about it, he said it was his *akeidah*.

Ultimately, a high-ranking Hungarian officer was bribed to smuggle the Rebbe and his brother, the Rebbe of Bilgoray, into Hungary. Eyewitnesses testified to a series of miracles during the harrowing trip. From Hungary he came to *Eretz Yisrael* in 1944.

In the Holy Land, the Rebbe immediately undertook to rebuild, and multitudes gathered around him. He resided in Jerusalem and built a yeshivah in Tel Aviv, and later in Jerusalem. The Rebbe lived almost ascetically, eating very little and liberally sprinkling salt on his food, but he did everything possible to lighten the burdens of his followers. He passed away without an heir, and his young nephew, Reb Yissachar Dov, the son of the Bilgoray Rebbe, was chosen to become Belzer Rebbe. Under his leadership the movement is growing vigorously.

Bobov

Bobov was a major Chassidic movement in Galicia with a network of yeshivos. The pre-War Bobover Rav, Reb Ben Zion Halberstam was captured by the Nazis, forced to dig his own grave and murdered. His son, Reb Shlomo, survived the Holocaust and came to the United States. At first, he had difficulty even having a *minyan*, but with dedication to Torah and Chassidus, charisma, and an unexcelled love for Jews, he attracted a very large and devoted following. Bobov today is the largest Chassidic community in Boro Park and has branches in cities throughout the world. Like his forerunners in Galicia, the Bobover Rav built yeshivos and girls' schools.

The Bobover Rav would not permit himself to be drawn into controversies; his *ahavas Yisrael* (love of fellow Jews) was legendary, and he transmitted it to his Chassidim. Kindness, dedication to Jewish education, and joy in the service of God were his hallmarks. He passed away in 2000, and was succeeded by his son, Reb Naftali.

Rabbi Aharon Rokeach of Belz

Rabbi Shlomo Halberstam of Bobov with the child of a Chassid

Ger

The Gerrer Rebbes were giants of Chassidus and Torah scholarship. They are known by the names of the *sefarim* they wrote. The first Gerrer Rebbe was the Chiddushei HaRim. His grandson and successor was Rabbi Yehudah Aryeh Alter, known as the S'fas Emes, and his son, the Imrei Emes succeeded him. The Gerrer Rebbes had hundreds of thousands of Chassidim throughout Poland. Miraculously the Imrei Emes, Rabbi Avraham Mordechai Alter, escaped the Gestapo and arrived in *Eretz Yisrael*, where he reestablished today's thriving Gerrer community. He was succeeded by his sons, Rabbi Yisrael, Rabbi Simchah Bunim, and Rabbi Pinchas Menachem. Today's Gerrer Rebbe is Rabbi Yaakov, the son of Rabbi Simchah Bunim.

Ger was always distinguished for its emphasis on intense Torah study, not only in its many yeshivos, but also as the lifelong pursuit of every Jew. Historically, although Rabbi Meir Shapiro introduced the Daf Yomi concept, it was the Imrei Emes who made it a mass movement, when he publicly began its study. As a result, many thousands of his Chassidim followed suit.

Klausenburg

The Klausenburger Rebbe, Rabbi Yekusiel Yehudah Halberstam, lived through the Holocaust — despite great suffering in slave labor camps — but his wife and eleven children did not. Despite his personal tragedy, the Rebbe was the main source of encouragement for his fellow emaciated survivors in the Displaced Persons' Camp after the War. Settling in the United States, he remarried and built a thriving community and a new family in Williamsburg. Later he established his community in Union City, New Jersey. The Rebbe ultimately settled in Netanya, Israel, where he continued his work of caring for the Jewish people. During the War, when the Rebbe was on the verge of death with no basic medical care available, he prayed to God, promising that if he survived he would provide medical care for Jews. Among his many achievements, the Rebbe built the famous Laniado Hospital in Netanya. The hospital strictly follows Jewish law and is recognized as one of Israel's finest institutions.

Munkatch

A grandson of the Minchas Elazar (see p. 189), Rabbi Moshe Leib Rabinovich was born during the Holocaust and, with his father, survived the war. He grew up in South America, and studied in the Telshe Yeshivah and Beth Medrash Elyon in the United States. As a young man, he was selected by the Chassidim of Munkatch to be their Rebbe. An outstanding Torah scholar and charismatic leader, he established a flourishing court, as well as growing schools for boys and girls. The Boro Park section of Brooklyn is now the new center of historic Munkatch.

Ruzhin

Rabbi Yisrael of Ruzhin was one of the great leaders of his time, and his sons and sons-in-law were Rebbes in their own right. Of the family dynasties that survived the Holocaust, the most prominent are Sadigora and Boyan. The Sadigora Rebbe, Rabbi Avraham Yaakov, settled in *Eretz Yisrael* in 1938. His son succeeded him and maintains centers in Jerusalem and Tel Aviv.

The Boyaner Rebbe, Rabbi Mordechai Shlomo Friedman, settled on the Lower East Side of New York in 1933, and immediately became recognized as a wise and holy man. He passed away in 1971. He was succeeded by his grandson,

Rabbi Yekusiel Yehudah Halberstam

Rabbi Avraham Mordechai Alter of Ger

Did you know that?

ஃ The distinctive tall fur hat worn by Gerrer Chassidim on the Sabbath and festivals is called a "spodek."

Did you know that?

§✹ The Satmar Rebbe was a great and pious leader who represented the great Chassidic Rebbes of Europe to American Jews. The Rebbe studied Torah day and night. For forty years, starting from his bar mitzvah, he did not lie down on a bed to sleep, except for Friday nights. He spent many hours a day helping his numerous visitors, giving them encouragement, advice and financial help. Thousands came to receive his blessings, which were known to be powerful.

§✹ Upon his passing in 1979, 100,000 people — Chassidim, yeshivah students, European and American-born Jews — came to pay homage to the Satmar Rebbe at his funeral.

§✹ The Satmar Rebbe was opposed to the creation of the State of Israel. In additon to his objection to the fact that most of its leaders were anti-religious, he believed the Jews must wait for Mashiach before founding their own state.

Rabbi Nochum Dov Brayer, who lives in Jerusalem, where he leads a large and growing Boyaner synagogue and a very highly regarded yeshivah.

Both Sadigora and Boyan have been distinguished for generations for their dignity, generosity, sensitivity, and promotion of Torah study.

Satmar

A miraculous survivor of the notorious Bergen-Belsen death camp, Rabbi Yoel Teitelbaum had been the Rav of Satmar, Rumania before the War. After the War he established his Chassidic center in Williamsburg, Brooklyn. Within a few decades he and his followers had built a huge Satmar neighborhood there, with yeshivos, synagogues, shops, its own emergency ambulance service, a matzah bakery and more.

Some time later the Satmar Chassidim established an independent village, Kiryas Yoel, near Monroe, in Upstate New York.

Satmar's *Bikur Cholim* society is famous throughout New York for its many activities to aid all Jews in need of help, without regard to their background or affiliation.

The Satmar Rav was a very great Torah scholar who learned virtually the entire day. His personal generosity was bound-

less and he communicated this trait to his Chassidim.

Skvera

Skvera was a small town in Ukraine. Its Rebbe, Rabbi Yaakov Yosef Twerski, came to the United States after the War and settled in Williamsburg. Though his Chassidim did not survive the Holocaust, he was soon recognized as a pious man and developed a large following.

He pioneered the concept of establishing a Chassidic community where the inhabitants — especially children — would be sheltered from harmful influences. Thus "New Square," a Chassidic village in Upstate New York, was born. Beginning with just a few houses, New Square has blossomed into a large community. This concept was followed by other Chassidic groups.

The present Rebbe, Rabbi David Twerski, is an inspirational leader of a growing community and offers guidance and blessings to streams of people who come from near and far.

Vizhnitz

Rabbi Chaim Meyer Hager, the Rebbe of Vizhnitz, came to America after the War and settled in Williamsburg. He was warm and charismatic, kind and outgoing, the composer of many Chassidic melodies and an inspiring *chazzan*.

As a result, his community of Chassidim grew quite large, but his heart was in *Eretz Yisrael*.

He settled there in 1950, leaving his younger son, Rabbi Mordechai, to lead his chassidim in America. Rabbi Mordechai later established a community in Monsey, New York, known as Kesser.

Rabbi Chaim Meyer established Kiryas Vizhnitz in Bnei Brak, and he became a prime leader of Orthodox Jewry in Israel. When he passed away in 1972, his older son, Rabbi Moshe, assumed his mantle.

The two brothers each have large communities of followers throughout the world, and they are both known as exceptional Torah scholars, distinguished for their diligence in study.

Rabbi Yoel Teitelbaum of Satmar

Rabbi Chaim Meyer Hager of Vizhnitz

THE U.N. VOTES TO CREATE A JEWISH STATE

5708 1947

On *Motza'ei Shabbos*, all over Israel, Jews living under the British mandate sat with their ears glued to radios. They were listening to a live broadcast of a vote taking place in the United Nations General Assembly thousands of miles away. The issue on the General Assembly floor was a plan to split Palestine into separate Arab and Jewish countries. In a dramatic vote of 33 - 13, the U.N. voted, on November 29, in favor of the creation of an independent Jewish state. In an unusual turn of events, even traditionally anti-Semitic Russia voted "yes." Overcome with joy at the news, Jews in *Eretz Yisrael* celebrated until late in the night, dancing in the streets.

1947
Radios become portable — the transistor is invented.

ISRAEL'S WAR OF INDEPENDENCE

5708 1948

In Haifa, the last British flag still fluttering over Palestine was lowered. Saluting from the deck of a British navy ship stood Lieutenant General Sir Alan Cunningham, the British High Commissioner of Palestine. This signaled the end of British occupation of *Eretz Yisrael*. Britain became the last foreign power to rule *Eretz Yisrael*.

In Tel Aviv, on the 5th day of Iyar (May 14), a few hours before the start of the Sabbath, David Ben Gurion read Israel's Declaration of Independence. In it, the State of Israel was established. The first act of the temporary Israeli government was to legalize unrestricted immigration. Finally, the doors of *Eretz Yisrael* were opened to any Jews wishing to return. The Jewish homeland was immediately recognized by President Truman. The United States was the first major country to grant such recognition. Five Arab nations quickly declared war on the newly declared state. This war would engage the Jews and Arabs in a year-long, bloody struggle.

The first few weeks of war looked very grim. Egyptian planes bombed Tel Aviv. In the north, Syrian tanks thundered into the Galilee. Within two weeks the Old City of Jerusalem had surrendered to Jordan's Arab Legion after a bitter fight. The rest of the city was besieged. Arab forces would not allow supplies of food and water to enter Jerusalem. The entire city was in danger of falling to the enemy. The Egyptian army had advanced

A captured Syrian tank at Kibbutz Degania

to within sixteen miles of Tel Aviv. Many Jewish settlements had to defend themselves against attacks from neighboring Arab villages and sometimes from regular Arab army units. To defend their people and their land, all able-bodied people — young teens, women, and newly-arrived Holocaust survivors — with memories of death still burning within themselves — went to battle. There was little ammunition to defend and protect the 600,000 Jews of *Eretz Yisrael* against the Arab armies. The Jews had a few thousand rifles, 10,000 homemade Sten guns, 1,000 light machine-guns and an air force of six propeller planes whose pilots dropped bombs by hand. There were no tanks, fighter bombers, or adequate ammunition. The Jews fought bravely and courageously. They defended every settlement, every inch of land, sometimes to the last man, and often turned back the attackers. The hand of God was particularly apparent as the Jews, against all possible odds, not only held back Arab invasions, but successfully counterattacked and were often victorious.

In the months before the war formally began, tensions between Jews and Arabs escalated. As it became evident that the state would declare its independence, Arab residents of many cities — including Jerusalem, Safed, Jaffa, Tiberias and Haifa — were urged by the Arab leadership to abandon their homes. The leaders promised that those leaving would soon be allowed to return — once the Jews were routed from Palestine.

Colonel Mickey Marcus was a Jewish West Point graduate who had fought in the American army during World War II. Now he came as a volunteer to Israel to help train and fight with the

Did you know that?

- Throughout the 1948 war there were many miraculous events. Here are some samples:

- In Kibbutz Degania stands a Syrian tank put out of commission by a lone Jew who attacked it with a Molotov cocktail.

- In a Negev kibbutz, 144 men resisted an Egyptian army unit of 2,000 men for five days. After the war, a visiting American army officer commented that he couldn't understand why the Egyptians had failed. He said he could have taken over the kibbutz in one hour, had he been in command.

- In the cities of Jerusalem and Tiberias stand monuments erected to a homemade weapon used by the Jews during the War of Independence. It was called the "Davidka." It was a small artillery piece that couldn't do much damage, but made such a terrible sound that it frightened off attacking Arabs. It was named for its inventor, whose name was David.

- Colonel Mickey Marcus was killed accidentally by an Israeli soldier. He is the only soldier buried in the West Point cemetery who died fighting a war for a foreign country.

1948

Mahatma Gandhi, Indian leader, is assassinated.

Jew Stats:

In **1948, 600,000** Jews lived in Israel. In **1950,** the population of Israel topped **one million.**

A "Haganah" member during Israel's War of Independence

Israeli army. He was appointed commander of the Jerusalem front. The lone highway leading to Jerusalem was under Arab control. The city was starving, with no food or water. Colonel Marcus derived an ingenious plan. His men blasted a road through the Jerusalem hills. Convoys of trucks could now bring food and water to the city. Jerusalem could now survive! This road was called the "Burma Road," and it broke the siege of Jerusalem.

On June 11 the fighting stopped. Both sides agreed to a month-long U.N. truce. During the following months, planes, tanks, and artillery poured into Israel from France and Czechoslovakia. Jewish war veterans from the air forces of the United States and England illegally flew bombers to Israel to create a real air force. When the war resumed over the next months, Nazareth and Lod Airport were captured by the Jews, Cairo was bombed, and the Negev was conquered up to the southernmost tip of Israel, the port of Eilat.

In January, armistice talks opened. They concluded in July 1949, officially ending the war. Israel had conquered territory that had not been allotted to it by the original U.N. partition plan. Tragically, access to the *mekomos hakedoshim* (holy places) such as Rachel's Tomb and the *Kotel,* the Western Wall, had been cut off from the Jewish people and would remain inaccessible to Jews for the next eighteen years, until Israel's victory in the 1967 war. The toll of war had been great: 6,000, or one out of *every* hundred Jews living in Israel, lost their lives. (A comparable death toll in the United States today would be 2.7 million!) However, the Jewish state was born.

FIRST KNESSET ELECTED

5709

1949

For the first time in Jewish history, Jews voted to elect their own government in *Eretz Yisrael*. The country's first prime minister was David Ben Gurion.

Focus: Immigrants to Israel

Can anyone imagine the United States absorbing 250 million new immigrants in a few years? Israel's population of 600,000 performed a comparable feat in the first several years of the country's existence. Survivors of the Holocaust came. Hundreds of thousands of refugees came from the Arab lands, in order to escape anti-Semitic persecution. These Sephardic refugees had to leave all their possessions behind, so both the Ashkenazic and Sephardic immigrants were penniless. Their Jewish brethren in Israel accepted them with open arms and helped them become established.

Did you know that?

- Ben Gurion believed in a socialist society. When asked what salary the prime minister of Israel should draw, Ben Gurion answered: whatever has been allotted to the Knesset's cleaning lady.

David Ben Gurion reading Israel's Declaration of Independence

David Ben Gurion

Did you know that?

§ In 1949, the Israeli government organized the mass *aliyah* of thousands of Yemenite Jews. This project was called "Operation Magic Carpet."

Focus: David Ben Gurion

David Ben Gurion was born in Plonsk, Poland in 1886. He immigrated to *Eretz Yisrael* at the age of 20, and changed his name from Green to Ben Gurion. He worked as a field laborer and eventually became the secretary-general of the Histadrut, the federation of all the labor unions in Palestine. He was active in the resistance to the British occupation of *Eretz Yisrael*. He believed very strongly that all Jews should be allowed to move to Israel, and he organized illegal immigration activities. He also led the armed struggle against the British through his unofficial army, the Haganah, which would later turn into Israel's army.

After the State was declared, Ben Gurion became Israel's first prime minister. He was responsible for the creation of the Israeli army and the defense of the Jews in *Eretz Yisrael* during its war of independence.

Unfortunately, Ben Gurion was thoroughly secular, and disparaged the Jewish religion and Torah learning. Yet, he recognized that the religious community's concerns for the newly-declared State could not be ignored. He made an arrangement with the representatives of Torah Jewry that has come to be known as "the Status Quo Agreement." This agreement was meant to retain the Jewish character of the State. The four points of the agreement were: There would be a religious school network in addition to a secular network; marriage, divorce, and personal status issues would be governed by the Chief Rabbinate; the Sabbath would be the official day of rest; all government bodies such as the army, embassies, etc. would be kosher.

In its first years the State of Israel absorbed huge numbers of new immigrants. Ben Gurion's government saw to their material needs. Unfortunately, in the process, his government was responsible for depriving hundreds of thousands of religious Sephardim and their descendants of their rich Torah heritage.

Ben Gurion was convinced that the Negev was the key to Israel's economic future, and poured government funding and efforts into the desert. He spent his last years on Kibbutz Sde Boker in the Negev, dressing simply and living in a modest kibbutz dwelling.

A young Jewish Yemenite, in a refugee camp near Aden

A Yemenite Habani family celebrating the Passover Seder at their new home in Tel Aviv

RABBI MENACHEM MENDEL SCHNEERSON BECOMES LUBAVITCHER REBBE

5711 1951

Rabbi Menachem Mendel Schneerson became Rebbe of Lubavitch following the death of his father-in-law, Rabbi Yosef Yitzchak Schneerson. Rabbi Menachem Mendel was a brilliant man. His charismatic personality and overpowering love for Jews of every background attracted thousands of visitors from all walks of life, from countries around the globe.

The Lubavitcher Rebbe developed a worldwide network of schools, synagogues, adult-education programs and charitable institutions in hundreds of cities, as diverse as Rochester, New York; Sao Paulo, Brazil; and Katmandu, Nepal. The Rebbe established "Chabad Houses" in the four corners of the world. These were centers of Jewish outreach and Jewish community service.

His efforts touched the lives of millions of Jews, and caused tens of thousands to rediscover their Jewish heritage. His talks and "farbrengen" (get-together of Chassidim) were the first Torah lectures to be internationally broadcast via sattelite to large audiences. The Lubavitcher Rebbe passed away on 3 Tammuz, 1994, and is buried in Queens, New York, near his father-in-law.

Did you know that?

- Israeli bus and taxi drivers, even non-religious ones, often hang the Lubavitcher Rebbe's picture in their vehicles.

- During World War II the Lubavitcher Rebbe worked as a marine engineer for the U.S. Navy on secret military projects.

- One of the largest Seders in the world takes place in Thailand, where Chabad caters a Seder for hundreds of Israeli tourists in the country.

1952
First hydrogen bomb exploded.

The Lubavitcher Rebbe and Menachem Begin, Prime Minister of Israel

5714
1953

BEN GURION MEETS THE CHAZON ISH IN BNEI BRAK

A great conflict between the religious and non-religious sectors of Israeli society erupted over the drafting of women into the army. The great Torah leaders, including Chief Rabbi Yitzchak Isaac Halevi Herzog, ruled that it was forbidden for women to serve in the army.

To reach an accommodation with the Israeli religious community, Ben Gurion went to Bnei Brak to meet with the great Torah sage, Rabbi Avraham Yeshaya Karelitz, the Chazon Ish.

Ben Gurion presented the State's manpower needs, and explained why he felt women should be conscripted. The Chazon Ish responded: "When two wagons, one empty and one full, must both pass through a narrow road, the empty wagon must move to the side and yield to the full one.

"Torah Judaism is a full wagon, with thousands of years of history, heritage, and experience. The new State has not yet withstood the test of time; it is still an empty wagon."

The "empty wagon" did, indeed, yield, and, even today, religious women are not drafted into the Israeli army.

Chazon Ish

Focus: The Chazon Ish

Rabbi Avraham Yeshaya Karelitz was born in Lithuania before the beginning of the 20th century. In 1920 he and his wife moved to Vilna. There he was close to Rabbi Chaim Ozer Grodzenski, the acknowledged leader of pre-war European Jewry. With the help of the Chief Rabbi, Rabbi Abraham Isaac Kook, the Chazon Ish was granted papers that allowed him to be one of the few legal immigrants whom the British allowed into Palestine. He arrived in *Eretz Yisrael* in 1933 and settled in Bnei Brak, where he shared a small apartment with his brother-in-law, the Steipler Gaon. The Chazon Ish soon became the unchallenged leader of Israel's *chareidi* Jewry. Thousands came to his home in Bnei Brak for his blessing and advice.

He wrote many volumes of *Chazan Ish,* which is a penetrating commentary on the Talmud. His *Emunah U'Bitachon* explores the concepts of belief and faith in God. His published letters

present his rulings, advice, and guidance on a wide array of issues. The Chazon Ish taught that every facet of Jewish life must adhere strictly to the requirements of halachah. He took great pains to determine halachic requirements. With great genius, he revitalized the *halachos taluyos ba'Aretz,* laws dealing with agriculture in *Eretz Yisrael.* These laws had not been practiced for centuries, because there had been hardly any Jewish farmers in Israel. He provided clear guidelines for the Jewish people, after centuries of exile, on how to once again properly perform the mitzvos of *terumos* and *maasros* (tithes) in *Eretz Yisrael* and how to properly observe the *Shemittah* (Sabbatical) year.

Through he never held a formal position as *rosh yeshivah* or synagogue rabbi, people from around the world — from all walks of life, and of all levels of Torah observance — sought his wisdom, counsel, guidance, blessing and halachic direction.

THE SINAI CAMPAIGN

5716 1956

Egypt had allowed its border with Israel to become an open gate for Arab terrorists attempting to enter Israel. It also closed off the Suez Canal to Israel shipping. It was obvious that Egypt was preparing to invade Israel, so Israel decided to attack Egypt, with the cooperation of Britain and France, who wanted to occupy the Suez Canal. Called the Sinai Campaign, in eight days the Israeli army conquered the Gaza Strip and the entire Sinai Peninsula. Providentially, the Israelis suffered relatively few casualities, while 3,000 Egyptian soldiers were killed and 6,000 taken prisoner. Under pressure from United States President Eisenhower and the Soviets, who sent submarines to the Mediterranean as a warning, the Israeli government ordered its soldiers to retreat and return the captured territories to Egypt.

1957
The Russian Sputnik, the first satellite, is launched into space.

Israeli soldiers prepare their weapons during the Sinai Campaign

5718 1958 ALEPPO CODEX SMUGGLED OUT OF SYRIA

The Aleppo Codex ("codex" is the Latin word for "book") is a 1,000-year-old manuscript of the complete Bible. It was written under the supervision of Aaron ben Moses ben Asher, the leading masoretic scholar living in 10th-century Tiberias. Masoretic scholars devoted their energies to studying and preserving the *mesorah* — the correct spelling, vowelization, and cantillation of the Bible. Ben Asher added the vowelization and cantillation marks in the Aleppo Codex.

From Tiberias the book was taken to Jerusalem and from there to Cairo. When Rambam arrived in Cairo he used this manuscript as the basis for the precise instructions for writing a Torah Scroll.

According to legend, some time in the 13th century, a great-great-grandson of Rambam brought the Codex to Aleppo, Syria, where it was kept in the Great Synagogue. During the Arab riots protesting the establishment of the State of Israel, this ancient manuscript was partially destroyed. To preserve the Codex from further destruction, the Jews of Alleppo hid it and eventually, at great risk, smuggled it out of Syria. The Codex was then returned to the country in which it had originally been written: *Eretz Yisrael*. Today the Aleppo Codex is kept in Jerusalem.

1959

Alaska and Hawaii become the 49th and 50th states of the United States of America.

224

RABBI MOSHE FEINSTEIN'S RESPONSA

5719 1959

Rabbi Moshe Feinstein, *Rosh Yeshivah* of Mesivtha Tifereth Jerusalem on the Lower East Side of Manhattan, was universally recognized as the premier halachic authority of the last two generations. His eight volumes of *Igros Moshe* contain his written responses to thousands of complex halachic inquiries sent from the four corners of the world. He dealt with an incredible variety of questions, applying eternal principles to modern life. Although the world relied on him as its halachic authority, he considered himself to be primarily the teacher of his students and the author of *Dibros Moshe* on the Talmud.

Rabbi Moshe Feinstein

Focus: Rabbi Moshe Feinstein

Moshe Feinstein was given the name Moshe became he, like Moses of the Bible, was born on the 7th of Adar. Rabbi Feinstein dedicated his life to teaching Torah to *klal Yisrael* devotedly and unselflessly. As a youngster in his hometown of Uzda, a suburb of the Russian city of Minsk, he was educated not in yeshivah, but by his father and a private tutor. Shortly before reaching the age of bar mitzvah he went to the yeshivah in Slutzk. From a young age his brilliance and phenomenal memory were apparent. He knew the entire Talmud and all four sections of the *Shulchan Aruch* by the time he was 17, yet he never became haughty and proud. All his life he

remained "a man of the people," caring and considerate of others. His incredible concern extended to every human being. Even the non-Jewish hospital nurses who had cared for him, and to whom he had shown appreciation and kindness, broke down and cried when he passed away.

Reb Moshe answered everyone's questions, from complex queries put to him by the great *roshei yeshivah*, to those of the woman in his neighborhood who called him on Friday afternoons to find out what time the Sabbath candles were to be lit.

In Luban, Russia, where Reb Moshe was Rabbi, the Communists and evil Josef Stalin were in power.

Did you know that?

🐾 During World War I, Reb Moshe was in danger of being drafted into the Russian army. He went to meet the Chafetz Chaim to receive his blessing.

1961

First man in space is a Russian "cosmonaut."

Jew Stats:

In **1960,** New York City had over **2 million** Jews. Sixty years earlier, in **1900,** only **600,000** Jews lived there.

With brutal force, the cruel Russian regime wanted to destroy all religious institutions, hoping to extinguish all religious belief and practice. Their goal was to create a purely atheistic state, whose citizens would not believe in religion or God. Reb Moshe resisted the official persecution and for six years remained at his post in Luban. Despite harassment from government officials he refused to resign. He was evicted from his home, taken from the house in the middle of the night and interrogated. Yet, while resisting the Communists, he was able to trick them into building a *mikveh* for his community.

Circumstances finally forced Reb Moshe to leave Russia. He arrived in the United States in 1937, at the age of 41, and became *Rosh Yeshivah* in New York's Mesivtha Tifereth Jerusalem, one of the oldest yeshivos in the United States. He expanded the yeshivah's programs and created its resident division, the Yeshiva of Staten Island, in 1966. In 1962, with Rabbi Aharon Kotler's passing, he became the chairman of the *Moetzes Gedolei*

HaTorah, Agudath Israel's Council of Torah Sages. He was leader of other national institutions as well. He worked tirelessly for the development and expansion of Torah Jewry in America and throughout the world

Reb Moshe passed away on *Taanis Esther* at the age of 91, in a New York City hospital. At the moment of his passing, miles away, at the Yeshiva of Staten Island, the light over his chair in the study hall flickered and went out.

His funeral in New York attracted well over 100,000 people.

When his bier arrived in Jerusalem for burial, Purim festivities were postponed as 250,000 people accompanied him to his final resting place on *Har HaMenuchos*. The large numbers that attended the funerals are not surprising when one considers that this was a man who, when once asked in what merit he had become so famous, responded, "All my life I never hurt a human being."

5722 1962

MOSSAD COMMANDOS CAPTURE SS OFFICER ADOLF EICHMANN

Did you know that?

§ Adolf Eichmann was the only person ever to receive the death penalty in Israel.

§ After the war, Eichmann surrendered to the Americans under a false name. He was kept in a prison camp from which he escaped.

On a Buenos Aires street a balding, ordinary-looking middle-aged man stepped down from a bus. He was returning home from his job at the Argentinian branch of Mercedes-Benz. As he walked down the street he was accosted by two men who pushed him into a waiting car and drove him to an isolated villa. The Mossad, Israel's intelligence agency, had just captured one of the century's most notorious criminals — Adolf Eichmann.

As the officer in charge of Nazi Germany's Jewish Section, Eichmann orchestrated the deportation of millions of Jewish men, women, and children to the Nazi death camps. After the War, he disappeared. Some years later his "widow" emigrated to Argentina, where she "married" a man named Ricardo Klement. As a result of efforts by Nazi hunters such as Simon Wiesenthal and others, the Mossad sent a team to investigate "Mr. and Mrs. Klement." When "Mr. Klement" brought home flowers on the day that Adolf Eichmann had married his wife twenty-five years earlier, the Mossad knew they had found their man, and seized him.

Surrepitiously boarding an El Al plane with their prisoner, the Mossad agents whisked Eichmann out of Argentina and brought him to Israel.

An Israeli court tried him for his crimes against the Jewish people. In the courtroom, the defendant sat in a special booth made of bulletproof glass, to protect him from a possible assassination attempt by people who had suffered at his hands during the Holocaust. Holocaust survivors were brought as witnesses and his prosecutor was a Polish born Jew.

Eichmann was found guilty, and was hanged. His remains were cremated and his ashes scattered in the sea, lest his grave become a shrine for anti-Semites.

Nazi war criminal Adolf Eichmann in his bullet-proof booth during his trial in Beit Ha'am in Jerusalem

1963

President John F. Kennedy assassinated.

5727
1967

SIX DAYS TO VICTORY

From secret air-force bases, 400 Israeli pilots flying fighter bombers flew off into the early morning sky. It was sunrise, and a new dawn was about to break over the Middle East. Flying at high speeds only 500 feet above the Mediterranean to avoid Egyptian radar, they entered Arab airspace and proceeded to their targets. They dropped their payloads of destruction over about twenty-five Egyptian, Jordanian and Syrian airfields, destroying 452 planes. In a mere three hours the threat to Israel's safety from the air was gone. The Six Day War had begun. The date: Monday, June 5, 1967.

For months before, under the leadership of Egyptian Prime Minister Gamal Abdul Nasser, the Arab world had been preparing its forces for war. The Arabs had been constantly

Destroyed Egyptian planes litter the ground after an Israeli air strike against their base

broadcasting threats to destroy Israel. They said they would push the Israelis into the sea, and asked all Arabs to join in a *jihad*, a holy war against the Jews. The combined Arab armies boasted over half a million soldiers, with 2,000 tanks. They represented an almost impossible challenge to the 300,000 soldiers and 800 tanks of the Israeli army. Badly outnumbered, the mood of the Jews was one of fear.

The Egyptians closed the Suez Canal and the Gulf of Aqaba to all ships traveling to Israel. This was against international law. They also blockaded the Israeli port of Eilat, an act of war. The rest of the world remained silent, and the Jews were convinced that they had to do something to defend themselves. Under the direction of Defense Minister Moshe Dayan, in a clearly miraculous six days of fighting, the Jewish armed forces defeated the Arab armies of five nations, capturing 50,000 square miles of territory, including all of *Eretz Yisrael* west of the Jordan, and the Sinai Desert.

In the north of Israel, infantrymen battled uphill against Syrian soldiers in bunkers, conquering the Golan Heights. In the south, churning up great clouds of desert sand, tank units thundered across the Sinai Desert. The Egyptian soldiers abandoned their tanks and equipment and retreated back across hundreds of miles of barren, arid land. In the west, jeeps rolled into Jordan.

Did you know that?

- Egyptian soldiers retreating in panic from the oncoming Israeli army littered the desert with their combat boots, which they removed in order to enable them to run faster through the desert.

- The victories in the north were assisted by intelligence reports that had been sent before the war by the courageous Israeli spy in Syria, Eli Cohen. He had earned the confidence and trust of the highest echelons of the Syrian government and military. Eli Cohen was eventually discovered and hanged by the Syrian government.

Defense Minister Moshe Dayan (center) flanked by *Aluf* Uzi Narkis and *Aluf* Rechavam Zeevi at the entrance to the Tomb of the Patriarchs in Hebron

On the second day of the war, Israeli units stood on the mountaintops overlooking the city of Jerusalem. The eastern part of the city, including the *Kotel*, had been occupied by Jordanians since 1948. Now, the soldiers were waiting for word from the Knesset to move forward; they realized they would be participating in a historic battle. For 2,000 years the

Israeli paratroopers, overcome by emotion, stand at the Western Wall in Jerusalem just after it was recaptured

Jewish people had yearned for the return of Jerusalem to Jewish control. The word was given and the Jews thundered down the surrounding hills. Paratroopers penetrated the Old City at the Lion's Gate as the infantry battled bravely, in desperate street-to-street and house-to-house fighting. All of them shared the same objective: to recapture the Temple Mount, holiest site in the world to the Jews. When the victorious Jewish paratroopers stood before the last remnant of the Temple on Wednesday 28 Iyar 5727 (June 7, 1967), the *Kotel HaMaaravi* towering above them, they broke out in tears of joy. Shoulder to shoulder they danced and sang. The sound of the *shofar*, which had not been heard at the *Kotel* since the Old City had been captured by the Jordanians nineteen years before, could be heard around the world. It resonated through the hearts of the entire Jewish people.

On *Motza'ei Shabbos*, June 10, all of Israel's borders were quiet. The war was over in six days, in one of the greatest miracles of the 20th century. Against overwhelming odds, Israel had survived, reconquered Jerusalem, and dealt the Arab world a devastating defeat.

Rabbi Shlomo Goren blows a *shofar* following the recapture of the *Kotel*

Focus: The *baal teshuvah* phenomenon

Israel's great victory in the Six Day War filled Jews of all backgrounds with Jewish pride. Jews in the Soviet Union began meeting to study Hebrew. Many even became religious and started learning Torah in secret and reuniting themselves with the faith of their grandparents. In America Jewish youth searching for a more meaningful life used to travel to Europe and the Far East. Now they started to come to Israel. They joined newly formed yeshivos created to serve people returning to their roots — or seeking knowledge of their heritage. Over the past decades these yeshivos have taught tens of thousands of Jews from assimilated homes, and guided them in their return to Torah living — the *baal teshuvah* movement.

1967
First heart transplant takes place in South Africa.

OFFICIAL END OF SPANISH EXPULSION

In 1968 Spain officially abolished the expulsion order that had banished the Jewish community from its borders in 1492.

5728 1968

Did you know that?

🌿 Though the Spanish Inquisition formally ended in 1820, the Edict of Expulsion remained in effect.

5729
1969

GOLDA MEIR BECOMES ISRAEL'S PRIME MINISTER

Prime Minister Golda Meir

1969
The first man lands on the moon.

In 1969, Golda Meir became Israel's first (and, to date, only) woman prime minister. She was the fourth prime minister since the establishment of the State.

Golda Meyerson was born in Russia, and, as a child, she witnessed pogroms. Her family immigrated to Milwaukee, Wisconsin, where she grew up and became a schoolteacher. At the age of 23, with a sense of idealism, she left the comforts of America for what was then primitive, backward *Eretz Yisrael*. She became an important political figure during the founding and early years of the State.

Disguised as an Arab, she secretly met with King Abdullah of Jordan to try and persuade him not to attack Israel in its War of Independence.

Over the course of her career she served as Israel's first ambassador to the Soviet Union and as Israel's foreign minister.

YOM KIPPUR WAR

5734 1973

Shortly after midday on the holiest day of the year, Yom Kippur, Israel was viciously attacked by Egypt and Syria. The Day of Judgment had arrived in more ways than one. Men left in the middle of prayer services to enter jeeps that would transport them to the war zone. Those who remained behind prayed with even greater fervor, seeing their fellow worshipers going off to war. For the next three days the State of Israel, its cities, towns, and citizens, teetered at the brink of destruction.

The Israeli government, headed by Prime Minister Golda Meir, had chosen to ignore intelligence reports of an impending attack by its enemies. Instead of strengthening its defenses, the army allowed many soldiers to go home for the Jewish holidays. When the attack came, Israel's borders were defended only minimally. On the Golan, 60 tanks were the only protection against an invasion of 1,500 Syrian tanks. In the Sinai, fewer than 100

Syrian soldiers holding their hands up as a sign of surrender in the Golan Heights, during the Yom Kippur War

A pontoon bridge erected by the Israel Defense Forces across the Suez Canal

An Israeli Centurion tank moving up to the battle zone

soldiers attempted to defend their country against an attack force of 70,000 Egyptian soldiers. *Hesder* soldiers, who combine Torah learning with army service, were particularly fierce and courageous fighters. However, in the face of overwhelming numbers, many were forced to surrender. In one Sinai outpost, though, the outnumbered Israelis fought so stubbornly that the Egyptians left them where they were and simply advanced around them.

The Egyptians moved into the Sinai toward Israel with 100,000 soldiers and 400 tanks. The Israeli air force, sent to stop the invasion from the air, suffered serious losses as its planes were targeted by Russian-supplied missiles. In the north, the Syrians advanced and took Mount Hermon, on Israel's northernmost border. When the Syrian troops arrived at the Kinneret, there was nothing to stop them from conquering the northern cities of *Eretz Yisrael*. Miraculously, they chose to stop at this point and not move on. Their attack and advance had been so easy that the Syrian command was sure the Israelis had set a trap for them!

In the face of these crushing defeats and danger, Jews all over the world prayed. Their prayers were answered, and the Israeli army was able to turn defeat into victory. On the sixth day of the war, during Succos, a counter-offensive was launched against Syria. Two armored divisions reconquered the north, advanced into the Golan, and pursued the retreating Syrian army to within 40 kilometers (about 25 miles) of the Syrian capital of Damascus. A few days later Mount Hermon was recaptured after a 12-hour battle against Syrian commandos.

A soldier saying his morning prayers before setting out to his base in Sinai

Did you know that?

§ One of the earliest images of the Yom Kippur War to be released by the Egyptians was that of a bearded, *kippah*-wearing Jewish soldier being taken captive, a Torah Scroll in his hand. The captured scroll was put on display in an Egyptian military museum.

§ In Orthodox Jewish neighborhoods in America, Jewish residents found out that Israel was at war not from radio or television newscasts — it was Yom Kippur! — but from non-Jewish neighbors. For many, rumors of the Arab attack were verified only after Yom Kippur when they could listen to the news bulletins.

§ In pictures of Israeli soldiers taken during the war, the long, thin object they are holding is not their weapon, but a *lulav*. For many, the *mitzvos* of *lulav* and *esrog* were performed standing next to their tanks.

§ The United States, under President Richard Nixon's direct order, airlifted massive amounts of military supplies to a desperate Israel.

1973
Last American troops leave Vietnam.

1974
President Nixon resigns because of Watergate scandal.

1975
United Nations votes to pass a resolution that equates Zionism with racism.

On October 15, General Ariel Sharon led his division behind the Egyptian lines in Sinai and penetrated into the Egyptian side of the Suez Canal. In one day he managed to ferry 2,000 soldiers and 30 tanks across the Suez. Israeli troops destroyed Egyptian missile batteries, allowing the air force to function effectively over the Sinai. The Egyptian Third Army was surrounded, its supply lines cut. Defeated and humiliated, Egypt appealed for a cease fire, which went into effect on October 24.

In twenty days of fighting the Arabs had lost 18,500 soldiers. Eight thousand had been taken prisoner. The Jewish casualties were high: 2,500 soldiers had died and 200 had been taken prisoner. The Jews were forcefully reminded of their vulnerability. The myth of the invincible Israeli soldier had been shattered.

In the aftermath of the war, Israel's goverment came under serious criticism for having ignored intelligence warnings that attack was imminent. Prime Minister Golda Meir and Defense Minister Moshe Dayan were forced to resign.

Rescuing a damaged helicopter on the Syrian front

OPERATION ENTEBBE

5736 1976

An Air France flight on its way to Israel from Paris was hijacked by Palestinian terrorists. They forced the plane to land in Uganda, which was under the dictatorship of Idi Amin. After separating the Jews from the non-Jews, the terrorists announced that they would kill the Jewish passengers within forty-eight hours

Model of Entebee Airport control tower and terminal building. This model is on display at *"Beit HaTzanchanim,"* the Museum of the Paratroopers, in Ramat Gan.

Segan Aluf Yonatan (Yoni) Netanyahu, the commander of Operation Entebbe and the only Israeli casualty of the rescue

Did you know that?

❧ The brother of the commando who was killed became an Israeli prime minister, Binyamin Netanyahu.

❧ News of the rescue at Entebbe reached the United States as its citizens were celebrating the 200th anniversary of American independence on July 4, 1976. President Gerald Ford became the first American president to officially congratulate Israel on a military action.

if Palestinians in jails in Israel and other countries were not released.

Israel's response was to organize an anti-terrorist commando team. Headed by Colonel Yoni Netanyahu, it consisted of elite paratroopers and Golani Brigade soldiers. Miraculously, the team flew undetected for 2,500 miles, some of it through enemy airspace, and landed at Entebbe Airport in Uganda. There they drove through the airport disguised as Idi Amin's entourage. Driving a Mercedes limousine, which was an exact copy of Idi Amin's, that had flown in with them in the belly of the large Hercules transport plane, they reached the air terminal where the hostages were being kept. Colonel Netanyahu led the charge to rescue the hostages. All the terrorists were killed in the first round of fire. During the short, fierce gun battle two of the hostages were killed. The passengers were transported to the waiting Israeli planes and flown to Israel to be reunited with their families. Tragically, there was one military casualty — Colonel Yoni Netanyahu, commander of the strike force, who was shot leading the charge against the terrorists. The world was astounded at the daring and bravery of the successful rescue, which had, through Divine Providence, been accomplished with relatively little loss of life.

Focus: The PLO and Arab terrorism

The Palestine Liberation Organization (PLO) began as an organization whose charter called for the destruction of Israel. Soon after the 1967 war Yasser Arafat became the leader of the organization. The PLO trained its members to kill innocent men, women, and children. They were responsible for the planning and execution of thousands of acts of terror. Acting under Arafat's orders, the PLO were responsible for airplane hijackings, and the bombing of buses and crowded streets. They proudly took credit for gunning down a group of schoolchildren in Maalot and for the killing of Jewish athletes at the 1972 Olympic Games in Munich, Germany. Other acts of terror for which they were responsible include: a grenade attack that killed airplane passengers in Lod Airport; suicide bombers attempting to blow up a busload of schoolchildren; throwing overboard of a wheelchair-bound elderly Jew on a hijacked ship; and the shooting of Jews on their way to pray in the Cave of the Patriarchs. In 1974 the Arab governments appointed the PLO as the sole legitimate representative of the Palestinian people. The blood of thousands of Jews, and the ruined lives of tens of thousands who have had to live with crippling injuries, is on the heads of the PLO and its leader, Yasser Arafat.

After the Oslo Accords were signed in 1993, the PLO became the governing authority of the Palestinian Autonomous Area, with Yasser Arafat as chairman.

PLO Chairman Yasser Arafat addressing the audience after the signing ceremony of the Oslo II accords at the White House

Israel's flag flies at half-staff at Lod Airport in anticipation of the arrival of remains of the Israeli athletes murdered by Arab terrorists at the Munich Olympics

Youthful victims of Palestinian terror. David Madar was 15 years old when he was killed during the Maalot massacre. The grave of his sister, Yehudis, is right behind his.

239

לע״נ
קל‬

כרם‬ יהודי פריבל ווַץ‬ יוסף חיי‬

זאב פרידמן‬ הי״ד

מרק סלבין‬ הי״ד

אליעזר חלפין‬ הי״ד

משה וינברג‬ הי״ד

יוסף גוטפרוינד‬ הי״ד

דוד ברגר‬ הי״ד

Scouts guarding line of torches above names of eleven Israeli athletes murdered in Munich,
during memorial ceremony on Yud Alef Square in Tel Aviv

Did you know that?

🐟 Sadat, who ordered Israel attacked on Yom Kippur 1973, was assassinated while viewing an Egyptian military parade on the anniversary of the Yom Kippur War eight years later.

🐟 Israel's Prime Minister, Menachem Begin, was the only head of state not to be driven in a chauffeured limousine to Sadat's funeral. He walked to the funeral, which took place on the Sabbath.

Focus: The *teshuvah* movement

In the early 1970's, sharply increasing numbers of young and old Jews began returning to their roots, and institutions were established to receive and teach them. Chabad had been engaged in such activities for many decades under the leadership of the late Rebbe, Rabbi Yosef Yitzchak Schneerson. His successor, Rabbi Menachem Mendel Schneerson, intensified the work exponentially, sending *sh'lichim* (emissaries) to the four corners of the world. Other major *baal teshuvah* institutions, founded in the 60's and 70's , were Ohr Some'ach, Aish HaTorah, and Neveh Jerusalem in Israel, and Hineni and Sh'or Yoshuv in the United States.

FIRST ARAB HEAD OF STATE TO VISIT ISRAEL

5737 1977

The President of Egypt, Anwar Sadat, was the first Arab leader who, after almost three decades of war with Israel, had the courage to try and make peace. He visited Israel and addressed the Knesset, and, over a three-day stay, pursued the possibility of a peace treaty — which was ultimately signed.

Prime Minister Menachem Begin (R) welcoming President Sadat, with President Ephraim Katzir looking on, at Ben Gurion Airport

President Sadat inspecting Knesset guard of honor after arriving in Israel

241

5739
1979

ISRAEL AND EGYPT MAKE PEACE AT CAMP DAVID

Did you know that?

In 1979, the Shah of Iran was overthrown and replaced by a fanatical Islamic fundamentalist regime under Ayatollah Ruhollah Khomeini.

On the invitation of President Jimmy Carter, President Anwar Sadat of Egypt and Prime Minister Menachem Begin of Israel met in Camp David, Maryland, along with the American president. In two weeks of negotiations, Egypt and Israel made a peace agreement. In return for the Sinai Desert, Egypt agreed to recognize Israel's legal right to exist, to normalize diplomatic relations, and to cease making war against Israel. Israel had achieved peace with its largest and most powerful Arab neighbor.

(L-R) President Anwar Sadat of Egypt, President Jimmy Carter of the United States, and Prime Minister Menachem Begin of Israel, in Washington at the ceremony marking the signing of the peace treaty between Israel and Egypt

Focus: Menachem Begin

Television cameras focused on Prime Minister Begin as he stood to speak at the historic signing of the Camp David Accords. He placed a black yarmulka on his head to say a blessing and a paragraph of Psalms — and the image of a European Jew, whose family had been killed in the Holocaust, burst into view on television sets across the world.

A Jew who had abiding respect for Jewish tradition, Begin survived the years he had spent in Stalin's Siberian slave labor camps.

He arrived in *Eretz Yisrael* in 1942, and soon became commander of the Irgun Zeva'i Leumi (IZL), which was more extreme than the Haganah in its battles for independence. He proceeded to fiercely battle the British occupation of

Eretz Yisrael. His vision was to see *Eretz Yisrael* governed by the Jews. In part due to his efforts, the British were forced to leave Palestine.

The Haganah, the larger unofficial army led by David Ben Gurion, very much opposed the Irgun. This opposition was so intense that the Haganah actually turned over Irgun members to the British, and sometimes attacked Irgun members. Only because of Begin's strong leadership and desire for the survival of the Jewish people was he able to stop the Irgun from retaliating against the Haganah, thus preventing civil war.

After the War of Independence in 1948, Begin became leader of the Herut party, which later absorbed another party and

Jew Stats:

In **1983** there were **30** Jews in **China** and **300** in **Kenya.**

Menachem Begin
as a young man

Prime Minister Menachem Begin greeting leaders of Agudath Israel's Council of Torah Sages at the home of Rabbi Moshe Feinstein. Rabbi Yaakov Kamenetsky is at left; Rabbi Yitzchak Hutner is in the center.

243

Did you know that?

§⋑ During the time that Menachem Begin was head of the Irgun, the British police in Palestine offered a very large reward for his capture. To escape them, Begin grew a beard and went into hiding in a religious neighborhood. He even attended Torah lectures.

was renamed the Likud. In 1977, the Labor party, which had ruled the state since its inception almost thirty years earlier, was voted out of office. The Israeli electorate voted for the leadership of Menachem Begin and his Herut party. As a statesman, Begin made peace with Egypt. To protect the Jewish people he ordered the destruction of Iraq's nuclear reactor, neutralizing Baghdad's nuclear warheads. He also approved the invasion of Lebanon to prevent terror attacks in the north. In 1983, in poor health, depressed by the death of his beloved wife, and upset at the course of the war in Lebanon, he resigned from public service.

He was succeeded as prime minister by Yitzchak Shamir, his former comrade in arms in the Irgun. Shamir was quiet and strong. He had no charisma, but he held the office longer than anyone else in Israel's history.

When Begin passed away nine years later at the age of 79, the world watched as the funeral procession snaked its way to the ancient Jewish cemetery at the Mount of Olives, and Begin's *tallis*-wrapped body was placed gingerly into the ground as his son said *Kaddish*. Menachem Begin's will specified that he wished to be buried in accordance with Jewish law.

1981

First space shuttle is launched.

1981

Ronald Reagan, a former movie star and governor of California, becomes the 40th president of the United States.

Did you know that?

§⋑ Knowing that Iraq was only a few years from having nuclear weapons, Prime Minister Begin sent fighter-bombers to destroy Iraq's nuclear reactor in 1981. The world protested furiously, but history proved that Begin was right.

§⋑ Egyptian President Anwar Sadat was assassinated by Islamic fundamentalists. He was succeeded by Hosni Mubarak.

The late Prime Ministers Menachem Begin and Yitzchak Rabin, on Mt. Herzl in Jerusalem

ISRAEL INVADES LEBANON

5742
1982

Lebanon, once the thriving financial capital of the Middle East, had become the headquarters of the Palestine Liberation Organization (PLO), which had been expelled from Jordan. Anarchy raged in much of the country as rival Muslim and Christian militias battled one another. The PLO used southern Lebanon as a springboard for terrorist forays into northern Israel.

Defense Minister Ariel Sharon, with Prime Minister Begin's approval, launched an incursion into Lebanon to drive out the PLO. The war was successful since it forced the PLO into exile in Tunisia, but it had unpleasant aftereffects. A Christian militia group entered the Palestinian refugee camps Sabra and Chatilla and massacred hundreds of helpless people. Israel was blamed for letting it happen and Sharon was held responsible and condemned by an Israeli commission of inquiry.

Israel withdrew, but continued to occupy a narrow strip of southern Lebanon to prevent terrorists from attacking northern Israel. In the 1990's, Hezbollah, an Arab terrorist organization supported by Syria and Iran, carried on a guerrilla war against the Israeli forces. In 2000, Prime Minister Ehud Barak withdrew unilaterally from Lebanon, in what was perceived as the first victory of Arabs over the Israel Defense Force.

CHANGE IN THE SOVIET UNION

5742
1982

Longtime conservative leader Leonid Breznev died in 1982. He was succeeded first by Yuri Androvov and then by Konstantin Chernenko, both of whom died after brief times in power. In 1985, Mikhail Gorbachev came to the helm. The decline and fall of the Soviet Union and the "Iron Curtain" was not far off.

5744 1984

DEADLOCK IN ISRAELI POLITICS

Did you know that?

In a secret airlift code-named Moses, Israel brought 8,000 Ethiopian Jews to the Holy Land in 1984. In 1991, in Operation Solomon, another 14,200 were brought to Israel in the space of 36 hours, in 40 flights!

The Labor Party (under various names) had dominated Israel's government and society until Menachem Begin and his Likud party broke its stranglehold in 1977. In the election of 1984, there was a virtual deadlock and it took months before a government could be formed, through an unusual compromise. Labor's Shimon Peres would be prime minister for twenty-five months and then Likud's Yitzchak Shamir would take over for the next twenty-five months.

New factors in Orthodox political life were the two parties created by Rabbi Elazar Menachem Man Shach. Degel HaTorah was the party of the so-called Lithuanian yeshivah world, and Shas was the party of Sephardic Jews.

Rabbi Shach founded Shas in order to give greater representation to Orthodox Sephardim. It developed into the voice of the traditional Sephardic community as well, guided by Rabbi Ovadiah Yosef, the leading Sephardic sage. Aryeh Deri, an unusually adept political tactician, made Shas one of Israel's major parties.

Degel HaTorah was established in 1988, and, though it has run together with Agudath Israel in several elections, it has retained its independence.

Yitzchak Shamir (L) and Shimon Peres (R).

246

Arab youth throwing rocks at Israeli troops

THE INTIFADA

During the 1980's, Palestinian Arabs grew increasingly resentful of Israel's rule. Terrorist activities became much more common, fanned by Yasser Arafat's PLO and the new Hamas organization. Hamas is a fundamentalist Islamic movement that refuses to accept the very existence of Israel. In 1987, a full-scale rebellion erupted. Known as the Intifada ("shaking off"), it consisted of riots and stone-throwing, primarily by young people. Unlike the Intifada that began in September, 2000, the first one did not include bombings and shootings, but more than 100 Israelis were killed. Minister of Defense Yitzchak Rabin employed force to put down the rebellion, but it mushroomed. Typically, world opinion was with the rioters and the United Nations, as usual, condemned Israel without mentioning the

Arab provocations. The intifada ended only in 1993, with th Oslo Accord and Israel's recognition of the PLO as the legitimate representative of the Palestinians.

The Intifada had unwelcome by-products. Israeli society was splintered, as segments of the polity and the public opposed the government's strong response to the rebellion. And in the United States there was a breakdown of the traditional Jewish support for whatever government was in power in Israel. There was publicly expressed opposition to the Shamir policies and new organizations came into being to pressure Israel and even to lobby in Congress against the elected government of the Jewish state. Palestinian opposition was emboldened, as the young stone-throwers gained the sympathy of the world and could not be subdued by Israel's army and police.

5749 1989 THE IRON CURTAIN FALLS; SOVIET JEWS ARE FREED

Seventy years of Communist rule had almost destroyed the connection between three and a half million Jews in the Soviet Union and their Torah heritage. For many, their only connection was the word *Yevrei* stamped on their identity cards, which identified them as Jewish. But Israel's remarkable victory in the Six Day War ignited the *"pintele Yid"*— the tiny Jewish spark that is never extinguished — into a bright flame. The Jews in Soviet Russia started to search for their tradition. Ultimately a mass movement began. Jews clamored to be allowed to leave Mother Russia to return to their land, *Eretz Yisrael*. Thousands applied for exit visas, even though it meant being dismissed from uni-

Did you know that?

In Soviet prison, religious refusenik Yosef Mendelevich was not able to mark the Sabbath with wine or special foods. To create a Sabbath spirit for himself, he would wear the one white undershirt given out by the prison only on the Sabbath — on top of his prison shirt. It kept up his spirit until his prayers were answered and he arrived in Israel, where he still lives.

Refuseniks gather for a clandestine lecture. Seated at the left is Rabbi Immanuel Jakobovits, Chief Rabbi of the British Commonwealth.

versity or losing one's job, years of economic difficulties, and harassment by the KGB, the Soviet secret police.

A secret *baal teshuvah* movement flourished, in defiance of the KGB, and despite great personal danger. Young men and women started keeping the Sabbath and *Yom Tov* for the first time in their lives. *Sefarim*, *tefillin*, kosher meat, and even *sheitels* were smuggled in by ordinary religious men and women who would visit Russia to help support their Jewish brothers. Rabbis were sent to Russia to answer halachic queries and to give lectures.

Outspoken Soviet Jewish leaders were known as refuseniks, because they were "refused" permission to leave the country. The Soviet authorities deemed these refuseniks to be very dangerous, and so they were often imprisoned, not heard from for years at a time, or sent far, far away, to the frozen Siberian wasteland.

Did you know that?

- Foremost among the secret heroes who kept Judaism alive under Communism were the Chassidim of Lubavitch. From the time of the Communist Revolution in 1917, the Soviets tried to stamp out Judaism, with great cruelty and efficiency, but the followers of Chabad worked secretly and with great courage — even risking death — to teach Torah and keep *mitzvos*.

- Eliyahu Essas, known as the Rabbi of the refuseniks, with daring and chutzpah created an education network of secret *baal teshuvah* cells. He ran a summer camp for families. For many of them it was the first time they could fully experience *Yiddishkeit*. Yet Essas did not know the *alef-beis* until he was in his 20's. Soon after beginning his Jewish studies, he was learning *Gemara*.

- Anatoly (Natan) Scharansky spent twelve years in prison, and many hours in a small cell, in solitary confinement. When his freedom was finally granted, he was informed that when he would be released he could take nothing with him. He refused to step into freedom unless he was allowed to take the book which had been a source of comfort and strength during his long years in prison — his Book of Psalms. In 1997, eleven years after his release, Scharansky returned to Russia, not as a prisoner, but as a minister of the government of Israel. Upon landing at the airport he was given the red carpet treatment. The Russian government, which had previously imprisoned him, now treated him with the greatest respect, as befitting a visiting dignitary. He even took the time to visit his former prison and reenter the solitary confinement cell.

Did you know that?

🔊 Jews from the former Soviet Union became an important political force in Israel, with their own political parties. Their votes have provided the margin of victory in recent Israeli elections.

🔊 There has been a resurgence of Jewish life in the countries of the former USSR. Chabad, which was active there even when it was very dangerous to espouse Jewish life, remains in the forefront. Among other groups is Karlin-Stolin. One of its disciples, Rabbi Yaakov Bleich, the Chief Rabbi of Ukraine, established and leads religious and social service organizations in his adopted country.

Prime Minister Mikhail Gorbachev

Outside of the Soviet Union, Jews prayed and demonstrated and used political influence to help free their brothers from behind the Iron Curtain. The great Russian bear was forced to bow, and in 1971 the gates opened a crack. Through that crack 100,000 Jews left over the next four years. But then the gates slammed shut.

When Mikhail Gorbachev came to power, he instituted a policy of *glasnost* that eased Communist rule, paving the road to the fall of Communism. With the end of Communist rule came the freedom of Soviet Jewry to practice Judaism openly and to live where they wanted. Over a million Soviet Jews emigrated, the majority settling in Israel or America. Today, Jewish children in Russia can attend Jewish schools. In the land where the sound of Torah study and prayer had been silenced, Torah and *tefillah* can be heard once again.

The Soviet Union collapsed and Gorbachev was replaced by Boris Yeltsin. All the republics of the USSR became independent countries and the Eastern European satellites broke free.

Rabbi Moshe Eisenmann (L), an American lecturer, speaking to refuseniks

Prisoner of Zion, Yosef Mendelevich, arrives at Ben Gurion Airport after being released from the U.S.S.R.

5751 1991

SCUD MISSILE ATTACK ON TEL AVIV — THE GULF WAR

Iraqi dictator Saddam Hussein ordered his army to invade its tiny neighbor, Kuwait. He threatened that if attacked by the United States he would attack Israel. In response to the invasion of Kuwait, the U.S. launched Operation Desert Storm. Saddam kept his promise: Twenty-four hours later, Scud missiles hit Tel Aviv.

The Scud missile attacks were a dangerous threat to Israel's citizens. People were particularly afraid of the possibility of the Scuds being armed with deadly nerve gas or other chemical or biological weapons that would spread in a killing cloud of death over Israel's cities. In the days before the war began, the government distributed kits including gas masks and hypodermic needles containing antidotes to poison gas. Windows were sealed shut with tape and covered with plastic sheeting, creating a sealed room to keep the poisonous gas out. Hospitals went on emergency status, preparing to handle the expected thousands of casualties.

On the first night of the war, sirens wailed through the darkness, signaling incoming missiles. All radio and television broadcasting was interrupted and an army spokesman ordered all citizens into their sealed rooms. Millions of Jews huddled together — men, women and children — in their sealed rooms, parents helping their children into gas masks and putting on their own. In many sealed rooms families sat together reciting Psalms. Doctors and nurses in hospitals continued to work, wearing gas masks while delivering babies, who were immediately placed into specially protected cribs. The streets were deserted; no one left their rooms until the radio sounded the "all clear," declaring that it was safe to leave.

As the days passed, whenever people went to synagogue or work they carried gas masks slung over their shoulders. To the delight of Israel's children, school was canceled. In all, thirty-nine Scud missiles fell on Israel; none of them contained nerve gas or chemicals. In the 7,000 apartments destroyed by the missiles, only one life was lost! (In comparison, when a single Scud fell on an American military base in Saudi Arabia, twenty servicemen were killed.) People and infants wondrously survived buildings that collapsed over them. Miracles were a daily occurrence — like the gas line that was hit by a missle, but had no gas because it had been shut that morning for repairs.

As a further sign of Divine Providence, the war ended on Purim. The Jews celebrated the defeat of the Iraqi Haman, which came about despite the fact that the Israeli army had never even fired a shot.

Speaking on a cordless phone while wearning a gas mask during an alarm

Did you know that?

At the request of President George Bush, Israel refrained from responding to the Scud attacks. It was the first time Israel had come under attack without striking back in self-defense. Bush was afraid that if Israel defended itself, the Arab countries would refuse to support Operation Desert Storm.

Michael Diyar trapped, but only injured, beneath the ruins of his Savyon home moments after a Scud exploded in the yard

A resident of Abba Hillel Street, in Ramat Gan, searching through the ruins of her home

5753
1993

YASSER ARAFAT AND PRIME MINISTER RABIN SHAKE HANDS

In Oslo, Norway, secret negotiations were taking place. Representatives of Palestinian Authority Chairman Yasser Arafat and representatives of Israeli Foreign Minister Shimon Peres were trying to agree on a formula to bring peace to Israel. At the conclusion of these talks, Rabin, Arafat, and United States President Bill Clinton gathered on the lawn of the White House for a ceremony to mark the signing of a Declaration of Principles between Israel and the Palestinians.

The agreement called for Israel to withdraw from the Gaza Strip and the city of Jericho, and for the PLO to stop terror attacks and recognize Israel's right to exist.

The internationally broadcast Arafat-Rabin handshake was thought to be a precursor of a process that would lead to peace in the Middle East and the end of terror attacks on Jews in *Eretz Yisrael*. This hope was disappointed, as terror did not end and Palestinian incitement in the media and the schools brought hatred of Israel to a new peak.

Did you know that?

President Bill Clinton was widely regarded as the best friend Israel ever had in the White House. Later in his term this image was tarnished as he tried harder and harder to make concessions to Arafat.

Israeli Prime Minister Yitzchak Rabin shaking hands with PLO Chairman Yasser Arafat on the White House lawn, as United States President Bill Clinton looks on

5755 1995

RABIN ASSASSINATION

Did you know that?

In October 1994, Rabin and King Hussein of Jordan signed a peace treaty. This made Jordan the only Arab nation other than Egypt that made peace with the Jewish State.

Prime Minister Yitzchak Rabin was assassinated as he returned to his car after addressing a peace rally in Tel Aviv. He was shot in the back by Yigal Amir, a law student who opposed returning territory to the Palestinians. Three bullets entered Rabin's body at point-blank range, and he died on the operating table. A terrible, horrific crime had been committed: A Jew had killed another Jew. At the funeral, attended by many heads of state from all over the world, President Clinton of the United States ended his eulogy with the Hebrew words, "Shalom, *chaver* — Goodbye, friend."

Prime Minister Yitzchak Rabin

Teenagers gather at Rabin Square in Tel Aviv, the site of the prime minister's murder

256

Members of the American delegation who attended the funeral of slain Prime Minister Yitzchak Rabin, from left: former Presidents Jimmy Carter and George Bush, former Secretary of State George Schultz (standing behind Mrs. Clinton), First Lady Hillary Rodham Clinton, President Bill Clinton, and Secretary of State Warren Christopher

Focus: Yitzchak Rabin

Yitzchak Rabin was born in Jerusalem. A brave soldier, during the War of Independence he was the commander of the Harel Brigade, one of the units fighting to capture Jerusalem. He was Chief of Staff of the Israel Defense Forces when Jerusalem was recaptured during the victorious Six Day War. After a short term as Israel's ambassador to the United States, Rabin entered politics and became prime minister for the first time in 1974. He became prime minister once again in 1992. Rabin pursued a policy of negotiating for peace with the PLO and with neighboring Arab countries. For his efforts, he was honored with the Nobel Peace Prize, together with Shimon Peres and Yasser Arafat.

Focus: Shimon Peres

Born in Poland and brought to Palestine as a child, Shimon Peres has been a public servant since the founding of the State. He is credited with a major role in creating the Israel Defense Force in the 1950's and with halting a disastrous inflation in the 1980's. Although he has served as prime minister, he was never able to win a national election. For the last decade he has been the main proponent of negotiations with the PLO and of a vision of a "new Middle East," where Israel and the Arab countries would cooperate economically and socially.

Shimon Peres

Binyamin Netanyahu

5756 1996

BINYAMIN NETANYAHU DEFEATS SHIMON PERES

Shimon Peres became prime minister after the Rabin assassination. Basking in the glow of Rabin's martyrdom, he seemed to be a certain landslide winner in the election of May 1996. For the first time, there would be a direct election for prime minister and a separate one for the Knesset.

But early in the year, there were several terrorist bombings of crowded buses in Jerusalem and Tel Aviv, costing dozens of lives. Peres, the architect of the Oslo Accord that gave legitimacy to the PLO, commented,

"Instead of thanks we got bombs." The treachery of the Palestinians made Peres vulnerable in a very bitter election campaign. Binyamin Netanyahu of the Likud was a relative newcomer to the political arena, but he was a gifted speaker who had served with distinction as Israel's UN ambassador. In the election, Netanyahu came from behind to defeat Peres by less than 1 percent of the vote.

The Knesset was hopelessly fragmented by more than a dozen parties and deeply divided between right and left, secular and religious, Sephardi and Ashkenazi. This made it extremely difficult for Netanyahu to cobble together a coalition in the Knesset and to rule effectively.

At the begining of his administration, Netanyahu gave a hugely successful address to a joint session of the U.S. Congress. Unfortunately, it was mostly downhill after that, as his slim majority and cabinet bickering dogged him throughout his term.

Did you know that?

🔖 Netanyahu was considered a hard-liner and he demanded performance from the Palestinian Authority before he would make further concessions to Arafat. Nevertheless, it was he who ceded Hebron to Arab control. He also ceded more of the West Bank to the Palestinian Authority. These gestures for peace cost him dearly in right wing support, and did not lessen Palestinian hostility.

🔖 The American administration put heavy pressure on Netanyahu to make "sacrifices for peace." He and Arafat were brought to the Wye River Plantation in Maryland for negotiations. Netanyahu agreed to give up more land in return for Arafat's promise to "fight terror" and live up to his commitments at Oslo. The land was given but the promises were ignored.

The aftermath of a terrorist bombing at Jerusalem's Machaneh Yehudah market, which left many civilians dead or injured

Focus: The spread of terrorism

Traditionally wars had been fought by armies. The second half of the 20th century saw the rise of a new kind of warfare: terrorism. Whereas international law prohibited attacks against civilians, terrorists targeted civilians as well as soldiers. Their intention was to gain their political goals by frightening populations and demoralizing governments. In Ireland and England, the Irish Republican Army attacked its opponents indiscriminately. Islamic terrorists exploded a huge bomb, intended to cause the collapse of New York's World Trade Center, and Libyan terrorists brought down a Pan Am airliner over Lockerbie, Scotland, killing 270 innocent people. In many countries — Colombia, the Phillipines, Germany, Japan and others — terror attempted to do what rational discussion and political activity could not. Israel was the primary victim of terrorism, but it was the only country condemned for trying to defend itself.

The American embassy in Nairobi, Kenya, destroyed in a terrorist bombing

The Tenth *Siyum HaShas* at Madison Square Garden in New York City, organized by Agudath Israel of America

GRAND CELEBRATION UPON COMPLETION OF THE TALMUD FOR THE TENTH TIME BY *DAF YOMI*

5757 1997

Madison Square Garden and the Nassau Coliseum are places where basketball and hockey games are usually played, or where concerts take place. But on September 28, 1997, tens of thousands of people came together to fill both arenas and celebrate the tenth *Siyum HaShas* of

Did you know that?

- Taped lectures of every page of *Gemara* are available on cassette tapes. That's over 2,700 tapes!

- There is a *Daf Yomi* site on the Internet, as well as CDs that feature lectures and many visual aids on every page of Talmud. One can access *Daf Yomi* lectures by phone, twenty-four hours a day.

- An important factor in the astounding increase in the numbers of people studying *Daf Yomi* is the Schottenstein Edition of the Talmud, in English and Hebrew, dedicated to the memory of Mr. Jerome Schottenstein of Columbus, Ohio, and published by Artscroll / Mesorah. The English and Hebrew editions are now being joined by a French edition.

Daf Yomi. For the tenth time since it was begun by Rabbi Meir Shapiro in 1923 (5683), Jews completed the study of the entire Talmud, at the rate of a *daf* (two pages) a day.

Rabbi Meir Shapiro had proposed the *Daf Yomi* concept at the first congress of Agudath Israel, in 1923, so that every day the same page of Talmud would be learned by Jews all over the world. To finish the 2,711 folio (two-sided) pages of Talmud, at the rate of a page a day, takes approximately 7½ years.

At the *siyum* celebration, immediately upon completion of the cycle with the last page of the Talmud, the first page of the Talmud was started anew. The gatherings were addressed by leading rabbinic figures. The celebrations took place on a Sunday evening, only three days before Rosh Hashanah. They began with *Ma'ariv*, the

A group of commuters study the *Daf Yomi* aboard the Long Island Railroad

evening prayer. Via satellite hookup, the 22,000 Jews in Madison Square Garden, the 18,000 in Nassau Coliseum, and Jews in thirty-five other cities around the world, including faraway Australia — a total of 70,000 people — celebrated this *kiddush Hashem* together. The large Madison Square Garden and Nassau Coliseum auditoriums vibrated not with the hysterical cheering at an athletic event, but with the sound of *Shema* being said by 40,000 Jews and the spontaneous dancing in the aisles when the last page of Talmud was completed.

Looking out over the large numbers of people swaying together, praying together, it looked like the waves of the sea. The evening was dedicated as a living memorial to the six million Jews, victims of the Nazi Holocaust.

Focus: Rabbi Meir Shapiro

Known as the Lubliner Rav, he was one of the great leaders of pre-World War II Polish Jewry. He was able to trace his lineage back to King David. A powerful speaker, full of energy, he became president of Agudath Israel in Poland and was one of the Orthodox Jewish members of the Polish parliament, the Sejm. Rabbi Meir Shapiro proposed the *Daf Yomi* concept in 1923.

After becoming Rabbi in Lublin he devoted his life to the creation of Yeshivah Chachmei Lublin. He built an impressive building to be the home of a very special yeshivah, the first in Poland to have dormitory facilities. Until then, yeshivah students were forced to rent rooms in various homes throughout the village where the yeshivah was located, eating dinner in different homes each day. In Rabbi Shapiro's yeshivah, all the boys learned, ate, and slept in the same building, together, under one roof. The yeshivah had an enrollment of over 500 students. Each one of them had passed a grueling entrance exam which required that he be well versed in several hundred pages of *Gemara*.

While still in his late 40's, Rabbi Meir took sick. Surrounded by a group of his students as he lay dying, he made a last request: that they sing and dance. As tears of grief streamed down their faces, they did as their *rebbi* had requested. In an adjoining room, hundreds of his students were saying Psalms. As the students in his room danced around his bed he whispered his final words on this earth: "*Nur mit simchah* — only with joy."

Rabbi Meir Shapiro

5759 1999

EHUD BARAK BECOMES PRIME MINISTER

Ehud Barak celebrates his election victory

Did you know that?

🔖 President Clinton's term was marred by a personal scandal which led to his impeachment by the House of Representatives — only the second President ever impeached. He was acquitted by the Senate, but his presidency was badly damaged and weakened. Many people thought that his strenuous effort to broker an Israeli-Palestinian peace treaty was an attempt to rehabilitate his reputation and win a Nobel Peace Prize.

🔖 Arafat had the gall to call Clinton as his term came to an end in January 2001, and congratulate him for being a great president. Clinton replied, "No, I was a failure, and you are responsible." In speeches since then, he blamed Arafat for killing the chance for peace and starting the Intifada.

Internal cabinet bickering, lack of trust, and vicious media criticism brought down Netanyahu's government. In the election for prime minister he was opposed by Ehud Barak, who had defeated Peres for leadership of Labor. Barak was intellectually brilliant, a former commander of Israel's military, and the most decorated soldier in its history. He made many promises in the campaign — including a pledge to institute a "secular revolution" — and trounced Netanyahu by a 12 percent margin.

Barak wasted no time entering into negotiations with both the PLO and Syria. In both cases he made daring offers of concessions beyond what any other Israeli leader had contemplated. Yet, even a personal, face-to-face appeal by President Clinton failed to move Syrian dictator Hafez al-Assad.

The Syrian option closed, Barak turned to the Palestinian front. As it became known that he was offering more than the Israeli public would accept, he lost support in his cabinet and Knesset until his government fell. Still, he continued to negotiate, even though a new deadly Intifada broke out in September 2000. This time the Intifada was not confined to stone-throwing. It was based on shooting and bombing.

Through it all, Barak continued his quest for peace and a settlement, with the backing and active support of President Clinton. During the Clinton presidency, Arafat was invited to the White House more often than any other leader.

Finally, Barak and Clinton offered Arafat about 95 percent of the West Bank and Gaza and control of East Jerusalem and the Temple Mount. Israel was in an uproar, but Arafat saved the country from serious internal conflict by rejecting Barak's offer. As Abba Eban once said, "The Palestinians never lose an opportunity to lose an opportunity."

L-R: Ehud Barak, Bill Clinton, and Yassir Arafat meet in Oslo, Norway

Focus: The Intifada

Whereas the 1987 Intifada began spontaneously and grew, the new Intifada was planned in advance. It began just before Rosh Hashanah 5761/2000. It was planned as a classic terror campaign, designed to destroy the morale of the citizenry and thereby force the government to move back to the pre-1967 borders. At this writing, nineteen months after it began, it rages on unabated, and has even intensified as the months passed.

There are daily shooting on the roads, in settlements, and even in the major cities. Then, as time went on, it assumed the most shocking dimension ever, as years of PLO and Hamas incitement bore bitter fruit. Young Palestinians — and even girls — became human bombs. They strapped explosives around their waists and blew themselves up in crowded places, taking many Jewish lives and injuring and maiming hundreds more. The most shocking and lethal such suicide bombing took place in Netanya as hundred of Jews were seated in a hotel ballroom, ready to begin the Pesach Seder. A suicide bomber killed twenty-seven people and injured well over a hundred. Although the army and police prevented most such bombings, too many slipped through.

The army retaliated forcefully, but was not able to subdue the rebellion. Arafat, for his part, lauded the "martyrs" and encouraged his people to kill themselves and go to Paradise.

Meanwhile over 400 Israelis have been murdered and over 1,400 Palestinians killed, the great majority of the latter terrorists and gunmen.

Arabs on the Temple Mount catapulting stones at Israelis

265

5759 1999

MORE THAN HALF A MILLION JEWS JOIN IN PRAYER

In a unique moment of modern Jewish history, more than half a million Jews assembled to pray together in the streets of Jerusalem. Under the clear blue sky of the holy city, the sound of *shofars* echoed through the streets over the heads of yeshivah boys in black hats, national-religious men and youth in knitted skullcaps, Chassidic Jews in wide-brimmed hats, and Sephardim. The gathering was graced by the presence of many great rabbinic leaders of the different circles of the Torah-observant population of Israel: Rabbi Ovadiah Yosef, the leader of Sephardic Jewry; the Israeli Chief Rabbis, Rabbi Lau and Rabbi Bakshi-Doron; the Chassidic Rebbes of Ger and Vizhnitz; Rabbi Yosef Shalom Elyashiv, the world's pre-eminent *posek,* and many others. Never in the history of modern Israel had anyone witnessed such a large gathering of different types of Torah-observers standing in unity, reciting the afternoon prayers as well as special supplicatory prayers, *ke'ish echad, b'lev echad* — like one man, with one heart. All were praying for God to grant that the State of Israel not forsake its Jewish identity. The assembly of more than half a million ended with a resounding declaration: *Shema Yisrael* — Hear, O Israel, Hashem is our God, Hashem is the One and Only, and *Hashem hu Elokim* — Hashem is the Lord.

Over 500,000 Jews gather in prayer

And so Jewish history goes on,
to the end of time, to the Final Redemption,
world peace and the coming of the Messiah.
Until that time, the Jewish nation continues
its wondrous journey through time with
emunah and *bitachon* —
faith and trust in God.

Bibliography

Baron, Salo W., *The Russian Jew Under Tsars and Soviets*, Schocken Books, New York, 1987.

Bloch, Abraham P., *Day by Day in Jewish History,* Ktav Publishing, New York, 1983.

Bromberg, Rabbi A.Y., *Rebbes of Ger,* Mesorah/Hillel Press, New York, 1987.

Burstein, Aviezer, *Adirei De'ah*, Beit Hillel, Jerusalem, undated.

Davis, Mac, *Jews Fought Too,* Hebrew Publishing Company, New York, 1950.

Encyclopedia Judaica, Keter Publishing House, Jerusalem, 1972.

Finkelman, Shimon, *Reb Moshe*, ArtScroll/Mesorah, 1986.

Frenkel, Rabbi Isser, *Men of Distinction*, Sinai Publishing, Tel Aviv, 1967.

Gilbert, Martin, *Atlas of Jewish History*, Dorset Press, 1985.

Goldberg, M. Hirsh, *The Jewish Connection*, Stein & Day, Briarcliff Manor, New York, 1976.

Goldwurm, Rabbi Hersh, *History of the Jewish People: The Second Temple Era,* Mesorah/Hillel Press, New York, 1982.

Gross, Rabbi M.D., *Avot HaDorot,* Yavneh Publishing, Tel Aviv, 1957.

Holder, Meir, *History of the Jewish People: from Yavneh to Pumbedisa,* Mesorah/Hillel Press, New York, 1986.

Johnson, Paul, *A History of the Jews,* Harper & Row, New York, 1987.

Jung, Leo, editor, *Jewish Leaders 1750-1940,* Boys Town Jerusalem Publishers, Jerusalem, 1964.

Jung, Leo, editor, *Men of the Spirit,* Kymson Publishing, New York, 1964.

Kantor, Mattis, *The Jewish Timeline Encyclopedia*, Jason Aronson, Northvale, New Jersey, 1992.

Kaplan, Rabbi Aryeh, *The Chassidic Masters,* Moznaim Publishing, New York, 1984.

Klugman, Rabbi Eliyahu Meir, *Rabbi Samson Raphael Hirsch,* ArtScroll/Mesorah, New York, 1996.

Landman, Isaac, editor, *The Universal Jewish Encyclopedia* (Vols. 1-10), 1940.

Levin, Nora, *The Holocaust*, Schocken, New York, 1968.

Mirsky, Dr. Shmuel, editor, *Mosdos Torah B'Europa*, Morasha Publishers, Israel, 1956.

Mishal, Nissim, *Those Were the Years*, Yedioth Aharonoth, Tel Aviv, 1998.

Paretzky, Zev T., *The Chida*, Targum Press, Southfield, Michigan, 1998.

Pett, Saul, editor, *Lightning Out of Israel*, The Associated Press, U.S.A., 1967.

Rabinowicz, Rabbi Tzvi, *Chassidic Rebbes*, Targum Press, Southfield, Michigan, 1989.

Rabinowitz, Rabbi Chaim D., *Da'as Soferim*, Israel, 1979.

Rakefet-Rothkoff, Aaron, *The Rav*, Ktav, Hoboken, NJ, 1999.

Rossoff, Dovid, *Where Heaven Touches Earth*, Guardian Press, Jerusalem, 1998.

Roth, Cecil, *The Jewish Contribution to Civilization*, Cincinnati, 1940.

Sachar, Howard M., *A History of Israel*, Knopf, New York, 1979.

Schappes, Morris U., editor, *A Documentary History of the Jews in the United States,* Schocken, New York, 1976.

Sorasky, Rabbi Aharon, *Great Chassidic Leaders*, Mesorah, New York, 1991.

Stern, Rabbi Yechiel Michel, editor, *Gedolei HaDoros*, Machon Minchas Yisrael, Jerusalem, 1996.

Wein, Rabbi Berel, *Echoes of Glory*, Shaar Press, New York, 1995.

Wein, Rabbi Berel, *Herald of Destiny*, Shaar Press, New York, 1993.

Wein, Rabbi Berel, *Triumph of Survival*, Shaar Press, New York, 1990.

Wein, Rabbi Berel, *Faith and Fate,* Shaar Press, New York, 2001.

Weiss, Rabbi Gershon, *The Holocaust and Jewish Destiny*, Targum Press, Jerusalem, 1999.

Wolpin, Rabbi Nisson, editor, *The Torah Personality*, Mesorah, New York, 1980.

Wolpin, Rabbi Nisson, editor, *The Torah Profile*, Mesorah, New York, 1988.

Wolpin, Rabbi Nisson, editor, *The Torah World*, Mesorah, New York, 1982.

Yoshor, Rabbi Moses M., *The Chafetz Chaim*, ArtScroll/Mesorah, New York, 1984.

Index

Photo Credits

Corbis Images: 11

Department of Public Affairs/Yeshiva University: 150

Israel Government Press Office, Jerusalem: 13, 47, 155, 171, 209, 210, 216, 218, 219, 220, 221, 223, 227, 228, 229, 230, 231, 232, 233, 234, 235, 236, 237, 238, 239 (top, and bottom – left), 240, 241, 242, 243 (bottom), 244, 246, 247, 253, 254, 255, 256, 257, 258, 259, 260, 264, 265, 267

Eli Kroen: 212 (right)

Zvi Pesach Olesker: 35

Orthodox Jewish Archives of Agudath Israel: 152 (bottom), 163, 174 (top), 181(left and right), 183, 202, 203 (top), 213 (left), 261, 262, 263

Universal Jewish Encyclopedia: 42, 43, 46, 49, 52, 53, 57, 60, 61, 62, 66, 74, 76, 77, 78, 80, 85, 86, 87, 88, 93, 94, 107, 111, 113, 121, 130, 135, 136 (top), 145, 146, 164, 171

Miriam Zakon: 3, 10, 15, 16, 17, 18, 39, 40, 69 (two bottom pictures), 72, 96

Nachman Zakon: 19, 33, 69 (top), 133